A MANUAL OF SOUND ARCHIVE ADMINISTRATION

A Manual of Sound Archive Administration

Alan Ward

Gower

Published by
Gower Publishing Company Limited
Gower House
Croft Road
Aldershot
Hants. GU11 3HR
England

Gower Publishing Company
Old Post Road
Brookfield
Vermont 05036
USA

British Library Cataloguing in Publication Data
Ward, Alan
    A manual of sound archive administration.
    1. Sound recordings. Collections. Administration
    I. Title
    025.1782

ISBN: 0 566 05571 6

Printed in Great Britain by
Dotesios Printers Ltd, Trowbridge, Wiltshire

CONTENTS

INTRODUCTION

This book aims to assist those who work to preserve and make available archival sound recordings. These 'sound archivists' are a mixed bunch. Since there are no full-time training programmes for them anywhere in the world, most have picked up what they need to know in the course of their work. Almost all will have started out as 'something else': as music librarians, 'conventional' archivists, radio station staff, teachers, subject specialists, researchers, musicians, record collectors, studio technicians etc.

Those with a technical background tend initially to know as little about archive and information work as the archivists and librarians know about technology. Yet this is a field in which a practical knowledge of both aspects is required. Reflecting my own position I have written this guide from the point of view of the technical layman, including, I hope, enough technical information to indicate the nature of the various media and their special requirements in language which people like me can understand. The technically knowledgeable may find this tedious, but I hope they in turn may appreciate my attempt to explain archival principles and practices while the documentalists yawn.

The pursuit of adequate, generally acceptable and compatible standards is an aim of this book, and for this reason its general arrangement is thematic rather than typological. My approach is based on the assertion that sound recordings preserved for reference may be categorized and processed by analogy with textual documentation, and that some therefore require 'archival' arrangement and treatment similar, if not identical, to that considered appropriate to textual archives.

As with textual archives, the subject matter of these recordings should not be used as the basis for their arrangement and documentation, and it does not dictate the arrangement of this book. Here, sound archives produced by broadcasting, musical, and oral history activities among others are seen as conforming and amenable to general rules regardless of content, and while the illustrative examples serve to show how principles work out in practice, there are no separate chapters on the various 'types' of sound archives.

Similarly, having arrived in Chapter 1 at a definition of sound archives by analogy with textual archives, the remainder of the book is concerned with such materials and not directly with other forms of permanently preserved sound documentation such as published gramophone records. Custodians of the latter may all the same find information which is of use to them, particularly in the conservation chapter.[1]

Because custodians of sound recordings share a number of problems, especially in the fields of conservation and documentation, whatever the extent, scope or status of their materials, it has been possible in some parts of the book to provide detailed information which is applicable in virtually any repository more or less worldwide. But some topics such as copyright are difficult to deal with 'internationally' in a general work of this scope and so information specific to the United Kingdom only will be found. Similarly, although much of the experience on which the book is based has been gained through my work at the National Sound Archive in London, and through contact with sound archivists who work in other big institutions such as the BBC and the National Archives in Washington DC, most sound archivists work in smaller repositories, or only deal with sound recordings as part of their work. So in order for the book to be of practical use to more than a few, its focus is on the small- or medium-sized repository or specialist section. Little attention is paid, for instance, to the design of expensive purpose-built accommodation or the management of large bodies of staff.

In preparing material of general usefulness I have benefited from contact with colleagues in the British Association of Sound Collections (the UK branch of IASA) and especially from experience gained in organizing and teaching on the sound archive training courses run by BASC. Nevertheless it is my view that however small an operation may be initially, it should be encouraged to adopt generally acceptable professional standards. With this in mind some of the practices and standards referred to and recommended in the following chapters reflect a more ambitious scale of operation than is typical of, say, the work of a small UK repository. What will also be clear, I hope, is the intention to assist with the relatively simple and modest by referring to the problems and experiences of more ambitious undertakings. All archivists should think in the long term and avoid basing their standards purely on today's patterns of use. The adoption of good practices need not be significantly more costly.

This is an old-fashioned book in several respects. It gives precedence to preservation over exploitation; it advocates 'conservation' rather than 'restoration' and does not recommend the early adoption of new technologies; it is not concerned (except indirectly) with publicity, publications, exhibitions or fund-raising, nor with recording activities or oral history project work except where the sound archivist looks after the results; and it does not assume the (for some inevitable) obsolescence of sound recording in the face of video. But paradoxically, by defining and examining only the archivist's essential knowledge, attitudes and responsibilities, the book appears to be breaking new ground, at least in English-speaking countries.

As knowledgeable readers will soon discover, the book is not based on new research but on a survey and assessment of existing sources and practices, published and unpublished, from various countries. By a fortunate coincidence a number of high quality publications appeared as my book was nearing completion, such as the joint FIAF/FIAT/IASA compilation, *Archiving the audio-visual heritage*, the ARSC/AAA's *Audio preservation: a planning study*, and the second edition of the British Library/Society of Archivists' *Manual of archival description*. In a field where almost every statement is in danger of immediate obsolescence, these studies have kept me a bit more up to date.

Certain terms used in the book require explanation. In common parlance 'sound archives' means both the recordings themselves and the facilities in which they are administered. Here 'sound archives' means only the recordings, and the time-honoured term 'repository' is used for the facilities, whether modest or lavish.

Sound archives are compared in many places to 'textual archives'. The latter means archives in the form of written or printed documents. I prefer this term to the more common 'conventional archives'.

Wherever 'cassette' appears without qualification the widely familiar Philips-type compact audio cassette is referred to.

The initials NSA stand for the British Library National Sound Archive.

In order to avoid unnecessary repetition of basic information parts of Chapter 5 refer to sections of British Standard 5454 *Recommendations on the storage and exhibition of archival documents*, while parts of Chapter 4 relate closely to the *Manual of archival description*. Readers may find it useful to obtain copies of both of these.

It is a pleasure to acknowledge the assistance received from many colleagues and friends. In the UK I should single out Peter Copeland, conservation manager at the NSA and incomparable sound recording buff, who read several chapters in draft and made many useful suggestions, prevented numerous errors, and generously drafted notes on noise reduction and aspects of disc and tape replay for my guidance. In the course of his NSA work he also wrote the acetate dubbing code which appears as Appendix III. Adam Green, now county archivist of Somerset, gave me expert advice on computer applications for the Documentation chapter which he also read in draft and criticized to its benefit. Other parts have been read by Rob Perks, recently arrived oral history curator at the NSA whose wide experience and knowledge I have also pillaged, and Anne Thurston of the London University Institute of Commonwealth Studies.

Several other present and former staff of the NSA have provided useful information or insight: John Sims (formerly assistant director) whose original paper on copyright eased me into this subject, in which I am not a specialist; Jonathan Vickers (formerly curator of spoken word recordings); Diana Hull (chief cataloguer); and Lloyd Stickells (chief engineer); and Paul Wilson (jazz and pop assistant).

Others in the UK to whom I am indebted are Mark Jones, head of the BBC Sound Library; Ken Howarth of the North West Sound Archive and Velson Horie of the Manchester Museum who have good ideas on preservation policy; Doc Rowe and Rosemary Dixon (London History Workshop Centre); Laura Kamel (Department of Sound Records, Imperial War Museum); Clifford Harkness (Ulster Folk and Transport Museum); Chris Jeens (Hammersmith and Fulham Archives); Tim Smith (Bradford Heritage Recording Unit); and Geoff Crabb, rights development officer at the National Council for Educational Technology; Michael Cook and Margaret Procter (University of Liverpool Archives).

Overseas my main debt is to the Associated Audio Archives Committee of the Association for Recorded Sound Collections, and particularly to the current ARSC president, Don McCormick, who allowed me to reproduce their draft glossary of sound archive terms which first appeared in *Audio preservation: a planning study* (1988). Mr McCormick also assisted me by showing me round and explaining the practices of the Rodgers and Hammerstein Archive in New York Public Library, as did Gerald Gibson (Motion Picture, Broadcasting and Recorded Sound Division, Library of Congress), Joseph Hickerson and staff of the Archive of Folk Culture, Library of Congress, Leslie Waffen, Charles Mayn and Charles de Arman of the Motion

Picture, Sound and Video Branch, US National Archives, and Dr Ronald Grele of the Oral History Office, Columbia University. Other useful information came from Ernest Dick (Canadian Broadcasting Corporation), Michael Biel (Morehead State University, Kentucky) and Nicholas Carolan (Irish Traditional Music Archive, Dublin). Several of the above have allowed me to reproduce forms used by their organizations, as have Grace Koch (Australian Institute of Aboriginal Studies), Ray Edmondson (Australian National Film and Sound Archive), and Dr Dietrich Schüller (Vienna Phonogrammarchiv).

Above all, however, I must thank the British Library and the National Sound Archive for allowing the use of photographs and copies of documentation, and for providing much of the literature needed in preparing the book and word-processing facilities on which to write it.

This is the first single-author work on the administration of sound archives. There will be many imperfections, which the publishers and I will be happy to have pointed out to us in a friendly way.

Alan Ward

References

1. For approaches to non-archival recordings collected by libraries see, for example, R. Fothergill and I. Butchart, *Non-book materials in libraries*, 2nd ed., Clive Bingley, London, 1984; or G. H. Saddington and E. Cooper, *Audio cassettes as library materials*, 2nd ed., *The Audiovisual Librarian*, London, 1984.

Chapter 1

WHAT ARE SOUND ARCHIVES?

What are archives?

The term 'archives' as commonly used in Europe and North America has both informal and formal meanings. To the man in the street archives are old documents kept in dusty basements and occasionally used for research. To the professional archivist, they have a specific definition which is not dependent on age or physical form but on functional origin.

The essentials of this concept were described by Sir Hilary Jenkinson in 1922. For a document to be regarded as archival, he says, it must have been 'drawn up or used in the course of an administrative or executive transaction . . . and subsequently preserved in their own custody by the person or persons responsible for that transaction or their legitimate successors'. To this he adds: 'Archives were not drawn up in the interest or for the information of posterity.'[1] Jenkinson saw the role of the archivist as custodian of existing accumulations of documents, but since World War II archivists have increasingly taken on an additional function, within the context of the organizations which employ them, as selectors of recently produced documentation (including new formats such as microfilm, computer data and even sound recordings) for long-term retention. Modern archives, as well as fulfilling at least the spirit of Jenkinson's definition, must usually also have been 'selected for permanent preservation'. Postwar writers[2] have also stressed the widely recognized legitimacy of archives selected and preserved purely on the basis of research applications which may be unrelated to the needs or functions of the originators.

The circumstances under which documents were produced and

1

subsequently kept are crucial in determining their status: one of the archivist's main responsibilities is to preserve or reestablish the 'provenance' of the documents in his care so that these circumstances will remain clear to future users. As life goes on so archives naturally tend to form series whose parts are interrelated and interdependent. Much of the evidential value of archives is lost if these series are split up and rearranged according to some scheme unrelated to their provenance. The arrangement and initial description of archives should always reflect their provenance and function, rather than their physical form or their subject content. The inextricable relationship between archives and events also dictates that, as all events are unique, so the related archives will also be unique. Recognition of the uniqueness of individual archival documents has involved archivists in elaborate measures to preserve originals permanently, since some element of archival authenticity must always be lost in the production of duplicates.

Archives as defined by professionals are thus a recognizably distinct, though nevertheless extremely commonplace, form of documentation which, because of the circumstances of their creation and subsequent custody, can – at least on the face of it – provide reliable evidence because their authenticity is 'built in'. Everyday examples of archives are title deeds to property, business contracts, case files built up by government and local authority departments, minutes of meetings, taxation and rating accounts, census returns, architects' plans etc. These archives were, and are, not created for publication and/or retrospective scholarly research, and thus differ fundamentally from library materials; systems used in the organization of libraries, particularly Dewey-type classification schemes, are inappropriate to them.

In recent years the computerization of much institutionally based information supply has permitted the amalgamation of data emanating from both 'archive' and 'library' sources among others. This development relates only to the manipulation of lists, catalogues and indexes already entered on machines; a change in basic organizational concepts has not taken place and should not be assumed. In Britain at least the last fifty years have seen the gradual establishment of specialist archival repositories and departments, particularly under local authorities, with functions and methods separate from the much larger and longer-established public libraries. The distinct character of archives is now well understood and accepted by the library profession and each speciality is represented by its own professional association.

Other types of historical evidence

As part of a study on oral history and oral tradition William Moss identified five types of source material used in historical research, and arranged them in a hierarchy according to their evidential value.[3] According to this the most reliable evidence is provided by 'transactional records' which are essentially archives as described above. (Professional archivists, incidentally, use the term 'records' to mean documents which have yet to go through the process of archival selection or designation. Only those designated for permanent preservation become archives.)

Below them come 'selective records'. These are 'attempts to preserve and to communicate to others descriptions of what is happening at a given time', such as 'audio, video or cinematic recordings of actions and events as they unfold, stenographic notes of conversations as they are taking place, still photographs, and even recorded running descriptions (such as that of a sports broadcaster on the radio)'. The evidential value of these is lower than that of transactional records because they are the product of a third party's observations of events, albeit concurrent, rather than of the events themselves; and it has to be said that the essential function of archivists faced with rapidly accumulating bulky documentation in selecting only a small proportion for permanent retention comes perilously close to reducing these archives to the status of 'selective records'.

On the other hand, as Moss indicates, these and his other forms of non-transactional documentation may provide more *useful* evidence because of the third party's intervention. This point is central to the thesis of Trevor Lummis's recent book in which he exhorts oral history interviewers not to 'duck their responsibility for deciding how evidence should be collected in the most historically useful manner'.[4] This serves to emphasize that in assessing evidence, definitions are of value only in establishing the *prima facie* status of documentation. No category can necessarily be taken at its face value. On the other hand, this status must be established, defined and adhered to throughout processing if custodians are to avoid distorting the evidence still further.

Moss's 'lower' categories are 'recollections', whose evidential value is clearly contaminated by such factors as the inclusion of hearsay, subjective (though unwitting) emphases and omissions, deliberate distortion etc.; 'reflections' (a person's spontaneous thoughts and impressions of the past); and 'analyses and reconstructions' (the products of systematic research).

Archive repositories in the UK and their holdings

Most archive repositories in the UK were established by, and serve the needs of, large organizations such as local authorities or commercial companies. The largest of this type is the Public Record Office which holds the records and archives of government departments. These repositories primarily exist to administer the archives (as defined above) of their organizations and their predecessors, and may also hold archives deposited by outside bodies or individuals. In addition they may hold documentation of the other types described by Moss, particularly in the form of collections of personal correspondence, diaries, research notes and so on, and process and keep them by methods similar to those used on the archives. The use of such respositories for research by the public depends on the function and attitude of the organization overall and whether it is obliged by legislation to provide a service.

Another less numerous form of archival repository exists primarily for the benefit of researchers and acquires virtually all its holdings by deposit or purchase. The manuscript collections of the Bodleian Library or the British Library fall into this category, as do some more recently established bodies such as the Modern Records Centre at the University of Warwick or the Churchill College Archives Centre. The latter generally 'collect' documentation of interest in a defined subject area, much of which will fall into Moss's 'selective records' or 'recollections' categories. Methods of processing tend to reflect the background and experience of the staff. Among the majority of professional archivists there is discernible prejudice against the approach of these subject-based repositories, because the formation of their collections has in the past resulted in the disruption of archival groups and series.

Analogies

In defining sound archives there appears to have been little progress beyond the 'man in the street' stage, but since the formal definition of textual archives is so widely understood and accepted, it is possible to categorize and define sound documentation by analogy. Thus many recordings may be regarded as archival if they are or were integral to the operations of an organization or created by individuals in the course of transactions, and kept permanently by the originators or by others because of the long-term value of their contents. On this basis recordings made by radio stations and kept

for reference or rebroadcast are archival, as are the original recordings made and kept by record companies in the course of their
commercial operations. Unedited recordings of parliamentary
debates, 'audio minutes' of meetings, interviews with suspects
recorded by the police, the roar of aircraft recorded by noise
abatement campaigners, and heart sounds recorded by doctors in
the course of experiments are all archival if selected for permanent
retention by the originators or 'their designated successors'. The
analogy between these types of recording and their equivalents in
textual archives is clear. Similarly, recordings which have been
processed and edited for publication, no matter how old, rare or
systematically collected or housed would not be archival; public
collections of them are analogous with reference libraries. The
inclusion of 'audio-visual resource centres' among sound archive
institutions is also clearly without justification and this is reflected in
the organizational practices of these bodies which are quite inappropriate to archival materials.[5]

Some forms of documentation may be difficult to place in a single
category. Of a piece of personal correspondence, for instance, Moss
writes: 'It is a record of the transaction of letter writing; but, that
does not mean that its content information is indisputable as
evidence of what it reports'.[6] Similarly the recording of an oral
history interview is a transactional record and if preserved might be
regarded as archival. But by their very nature the contents will
reflect the selective contribution of the interviewer and the recollec-
tive or reflective contribution of the informant. Oral history interviews are conducted entirely 'in the interest of or for the information
of posterity' which is not an archival function. (Moss, incidentally,
sees 'Recordings of oral history interviews and oral tradition nar-
rations' as 'selective records of those events' according to his scheme,
but if as is usual the oral history interviewer is also the recordist, his
participation in the event would appear to raise the recordings to the
transactional level.) In practice most repositories holding oral history
interview tapes adopt an 'archival' approach to them, arranging
them and listing their contents in chronological order, rather than
attempting an arrangement based on their often very varied subject
content.[7]

'Documentary' recordings of everyday events also incur a mixture
of definitions. It may be the commercial function of an organization
or individual to make such recordings, which are bound therefore to
be the product of numerous 'transactions', but in choosing to record
only one of a series of events, to leave at half time, or to concentrate

on one or other aspect of a complex occurrence such as a road accident or civil disturbance, a strong selective factor is introduced.

The approach to the organization of sound archives by analogy with textual archives and information carriers is followed throughout this book, though it is readily accepted that the analogy is not perfect.

Sound archives *v.* the rest

Moss's analysis of historical evidence is notable in that it quotes examples from various forms of documentation, both textual and 'audio-visual'. This functional approach which is rare in the UK and Europe but not uncommon in the US and Canada[8] enables us to compare the various media, and to reach the perhaps obvious conclusion that for certain purposes sound recordings provide better quality evidence than written records. Essentially the function of preserving sounds, whether speech, music, specific or ambient noise, animal cry or any other is better performed by recording than by annotation, enabling highly objective archival or 'selective' evidence to be preserved where otherwise only a subjective written evocation is possible. Researchers in the fields of musicology (particularly ethnomusicology), drama, politics, sociology and so on need only ask themselves how much more they would know if the era of sound recording stretched back into the nineteenth century and beyond (and the sound archives profession with it, of course) to realize the inadequacies of written documentation.

If this is true of the past and our knowledge of it, many aspects of the present will be totally inexplicable without 'audio-visual' archives to reflect modern patterns of communication. Today more knowledge is conveyed via the telephone, radio and television than by means of reading and correspondence; the pattern of archive retention must reflect this if a balanced view of the present is to be preserved for the future.

However, the potential of sound archives continues to be undervalued for a number of reasons. Prejudice and ignorance among scholars and archivists is the least excusable but is still widespread. Behind this may lie the feeling that materials and techniques which owe their development largely to the entertainment industry must be of ephemeral interest and cannot be taken seriously. On the other hand there are some genuine drawbacks which continue to put people off. The most serious results from the excellence of sound recordings as complete evidence: since everything has been preserved, everything has to be interpreted. Good old written archives on the other hand already represent a distillation, which is easily scanned and assessed by its appearance and diplomatic. Recording what is said at a meeting may provide a complete unbiased record, but duplicating this and sending it round the participants instead of written minutes will not serve the required purpose. Written minutes must therefore be drawn up using the recording as an *aide-memoire*. This sometimes happens, but most secretaries understandably prefer to get the job done while the meeting is in progress.

The only organization in the UK which considers all its meetings to be important enough to record in their entirety is Parliament, and this relatively recent development stemmed mainly from the decision to permit the broadcasting of debates rather than from an independently felt need to establish an 'audio-Hansard'.

Of course the contents of many sound recordings cannot be represented in written form but the costly process of listening, dependent on obsolescent machines and fragile media of relatively short life, remains inescapable and to many unwelcome. These cautious attitudes to the technical complexities and intangible form of sound recordings may well be altered as more archivists and researchers are forced to deal with machine readable documentation.

Sound archivists have never enjoyed the luxury of 'permanent' carriers like parchment and non-acidic paper: if sounds are to survive for ever they must be transferred to new carriers sooner or later. Many custodians therefore regard the *carriers* of sound archives as of little importance so long as the unadulterated *sounds* remain available, and there is logic in this, although it is not a view which this writer necessarily wishes to encourage.

Certainly carrier and sound are more divisible than paper and writing. Until the 1940s for example almost all sound recordings were made by one or other 'direct cut' process, which meant that the concept of 'editing' hardly existed, particularly in the preparation of commercially published discs. A singer might therefore record a song on wax from which a disc pressing master would be directly produced, with an identifying matrix number inscribed in it. All the pressings from this master would be identical to each other and to the original wax, although the wax would not usually be playable and was normally shaved for reuse. Here the sound recorded is unique but there are numerous identical carriers, all easily authenticated by the matrix number. Since the only unique element is the sound, this according to conventional principles must be the archival element.[9]

7

Such a situation would have been outside Sir Hilary Jenkinson's experience, and that of most archivists until perhaps ten or even five years ago; but no longer. With the need for permanent preservation of machine readable documentation, textual archivists have now to tackle information capable of such exact duplication that its carriers are relatively unimportant, certainly short lived (the computer industry regards the reliable lifespan of magnetic tape with much less optimism than the sound engineering fraternity) and entirely dependent on machines whose rate of obsolescence is staggering even by sound recording standards.

As a general statement, although sound recordings are easy to duplicate exactly they are difficult to alter without this interference being detectable – and owing to their complexity this applies equally to digitally stored recordings which are the most directly comparable with machine-readable textual archives.[10] No such check on authenticity is available with computer-dependent text; in fact, although one may administer machine-readable archives by analogy with their written predecessors, there appears to be no means at all of monitoring their status.[11] Sound archives are easier to authenticate, preserve and use than machine-readable textual archives.

Sound archives in Britain

A *Directory of recorded sound resources in the United Kingdom* has recently been published by the NSA.[12] Although the survey on which it was based is already in need of revision, the directory does give a clear indication of the nature and balance of activity. It is clear that the 'subject-based research collections', mostly small and narrow in scope, predominate. About 500 collections were identified altogether and these can be broken down into broad categories based on geographical and subject coverage.

National and international collections

These receive material relating to any part of the UK and, where appropriate, beyond. The largest is the *National Sound Archive* which became a department of the British Library in 1983, having been set up as the British Institute of Recorded Sound in the late 1940s. It holds recordings on all but the most esoteric media from all over the world and from all periods, but concentrates on British and Commonwealth or ex-Commonwealth material. Its approach is strongly subject-based and a very high proportion of its holdings consists of commercially published discs and recordings of BBC broadcasts. It also makes its own field recordings, mainly of performing arts events, but also wildlife and mechanical sounds, oral history, dialect speech etc., and has received a number of important archival collections from individual recordists, record companies and radio stations. It is shortly to become the repository for the relatively small 'official' government sound archives, including older Parliamentary Sound Archive material and recordings made by the Central Office of Information.

The Department of Sound Records at the *Imperial War Museum* has a similarly wide, though less bulky, range of recordings in its subject field: twentieth-century warfare involving the UK or Commonwealth. The core of its collection, however, consists of oral history interviews emanating from the numerous formally defined projects mounted by the Department since its inception in the 1960s.

The Centre of English Cultural Tradition and Language holds the main collection of English dialect and folklife recordings, consisting almost entirely of field recordings on tape, while the sound recordings departments of the *Welsh Folk Museum* at St Fagans near Cardiff, the *Ulster Folk and Transport Museum* at Cultra, Co. Down, and the *School of Scottish Studies* at Edinburgh University fulfil similar functions for Wales, Northern Ireland and Scotland. An *Irish Traditional Music Archive* has recently been established in Dublin which collects tape recordings and commercial discs, particularly in the field of traditional music, and the old-established collection of the Irish Folklore Commission, originally on wax cylinders and later on tape, of Irish traditional song, music and speech, is now housed at the Department of Irish Folklore, University College, Dublin.

There are also a number of significant smaller collections with a national brief, often run by organizations which collect literature and other documentation as well. Examples are the *British Music Information Centre* which is concerned with twentieth-century British classical music, and the *Department of Sociology, Essex University* (life history interviews illustrating early twentieth-century work and family experience).

Regional collections

There appears to be only one organization which really fits this description, the *North West Sound Archive* based at Clitheroe near Manchester, which holds archival recordings transferred from several local radio stations, oral history, dialect, music, and documentary recordings relating to the region, and a small amount of commercially published material. In addition the *London History Workshop Centre Sound and Video Archive* receives and processes oral history recordings made by individuals and groups in the Greater London area. At the time of writing the future of both these organizations is threatened by funding problems.

Local collections

These represent the most common form of sound recording collection in Britain. The vast majority consist of oral history interviews recorded and processed by local groups or institutions. Before 1980 a number of evening institute classes, local history societies etc. were carrying out interviews with older local residents on a small scale, and the staff of several local record offices, libraries and museums were undertaking oral history projects, some long established and very ambitious such as that based at *Walsall Archive Service*. A major expansion took place following the advent of Community Programmes funded by the Manpower Services Commission, however, through which interviewers could be employed and larger-scale projects undertaken. These projects continued to be based on local institutions, or were set up in some cases as independent organizations.

Prominent examples of the latter type are *Bradford Heritage Recording Unit, Kirklees Sound Archive*, the *Avon County Community Environment Scheme*, and the *Ilfracombe and District Community Archive*. With the change in the government's strategy on employment training, many of these organizations have been forced to shrink or close down. In most cases arrangements have been made for the recordings and documentation to be housed in local libraries.

Specialist collections

There are a number of collections covering narrow subject fields which consist of or embrace archival sound recordings. A random selection might include the collection of anthropological field recordings on wax cylinders at the *Pitt Rivers Museum*, the *British Antarctic Survey*'s oral history recordings, Countess von Staufer's privately-run *Christmas Archives*, the *History of Advertising Trust* collection and the *Britten-Pears Library*.

Sound archives built up by organizations in the course of business are less numerous in Britain than the subject collections, and are found mainly in the fields of radio broadcasting and commercial record production. The leading radio archive, and one of the great collections of sound recordings in the world, is of course the *BBC Sound Library* which was established c. 1933 and caters primarily for the BBC national networks. Its selection criteria and administrative procedures are geared to BBC production needs and the likelihood of rebroadcast, not to the requirements of researchers, for whom better access to broadcast material is provided at the National Sound Archive. The BBC also runs numerous local radio stations, and these together with their commercially-run competitors make local arrangements to preserve valued recordings, either on the premises, like *Radio Bristol* and *Radio Viking*, or at a local record office or library, like *Radio Stoke on Trent* at Stoke Central Library or *Piccadilly Radio* at the North West Sound Archive. There is no central sound archive for the local commercial stations, though the NSA houses a range of material received directly or indirectly from independent stations.

Britain also has an internationally famous record company collection: the *EMI Archive* which again exists primarily for commercial needs, although numbers of serious researchers and enquirers have enjoyed generous assistance over the years. Its holdings of recordings and related documentation go back to the turn of the century, a longevity with which no others can compete since the forerunner of the present company, the Gramophone and Typewriter Company, was the earliest record company established in Britain.

The only government-run recordings collection is the *Parliamentary Sound Archive* which was set up following the decision to broadcast portions of parliamentary debates; it receives a 'clean feed' of unedited recordings from the equipment set up by the BBC in the House of Lords and House of Commons. At present its holdings are not available to the public, but recordings more than seven years old are transferred to the NSA where anyone may listen to them.

Numerous recordings are made by commercial firms and other concerns, whether 'media' related (such as advertising agencies) or simply as alternatives to written documentation, but little of this appears to be thought worthy of permanent preservation, and those firms whose names appear in the NSA's *Directory* do so normally because they have begun to collect or record oral history interviews. Several orchestras and theatres maintain collections of recordings for musicians' and actors' reference, and/or record their rehearsals and performances, but because sensitive copyright issues are involved, these recordings are rarely available to outsiders.

The British Association of Sound Collections

One of the reasons for the great variety of approaches to the administration of sound archives in Britain, and for the predominance of subject-based collections, is the equally varied experience of those involved. Even in the large institutions there are few who trained as archivists; those with a background in librarianship are more typical. Some small collections are run by archivists or librarians as part of a wider range of duties. But probably the most common 'sound archivist' is the enthusiast or specialist in a particular subject area. A professional association like the Society of Archivists or Library Association would be inappropriate for such a small and miscellaneous group and for several years it was thought that a national organization of any kind would not be viable. Thus it was natural that a number of BBC and national collection staff should arrange to form a branch of the wider International Association of Sound Archives rather than an independent association as their counterparts in the USA had done. This arrangement continued almost unchanged from 1976 to 1986, when members renamed the branch the British Association of Sound Collections, reflecting the increasing number of collections in Britain and the greater need for specific local provision. A local subscription is now collected, more local events are staged, and the series of training courses started in 1985 has enjoyed increasing support. Membership has risen from around 35 to around 100, and while the variety remains, it is clear that the involvement of the MSC in particular has given British sound archives a distinct national character.

References

1. H. Jenkinson, *A manual of archive administration*, 2nd ed., revised by R. H. Ellis, Lund Humphries, London, 1965, p. 11. Although by no means the first to approach and define archives in this manner, Jenkinson's book has been the most influential among English-speaking professional archivists.
2. For example, T. R. Schellenberg, *Modern archives: principles and techniques,* University of Chicago Press, Chicago, 1956; M. G. Cook, *Archives administration*, Dawson, 1977.
3. The article originally appeared as W. W. Moss, 'Oral history: an appreciation' in *The American Archivist*, vol. 40, no. 4, October 1977, and was incorporated in a slightly revised form as the first chapter in W. W. Moss and P. C. Mazikana, *Archives, oral history and oral tradition:*

a RAMP Study, UNESCO, Paris, 1986. References here are to the RAMP study.

4. T. Lummis, *Listening to history,* Hutchinson, London, 1987, p. 43; and he later cites examples of impeccably Jenkinsonian archives, entirely transactional in character, which nevertheless convey false information (*ibid.,* ch. 7).

5. See also D. Roberts, 'Archives and sound archives – what's the difference?' in *Archives and Manuscripts* (Journal of the Australian Society of Archivists), vol. 12, no. 2, November 1984.

6. Moss and Mazikana, *op. cit.,* p. 6.

7. For the involvement of archivists in oral history see R. Lochead, 'Oral history: the role of the archivist' and R. Grele, 'Oral history and archives' in *Phonographic Bulletin,* vol. 37, November 1983, pp. 3 and 12.

8. See for instance L. C. Waffen, 'Recorded sound in the National Archives of the United States' in *Phonographic Bulletin,* vol. 14, 1976, p. 4.

9. The 'archival' character of published direct-cut recordings is reflected in postwar discographical practice relating to jazz 78s. Using matrix numbers as a starting point, the date and place of recording, personnel present, material recorded, and other circumstances can be established, and an accurate impression of a performer or band's career derived from this information. A note of the labels and catalogue numbers under which the recording may have been issued can then be provided as a secondary operation. As a starting point see Brian Rust, *Brian Rust's guide to discography,* Greenwood Press, Westport, 1980.

10. See T. Owen, 'Forensic audio and video – theory and applications' in *Journal of the Audio Engineering Society,* vol. 36, no. 1/2, 1988, pp. 34–41.

11. See, for instance, M. G. Cook, *Archives and the computer,* 2nd ed., Butterworths, London, 1986, ch. 4; and P. Emmerson, 'Some legal aspects' in M. G. Cook (ed.), *Approaches to problems in records management II: computer-generated records,* London, Society of Archivists, 1986.

12. L. Weerasinghe (ed.), *Directory of recorded sound resources in the United Kingdom,* The British Library, London, 1989.

Chapter 2

ACQUIRING SOUND ARCHIVES

Introduction

The function of sound archive repositories is to preserve sound recordings and make them available. These activities will take place in the context of local circumstances, which will dictate the repository's terms of reference. These terms should be written down at an early stage; they will be needed in communications with depositors or potential sponsors, in descriptive literature and publicity or whenever the repository's work has to be explained or justified. A principal element in this *raison d'être* will be the acquisitions policy: which agencies, departments etc. are served by the repository and on what authority; which geographical or subject areas are covered, and which are not; what present and future demands are being catered for; and so on.

The Australian National Film and Sound Archive is currently engaged in this process and examples of its general policy statements, and a draft version of its acquisitions policy statement, are given in Appendices VI and VII.

Repositories are set up and sound archives acquired in response to an administrative or cultural need. Recordings are being made which require permanent preservation for future use; present and future researchers (in the broadest sense) want access to recordings which may not otherwise survive. It is the archivist's job to provide the necessary facilities for storage and retrieval. Some sound archivists are also involved in making recordings, just as some textual archivists play a role in the management of organizations whose documentation they will subsequently care for. But this involvement should not be allowed to obscure the archival function, which is essentially reactive, though not usually passive.

Although the holdings of a repository are often described as 'collections', the popular image of collecting, as in collecting butterflies, antiques, or rare books, does not or should not apply to the role of the sound archivist. Collectors of recordings who have rifled through redundant series of tapes in order to remove the odd political speech or music performance by some personality, while discarding the rest, remind one of those collectors who have bought up old personal correspondence in order to cut off the Victorian stamps and postmarks, or the signatures of the famous or notorious. Archivists are there to prevent this sort of opportunism.

Sound archive repositories receive three main types of recordings: (a) those produced by the organization which runs the repository and employs the sound archive staff – borrowing a term from the textual archive sphere, these may be referred to as *inherited recordings*; (b) recordings produced by bodies and individuals outside the employing organization, which may be referred to as *deposited recordings*; (c) recordings commissioned by the repository.

While there are many textual archive repositories which receive both inherited and deposited materials, this is rare in the world of sound archives: either the repository is run by, say, a radio organization or record company and deals only with the materials produced by that organization, or it is supported by public or private funds to receive deposits of material in a specified geographical or subject area. But both types of repository are frequently involved in commissioning recordings.

Inherited recordings

Modern records management

In the field of textual archives many custodians nowadays play an expert role in the management of recently produced documentation, setting up systems through which office paperwork is systematically destroyed if no longer required, kept for a period until a decision to preserve or destroy can be made, or transferred immediately to 'the archives' for permanent preservation. This 'modern records management' is well established and there is plenty to read on its techniques.[1]

Some sound archivists working for record companies or radio stations, or with responsibility for recordings made by government departments, may find it useful to acquaint themselves with the practice of modern records management as a means of bringing

15

order to situations where large numbers of recordings are falling out of use. It is difficult to implement unless the archivist has sufficient authority to ensure that established systems are adhered to. The essential element in the technique is the 'transmittal' procedure. For this a form or its computer input equivalent is completed by the originator on which the material is described and its transfer to the 'records centre' authorized. A typical 'records transfer form' from the relatively small-scale system operated in the London Borough of Hammersmith and Fulham is shown in Figure 2.1 together with its functional successor, the form used to input the same information into the recently established computer system (Figure 2.2).

Further transmittal forms are reproduced in the Society of American Archivists' *Archival Forms Manual*.[2] In most systems the future of each type of material will already have been decided through consultation between its creators and the archivist, and a 'retention schedule' drawn up. In others an indication may be given on the transmittal form, and the latter arrangement may be best for transfers of sound recordings where individual decisions often have to be made. Either way the initial decision as to future usefulness and need for retention is taken by the creators, not in retrospect by the archivist.

The usual options available are immediate disposal, disposal after a specified period, review after a specified period, when the creators or their successors get a second chance to assess the material, and permanent retention. Most systems have an arrangement built in whereby the archivist can keep things which the creators are happy to have destroyed (though not vice-versa, of course). Here the broader selection criteria, as discussed below in 'Deposited recordings', will be needed, but it is rare for material seen as ephemeral by creators to be kept by the archivist, except perhaps as the product of a sampling exercise in which a small representation of a long series of similar material is kept.[3] Organizations big enough to benefit from formal transfer procedures such as these are likely also to have the resources to install online computer access to the documentation compiled. A suitable programme can then be written or adapted to indicate which material has been destroyed, which is due for review on a certain date, and which is for transfer to permanent storage.[4]

Recent developments at the BBC Sound Library

Records management techniques enable the archivist to become more involved in and knowledgeable about the organization, while creators play a part in deciding which material is to be kept and

LONDON BOROUGH OF HAMMERSMITH PUBLIC LIBRARIES: ARCHIVES DEPARTMENT

RECORDS TRANSFER FORM

For Archives Department's use	
Location	Consignment no.

To be completed by the officer transferring records and placed with records at Records Transfer Point

DEPARTMENT

SECTION

FUTURE RETENTION

This section to be completed if records are not already subject to an agreed destruction schedule.

Department's reference(s)	Description of records	Covering dates		Preserve permanently (tick)	Review after (insert no. of years)	Destroy after
		from	to			

Signature of officer transferring records ....:.................... Date ....

Figure 2.1

Hammersmith & Fulham

Archives Dept: Records Management System

RECORDS TRANSFER FORM

PAGE........ OF......

To be completed **in duplicate** by the officer transferring records and both copies placed with records at Records Transfer Point.

CL	DOCUMENT REFERENCE	DOCUMENT TITLE	FROM: D M Y	TO: D M Y	ACTION	ACTION DATE M Y	A.R.M.S. USE ONLY

A.R.M.S. USE ONLY		
Processed by:-		Consignment Number
Date		

RECORDS FROM:

Code ....

Name ....

Dept ....

Date ....

Signature ....

Figure 2.2

should therefore be able to rely on finding what they need. At the headquarters of BBC Radio however, such cooperation could not always be relied on until recently, despite the long existence and international recognition enjoyed by the Sound Library. Because recordings were selected in retrospect by Sound Library staff working outside production areas, some individual producers or departments tended to build up their own unofficial collections of recordings because they lacked confidence in (and sometimes even knowledge of) the library's ability to keep and retrieve valuable material.[5] A more integrated system involving greater cooperation and participation by producers is now steadily replacing the older methods.

The first phase in this does not have a clear equivalent in management systems for textual records: about five years ago the library took over the acquisition and issue of blank tape, together with responsibility for budgeting and stock control. A computer-based booking-out system was set up (it is currently being upgraded into an online form known as ECHO) through which the issue of numbered blank tapes to production departments is documented. After use in programme-making the tapes return to the library's control in the current recordings library (the equivalent of the interim storage facility in a modern records management system) and a note of their contents added to existing information on the computer. In consultation with departments, tapes used in interme-diate stages of production, for which there is no further require-ment, can be removed and recycled, while more significant tapes are kept for a period pending a decision on their long-term future.

In fact the system was set up primarily to monitor and control patterns of tape use by departments. By documenting the destina-tion of each individual tape, budgeting could be better directed and extravagance identified. Almost incidentally however the Sound Library began to play a practical role in day-to-day aspects of production, which could no longer be ignored. New channels of communication were established and the role and function of the Sound Library more widely acknowledged.

More recently further steps have been taken. It has been possible via the computer to draw up lists of material held in the current recordings library which producers can scrutinize and make decisions about. As backlogs have been reduced less time has been spent by the Sound Library in retrospective appraisal and more in liaising with departments in order to increase the efficiency of selection by involving production staff and building up confidence. By taking over the initial documentation and management of recordings, while continuing with its traditional role as the manager of 'historic' material, the Sound Library has increased its status and at present appears well placed to take effective control of all aspects of the retention and documentation of recordings.

Bulk transfers

Even if the sound archivist is able to set up a controlled system through which recordings are assessed and managed as they fall out of use, there may still be a mass of ill-sorted earlier material to deal with. An approach to these older recordings might be to carry out a survey using a standard form to gather information. Again this is a well-established procedure in the textual archives field and there is plenty of published guidance[6] And there will be some sound archivists without sufficient status to influence management policy, whose work will typically consist of sorting out bulk transfers of discarded tapes. For them the fact that they are actually employed by the organization which also produces the recordings counts for little; the best approach will be to appraise and process the material as if it were being offered by an outside body (see 'Deposited recordings' below), while taking suitable opportunities to alert senior managers to the savings and greater efficiency to be gained from better methods.

Deposited recordings

Appraisal

The sound archivist may at least have had a chance to influence policies governing the survival of inherited recordings, but decisions concerning deposits must be retrospective. For this purpose criteria need to be drawn up and the material on offer 'appraised' in the light of these. 'Appraisal' is an American term meaning the process of assessment and selection.[7]

The establishment of appraisal criteria, and many other aspects of appraisal in various contexts, has been usefully examined in the IASA compilation *Selection in sound archives*.[8] The following legitimate areas of concern, arranged in order of overall importance, should influence the repository's appraisal standards.

Obligations   Is the repository obliged to accept the material for legal or constitutional reasons, or as part of an existing agreement?

19

Appropriateness and relevance Does the material fall within the repository's brief? If not it may be worth referring it elsewhere. Will the material increase the usefulness of similar or related recordings already held?

Relative 'importance' Is the individual, organization or activity which produced the recordings of any significance in the context of the repository and the constituency it serves? The answer will depend on the repository's specific terms of reference.

Will the recordings provide information of interest or use to the repository's present or future users? If so, will they be sufficiently useful to justify the costs involved in keeping them? Any calculation of running costs will normally include salaried staff time, annual value of storage occupied, equipment costs etc., but figures are open to considerable manipulation, especially where premises are shared with a larger organization which pays most of the overheads, and would still have to pay them even if the sound archive repository did not exist.

Uniqueness and rarity Is the material the only source, or one of only a few sources, of information about its subject? Are there any or many other recordings like it? In this context an informed judgement can only be made if the sound archivist knows what is held elsewhere. As a start he could do worse in the UK than read the *Directory of recorded sound resources* and join the British Association of Sound Collections. In the oral history field the most useful initial moves are to contact the oral history curator at the NSA, and join the Oral History Society.

Status Are the recordings original or copies of recordings held elsewhere? Copies may still be of value if the originals are inaccessible to the repository's users owing to geographical remoteness or restrictive conditions of custody.

Condition If the material is in poor condition, is it sufficiently important to justify the conservation work required? If it is of marginal interest it may be worth keeping because it has been better looked after than other available sources.

Integrity Can the recordings be placed in context and provide a useful reflection of events as they took place? Do they form part of a series of recordings and interrelate with them? Or are they a miscellaneous accumulation of separate 'good examples'? Does this matter?

Availability of documentation   Undocumented or poorly documented recordings require so much time to process that the repository may never have the resources to make them available for use. On investigation undocumented recordings may turn out, against expectations, to be of little worth. Undocumented recordings should only be kept if they are of the greatest interest under other criteria, for instance because of their early date.

Functional aptitude   Recordings are time-consuming to process compared with written documents. If the recordings contain information which is also available in written form (e.g. autobiographical material in memoires and correspondence), only a small sample, if any, may be worth retaining.

Internal hierarchy and duplication   Within an accumulation of recordings not all may be originals; in fact a high proportion may be duplicates produced in the course of editing and research which contribute nothing of value and may therefore be discarded. On the other hand, where a number of original recordings have been edited down in the course of producing a final master tape for publication, the complete originals may be of greater long-term interest than the publication. Although the process of weeding out low-value material can sometimes take more time than it saves in the field of textual archives, with sound archives it is likely to be worthwhile because recordings take longer to process than their textual equivalents. Advice on the role and relative importance of recordings on offer from an organization or commercial concern is best sought from those who made or formerly looked after the recordings. A recorded interview can be an appropriate way to go about this.

Access and rights limitations   Certain acquisitions may be ruled out if the current owner will not agree to allow the material to be copied and studied in accordance with the normal policy of the repository. If a depositor wishes to impose conditions, the archivist should immediately weigh the value of the material against the resources needed to administer the restrictions. The material may also be subject to complicated copyright ownership which renders it 'not worth the hassle'.

Intrinsic character   Some recordings may be worth keeping as 'examples' or 'artefacts' even though their contents are available elsewhere or have no value, particularly if their personal associations, unusual appearance or technical form can be used in publicity to promote the work of the repository. The US National Archives and Records Service formulated a list of 'qualities and characteristics of records with intrinsic value' relating to archives on all media in 1982, as a guide to those faced with the problem of whether to retain records or archives in their original form after they had been copied or miniaturized.[9] The following summary of the characteristics listed which relate to sound archives may help in a situation where intrinsic value is being used as a criterion for retention:

- physical form as a subject for study, e.g. as evidence of technological development
- aesthetic or artistic quality
- unique or curious physical features
- age in that it provides the quality of uniqueness
- value for use as exhibits
- questionable authenticity, date, author etc. or other characteristic only ascertainable by physical examination
- general interest because of direct association with famous or historically significant people, places, events etc
- significance as documentation of the establishment or continuing legal basis of an agency or institution.

'Intrinsic value' should not be used as an appraisal criterion except on material which would otherwise be destroyed.

As a general rule the disposal of original recordings once their contents have been duplicated is not recommended.

Capacity of the repository   Unlike the above criteria which relate to the characteristics of the recordings on offer, this final criterion concerns the repository's capacity to house and deal with the material. The validity of this criterion is subject to debate. Those who value primarily the preservation aspects of the archivist's role may consider that mere practical circumstances, quite possibly temporary, should not influence appraisal except, perhaps, if acceptance and preservation would overwhelm all activity and lead directly to failure. The fact is, however, that most repositories can find *somewhere* to keep deposited material which they cannot process immediately. Sound archives by comparison with textual archives are very compact. But those who place more emphasis on the service role of the repository – 'What's the point of keeping it if nobody can use it?' – argue that archivists are actually doing themselves and their clients a disservice by taking on more than they can immediately cope with.

In practice the capacity of the repository should only be considered in conjunction with other factors such as the relative importance of the material. In a borderline case, shortage of space or processing capacity might tip the balance in favour of refusal or disposal. If the material is considered worth keeping, but because of its bulk or complexity it is impossible for the repository to handle it, additional resources should be sought, perhaps from grant-making agencies or through a public appeal. As a last resort attempts should be made to find suitable accommodation elsewhere.

Terms of deposit

Transfer documentation　When recordings are purchased the vendor is rarely in a position to impose conditions on the repository, so no formalities are likely to be needed beyond his invoice. When recordings are accepted without financial consideration a written agreement should be made with the depositor. In most cases the sound archivist should set out the terms in a letter to which the depositor will give consent in writing. If a number of similar deposits are received, a preprinted form of agreement could be drawn up, to be signed by both parties. In rare cases a legal document may be necessary. The circumstances will probably be similar to those surrounding the transfer of private papers to repositories, about which the Society of Archivists has recently published a useful leaflet.[10] In all cases the sound archivist should aim to negotiate conditions which are favourable to the repository, particularly with regard to access and use of the material.

Acceptable conditions　It is important to establish who owns the recordings and related copyright or other rights, and whether the depositor is entitled to transfer them to the repository. Ideally the recordings should be handed over as a gift, but if the depositor wishes to retain nominal ownership by describing the transfer as a 'permanent loan' this makes little difference in practice. Loans which are not permanent should be strictly avoided unless the material is very important and there is no alternative. It should be pointed out to depositors who suggest loan terms that the repository will incur considerable expense in storing and processing the recordings over the years, and that it cannot be expected to commit these resources without a return. A compromise may be possible: the repository may

23

agree to lend back a few of the items (preferably in the form of copies; the average number per year should be stated in the agreement), or in the case of a small accumulation to supply a complete set of copies. The archivist's poorest option is to make a set of copies for retention and hand the originals back, perhaps with an agreement that the originals will eventually reach the repository as a bequest. In the early days of a repository's existence it may be necessary to make these sorts of arrangements in order to encourage deposits and build up holdings, but the sound archivist should aim to cut down this essentially unproductive activity as time goes on. As the usefulness and prestige of the repository grows, depositors should be encouraged to see the transfer of their materials as a privilege.

It is not unknown for commercial companies to offer recordings to repositories in order to avoid high storage charges elsewhere. If this is suspected the recordings should be very carefully appraised and only accepted on terms which are completely acceptable to the repository.

Restrictions Limitations on the use of deposited recordings for research, publication, exhibition etc. may be required by depositors or initiated by the sound archivist. Such restrictions should not be imposed or conceded lightly as they are inconvenient and costly to administer and obviously reduce the usefulness of the recordings. The need for restrictions is normally confined to recordings of speech which contain personal references. Where the depositor is involved, the restrictions should be stated in the transfer documentation, together with an expiry date and, if possible, a statement of circumstances under which they may be relaxed.

Copyright Where possible sound archivists should try to achieve an assignment of copyright, in recordings and their contents, to the repository, though in practice this is usual only in the case of oral history interview recordings. Sample forms of agreement on access and copyright are given in Chapter 3, 'Copyright and access in practice', and in 'Commissioned recordings', below.

Accompanying paperwork It is essential that written material relating to recordings is acquired and retained, particularly if it includes contracts, licences and rights assignments. Recordings which can stand alone without the need for supporting paperwork, ranging from scribbled notes on containers and labels to filing cabinets full of correspondence and accounts, are virtually unknown. This will be obvious to archivists whose main work is with written documents, but receives less emphasis among custodians from other backgrounds.

A description of how written archives should be managed would be out of place here; for those in doubt advice is best sought from a local professionally staffed record office. Unless suitable accommodation is completely lacking it is best to keep the papers on the same premises as the recordings for ease of reference, but the shelving and containers required for each will probably be different and they should not be lumped together.

Notebooks and logs kept by field recordists and researchers should be acquired where they exist, if necessary in copy form. Where they do not, donors should be asked to write down all relevant information, perhaps on a form like the one illustrated in Figure 2.4 as used for collecting data from current project workers.

Commissioned recordings

Repositories which run oral history or 'event' recording programmes often commission interviewers or technicians to make the recordings. Alternatively students and researchers who wish to make recordings as part of their assignments may approach the repository for support, or offer to make recordings as an adjunct to other activities in a remote area. In appropriate cases a deal may be struck whereby the repository receives the original recordings to add to its collections in return for providing blank tape and possibly lending items of equipment. Whatever the arrangement care must be taken to document the materials provided and the undertakings given, and to obtain from the recordist detailed information about the circumstances of the recording, the equipment used, and the material recorded. It should be a condition of any arrangement or contract that documentation required by the repository must be provided. Long experience at the NSA, for instance, indicates that researchers and itinerant recordists frequently fail to answer correspondence and often disappear without trace once their projects are complete, so that the retrospective gathering of this or that vital piece of information is frustrated.

The Archives of Traditional Music in the Folklore Institute of the University of Indiana uses preprinted forms to gather the required administrative information systematically. On the two-page 'Application for blank tape loans' (see Figure 2.3) the nature of proposals, the likely quality of their outcome, and the procedures required by the archives are set out.

ARCHIVES OF TRADITIONAL MUSIC
Morrison Hall 117
Indiana University
Bloomington, Indiana 47405-2501
(812) 855-8632

APPLICATION FOR BLANK TAPE LOANS

NAME: _____

INSTITUTION: _____ DEPT.: _____

PERMANENT ADDRESS: _____

_____

_____

INSTITUTIONAL ADDRESS OVERSEAS [OR U. S. ADDRESS TO WHICH TAPE SHOULD BE SHIPPED]:

_____

_____

_____

PLAN AND PURPOSE OF FIELDWORK PROJECT [PLEASE ATTACH COPY OF RELEVANT GRANT PROPOSAL]:

PREVIOUS RECORDING EXPERIENCE?: YES ____ NO ____ HOURS ESTIMATED TO BE SPENT RECORDING:

BRAND NAME AND TYPE OF TAPE RECORDER(S):

AMOUNT AND FORMAT OF REQUESTED TAPE [LIMITED TO 20 AUDIO TAPES OR 10 VIDEO TAPES PER APPLICATION]:

     5" REEL _____ 7" REEL _____ 10" REEL _____

     60-MINUTE CASSETTE: _____ 90-MINUTE CASSETTE: _____

     VHS VIDEOTAPE: _____ BETA VIDEOTAPE: _____ OTHER: _____

DOCUMENTATION:
     WE EXPECT ALL TAPES TO BE ACCOMPANIED BY INDEXES, GENRE OR SUBJECT TITLES, AND BASIC INFORMATION ON DATES, LOCATIONS, PERFORMERS, AND PERFORMANCE CONTEXTS.

OTHER DOCUMENTATION: _____

     TEXT TRANSCRIPTIONS: _____ PHOTOGRAPHS: _____

     OTHER (SPECIFY): _____

Figure 2.3   Application for blank tape loans.

ACQUIRING SOUND ARCHIVES

Tapes being loaned to you are the physical property of Indiana University, and all tapes, blank, filled, or broken, should be returned to the Archives as soon after recording as possible, during or after the field research. A charge of $20.00 per open-reel tape, $10.00 per cassette tape, and $15.00 for videotape will be made for tapes not returned.

Tapes will be returned (date): _____

Collectors will receive one set of copies gratis if requested.
Collector's copies needed (yes or no): tape: _____ documentation: _____
Please note: Collector's copies will be withheld until appropriate documentation is received.

After your collection of materials is deposited, we will sign a contract with you whereby you may stipulate what restrictions you would wish to place on its use. You own the intellectual rights to the material collected, and are also responsible for any rights the performer/consultant holds.

It is the collector's responsibility to obtain a written statement from the performers/consultants concerning their rights to and use of recorded data.

It is also the collector's responsibility to determine if research permits require the deposit of copies of field recordings in archives or other institutions in the country in which the research is conducted.

REFERENCES:

1. _____
   (NAME)   (ADDRESS)   (PHONE)

2. _____
   (NAME)   (ADDRESS)   (PHONE)

SIGNED: _____

DATE: _____

_____

REFERENCES CHECKED: _____

ACTION TAKEN: _____

_____ DATE: _____
(SIGNATURE OF ATM DIRECTOR OR REPRESENTATIVE)

TAPES SHIPPED: _____ BY WHOM: _____

Figure 2.3   (reverse side)

Applicants also receive guidance on the repository's expectations prepared from a pre-prepared leaflet which prescribes tape recording speeds and other standards. The receipt of the recordings and documentation and other readily available information are entered on the 'Collection summary' form (see Figure 2.4)..

A 'Contract of deposit of materials' form (similar to the AIAS 'Deposit of materials' form Chapter 3, Figure 3.7., but suggesting fewer options) is also signed, enabling any restrictions applying to the recordings to be stipulated.

A form on which recordists can write up descriptive information, either in the field or on return to the repository, is also useful. Of several examples available, the NSA's version (Figure 2.5) could serve as a basis for designs to suit local requirements.

Repositories lending equipment to fieldworkers could follow the example of the world's first sound archive, the Phonogrammarchiv der Österreichischen Akademie der Wissenschaften, which uses a form on which the recorder, case, microphone, windshield, mic stand, battery, empty spools and sundries, as well as blank tape are described and signed for (see Figure 2.6).

Finally the copyright ownership in commissioned recordings needs to be clearly documented and forms for use by recordists are usually provided by the repository which may also cover performers' rights and access restrictions (see Chapter 3).

INDIANA UNIVERSITY
ARCHIVES OF TRADITIONAL MUSIC
COLLECTION SUMMARY

STAFF USE ONLY:

acc. no: _____   shelf nos: _____
ATL no: _____   _____
OCLC no.: _____   _____

collector/depositor: _____

address: _____

_____

_____

phone: _____   date collection received: _____

date contract signed: _____   option: _____

provenance (if not collector): _____

ORIGINAL MATERIALS IN COLLECTION

_____ reels: size _____ feet _____ ips _____ track configuration _____

_____ cassettes: 60-minute _____ 90-minute _____ other _____

_____ discs: 7" _____ 10" _____ 12" _____ 16" _____ other _____

_____ cylinders: 4" _____ 6" _____ concert _____ other _____

_____ videotape: b&w _____ color _____ beta _____ vhs _____ format _____

original recordings? _____ copies of originals? _____ generation _____

if copies, format of originals _____   duration: _____

COLLECTION DESCRIPTION [ATTACH ADDITIONAL SHEETS IF NECESSARY]

date: _____   country: _____

province/state: _____   city/town: _____

culture group: _____

language(s): _____

performers/informants: _____

_____

_____

genre(s): _____

_____

_____

atm-2/88

Figure 2.4

NSA 3

NATIONAL SOUND ARCHIVE : C SERIES RECORDINGS

Reference	Playback copy reference	Access
P.T.	Copy status	Recordist
Date of recording	Place of recording	Notes
Track	Performers, speakers, etc.	Authors, composers, etc.	Titles

Figure 2.5

30

ACQUIRING SOUND ARCHIVES

E n t l e h n f o r m u l a r für das Projekt

....

Name ....

Adresse ....

Rückgabetermin ....

Das Phonogrammarchiv unterstützt das oben genannte Forschungsvorhaben durch die
leihweise Überlassung der unten angeführten Aufnahmegeräte und Tonbänder. Der
Forscher übernimmt diese Gegenstände und behandelt sie schonend und fachgerecht.
Er haftet für die termingerechte Rückgabe der Gegenstände sowie für die Beschä-
digung durch unsachgemäße Handhabung, Verlust oder Zerstörung. Er bestätigt,
daß er die Gegenstände ausschließlich für das vereinbarte Forschungsvorhaben
einsetzt und bei vorzeitigem Abschluß umgehend retourniert.

	Rückgabebestätigung	techn.Bemerkungen, Betriebszeit (Aufn. und Wiedergabe)
Tonbandgerät	....	
Tasche	....	
Mikrophon	....	
Kabel	....	
Windschutz	....	
Stativ	....	
Netz/Ladegerät	....	
Leerspule	....	
Sonstiges	....	

Tonbänder: retour:

Datum:	ausgegeben:	leer:	bespielt:	Arbeitskopien:	Übernahme:
....	....	....	....	....	....
....	....	....	....	....	....
....	....	....	....	....	....
....	....	....	....	....	....
....	....	....	....	....	....

Der Entlehner: Für das Phonogrammarchiv:

Archiviert unter: ....

Figure 2.6

References

1. For example, E. J. Leahy and C. A. Cameron, *Modern records management*, New York, 1956; W. Benedon, *Records management*, Prentice Hall, Englewood Cliffs, N.J., 1969. See also F. B. Evans, *Modern archives and manuscripts: a select bibliography*, Society of American Archivists, Worcester, Mass., 1975.
2. Society of American Archivists, *Archival forms manual*, Chicago, 1982.
3. See F. Hull, *The use of sampling techniques in the retention of records: a RAMP study* (ref. PGI–81/WS/26), UNESCO, Paris, 1981.
4. See M. G. Cook, *Archives and the computer*, 2nd edn., Butterworths, London, 1986, pp. 56–80.
5. Lack of sufficient status and of suitable channels of communication were mainly to blame for this, rather than an actual inadequacy in the library's work, which has always been expertly systematic. See T. Trebble and M. Jones, 'Broadcasting' in D. Lance (ed.) *Sound archives. A guide to their establishment and development*, IASA, Milton Keynes, 1983, pp. 69–71; M. Jones, 'Selection in practice' in H. P. Harrison, *Selection in Sound Archives*, IASA, Milton Keynes, 1984, pp. 93–97.
6. For instance, J. A. Fleckner, *Archives and manuscripts: surveys*, SAA Basic Manual Series, Society of American Archivists, Chicago, 1977.
7. See, for instance, M. J. Brichford, *Archives and manuscripts: appraisal and accessioning*, SAA Basic Manual Series, Society of American Archivists, Chicago, 1977; N. E. Peace (ed.), *Archival Choices*, D. C. Heath, Lexington, Mass., 1984. Some use the term 'selection' as an equivalent to 'appraisal' (see H. P. Harrison, *The archival appraisal of sound recordings and related materials, a RAMP study*, (ref. PGI–87/WS/1), UNESCO, Paris, 1987, p. 4), but for once the jargon term has some point in conveying the specific archival function. 'Selection' in many contexts has a strong subjective choice connotation which is just what the archivist should be avoiding.
8. H. P. Harrison (ed.), *Selection in sound archives*, IASA, Milton Keynes, 1984.
9. Quoted in appendix D to L. C. Waffen, 'The art of appraisal and selection of sound recordings for archival retention' in H. P. Harrison, *Selection in Sound Archives*, pp. 68–78.
10. G. E. A. Raspin, *The transfer of private papers to repositories*, Information leafet 5, Society of Archivists, 1988.

Chapter 3

COPYRIGHT AND PUBLIC ACCESS

THE LAW OF COPYRIGHT IN THE UK

Introduction

The nature of copyright

Copyright is a property right which enables the owner to prevent other people from copying an original work. It must relate to something concrete rather than to an idea. Theoretically two identical works could be covered by separate copyrights owned by different people, as long as each work was produced by an independent process. Copyright holders are entitled to demand payment for granting others permission to copy. In practice therefore the main *raison d'être* of copyright legislation is its role in defining and protecting potential sources of income for copyright owners. Infringement of copyright is actionable by the copyright owner, and it is also a criminal offence to make for sale or hire, import, exhibit or distribute infringing copies, or to perform, show or play a copyright work in public without permission from the copyright owner.

The legislative basis

Copyright in the UK is now governed by the recent Copyright, Designs and Patents Act 1988, which came into force in August 1989 and supersedes the 1956 Copyright Act. In some respects the new Act has rendered superfluous the type of guidebooks and glossaries generated in large numbers in relation to the 1956 Act. With the major exception of the chapter on licensing, the copyright provisions of the Act are set out in a logical order in language which should be clear to the layman. Most sound archivists will need some acquaintance with current copyright law and should not hesitate to buy and read the Act. Having said this, the new Act leaves some matters unresolved or in an unsatisfactory state, particularly for sound archivists the question of tape copying.

Since the introduction of a levy on blank cassettes was dropped from the Act, the exemptions and 'fair dealing' provisions which were to go with it have also disappeared, leaving the whole matter unresolved. According to the letter of the Act as it now stands, no copying of copyright recordings, even for conservation purposes, is allowed without permission except where such recordings form part of a broadcast. However, although the Act might normally have been expected to remain current for twenty years or more, many copyright issues affecting the publishing and entertainment industries are already negotiated on a European scale. Particularly with the advent of the free European market in 1992 it seems likely that further changes to British law will be needed, including perhaps a tape levy and related provisions such as exist already elsewhere in Europe.

Works covered by copyright

Nine categories of work are covered by the new Act: original literary, dramatic, musical or artistic works; sound recordings, films, broadcasts or cable programmes; and the typographical arrangement of published editions. 'Literary work' means any work which is written, spoken or sung which is not a dramatic or musical work, and includes written tables and compilations, and computer programs; 'dramatic work' includes work of dance or mime, and 'musical work' means a work consisting of music, exclusive of any words or action intended to be sung, spoken or performed with the music.

In the wording of the Act 'Copyright does not subsist in a literary, dramatic or musical work unless and until it is recorded, in writing or otherwise . . . '. 'Otherwise' includes by means of sound recording, and therefore speakers such as oral history interviewees whose words are recorded become owners of the literary copyright in their words. This was not the case under the 1956 Act (see p. 48, 'Oral history – copyright'). Sounds which are not recorded in any form (e.g. improvised music), or which cannot be defined as works (e.g. the sounds of wildlife or machinery) are not protected by copyright.

'Sound recording' is defined as 'a recording of sounds, from which the sounds may be reproduced, or a recording of the whole or any part of a literary, dramatic or musical work, from which the sounds producing the work may be reproduced'. No attempt is made to define recording media, so recordings on any medium, including those still to be invented, are covered. 'Film' is defined as 'a recording of visual images, on any medium, from which a moving picture may by any means be produced' and thus includes video recordings. Copyright does not subsist in copies taken from original sound recordings or films, so when a published recording is reissued this does not result in an extension of the copyright period.

It is essential to remember that each of the nine categories of works is protected by a separate copyright under the Act, and so it is usually necessary to consider at least two copyrights in a sound recording: one relating to the recording itself and the other(s) to the contents. Provisions in the Act (e.g. regarding the duration of copyright) are not uniform across all the categories.

On top of this, although performers do not enjoy copyright in their performances, their rights are now defined and protected by the Act, and their permission must be obtained before recordings can be made or copied, except for private or domestic use (see 'Performers' rights' below). Therefore in order to make and sell a copy of an off-air recording of an independently produced opera broadcast (to take a 'worst case' example), the recordist would need to come to terms with the copyright owners (or their representatives) in the words, music, original recording and broadcast of the work (all likely to be different people), together with all the performers. This is the main reason why copyright is a costly, time-consuming and confusing business.

Copyright ownership

First owner

The author, i.e. creator, of a literary, dramatic, musical or artistic work will be the first owner of the copyright in that work unless the work was made in the course of employment, in which case the employer is the first owner subject to any agreement to the contrary. The 'author' of a sound recording, film or computer-generated work is defined as 'the person by whom the arrangements necessary' for making the work are made, and existing case law indicates that 'arrangements' essentially mean 'financial arrangements'. Thus copyright in recordings made on behalf of a repository by employees and contractors belongs to the repository, not the recordist. Where recordists are unpaid but are using tape or equipment provided by the repository, or if the repository pays their expenses, then the repository will have a strong claim on the copyright; but to avoid any possible disputes over who made the 'arrangements', the copyright ownership should be agreed in writing. This is essential where the repository wishes to be sure of obtaining copyright in recordings made on its behalf where it has not contributed to the 'arrangements'. The first owner of copyright in a broadcast will be the person making the transmission; in a cable programme, the person providing the cable service; and in a typographical arrangement, the publisher.

Copyright transfer

Copyright is a form of property and may be 'assigned' (i.e. given or sold), or bequeathed. Assignments need to be written and signed by the copyright owner or his representative. Future copyright in works as yet uncompleted may also be assigned in the same way. Any aspect or aspects of copyright may be licensed to another party, and these aspects will remain subject to the licence when the copyright is transmitted by inheritance or assignment to another party. Copyright may be transmitted many times during its currency and, since there is no system of registration in the UK, difficulties in tracing the current owner are often experienced. Repositories should try wherever possible to arrange for copyright in recordings and their subject matter to be assigned to the repository at the time of transfer. Otherwise difficulties in tracing the current copyright owner may be encountered later.

In relation to literary, dramatic, musical and artistic copyrights the Act does allow copying if it is 'not possible by reasonable enquiry' to trace the author, or if it is reasonable to assume that the author has been dead for fifty years or more, except where copyright is owned by the Crown. There is no mention of a similar concession in relation to copyright in recordings. Archival recording of folksongs, with the consent of the performer, is allowed under the Act as long as the words are unpublished and of unknown authorship. Single copies of such recordings may be supplied for research or private study.

Moral rights

A new provision of the 1988 Act which reflects longstanding provision elsewhere in Europe gives authors of copyright in literary, dramatic, musical or artistic works, and directors of copyright films a 'moral right' to be identified as the author or director of the work whenever it is published commercially or copied for issue to the public, although this 'paternity' right has to be 'asserted' in writing when the copyright is assigned or when permission to copy is given. The onus is on the author or director to assert his right; there is no infringement under the Act if the right has not been asserted. The Act also provides authors and directors with the moral right to object to 'derogatory treatment' of their works (i.e. additions to, deletions from, alterations and adaptations which amount to distortion or mutilation or which may prejudice their honour) and there appears to be no requirement for this right to be asserted. Thus if a repository wishes to publish commercially a recording of a copyright work (such as for instance an oral history interview) it must name any author or composer who has asserted his right to be identified – interviewees count as 'authors' – and must not edit the recording so as to subject the copyright work to derogatory treatment (see below 'Oral history – Ethics'). The 'moral rights' of authors and directors are similarly infringed if works are falsely attributed to them.

Duration of copyright

Literary, dramatic, musical and artistic works

Under the new Act, copyright in literary, dramatic, musical or artistic works will expire at the end of fifty years from the end of year in which the author dies. If the author is unknown, copyright will expire fifty years after the work is first made available to the public.

Sound recordings and films

In sound recordings and films copyright will expire at the end of fifty years from the end of the year in which they were made, or, if 'released' (i.e. published, broadcast etc.), fifty years from the end of the year in which they were released. Copyright in broadcasts and cable transmissions will expire fifty years from the end of the year in which the transmission takes place. This period is not extended by repeat transmissions.

For sound recordings this effectively restores the provisions of the 1911 Copyright Act under which copyright expires fifty years after the recordings were made. This Act still governs copyright in recordings made prior to the coming into force of the 1956 Act (June 1957), under which recordings have enjoyed copyright for fifty years after publication, or perpetually if they remained unpublished. Under the new Act, this copyright in unpublished recordings made between 1957 and 1989 will no longer be perpetual, but will

expire fifty years after the Act comes into force, unless the recordings are published during this fifty-year period, in which case
copyright will expire fifty years from the date of publication.

Therefore in 1989 no copyright subsists in sound recordings
published before 1939 or if unpublished, recorded before 1939.
Recordings published between 1939 and 1989 will fall out of
copyright between 1989 and 2039. Copyright in unpublished
recordings made between 1939 and 1957 will expire between 1989
and 2007. Copyright in all unpublished recordings made between
1957 and 1989 will expire in 2039, but if they are published before
2039, copyright will expire between 2039 and 2089.

No copyright subsists in films or broadcasts as such made before
June 1957, or in cable programmes made before January 1985,
though unexpired copyright may still subsist in their literary,
dramatic or musical contents, in soundtracks which are regarded as
'recordings', and in film footage which is regarded as 'photographs'.

Crown and parliamentary copyright

Literary, dramatic, musical or artistic work created by an 'officer or
servant of the Crown' remains in copyright for 125 years from the
end of the year of creation. If published commercially within the
first seventy-five years of this period, copyright will expire fifty years
from the end of the year of publication.

There are no separate provisions concerning the duration of
Crown copyright in recordings and films.

The Houses of Parliament own copyright in all works made by
them or under their control (including sound and video recordings
of their proceedings) for fifty years from the end of the year in which
they were made. They do not enjoy copyright in works which are
merely commissioned by them or on their behalf.

Restricted Acts

Subject to the exceptions indicated under 'Permitted Acts relevant to
sound archives' below, the Copyright Act confers on copyright owners
the exclusive right to copy works and issue copies to the public; to
perform, show or play works in public; to broadcast them or include
them in a cable programme service; and to make an adaptation of
them. Anyone who carries out any of the above acts without permission
from the copyright owner will infringe the copyright.

Under the Act there are also a number of 'secondary infringements': importing an infringing copy without permission from the copyright owner, or possessing such a copy in the course of trade, hire or distribution; making, importing, hiring or selling equipment to be used for making infringing copies; permitting a place of entertainment to be used for an infringing performance; or providing equipment for playing recordings, showing films etc. which would constitute an infringing public performance.

Permitted Acts relevant to sound archives

Fair dealing

The new Act provides for 'fair dealing' with literary, dramatic, musical or artistic works, which may be copied for private study and research without infringing copyright. The Act indicates that librarians and archivists may rely on a signed declaration from the person requesting the copy that it will only be used for purposes which will not infringe copyright. If, having signed this declaration, the client then uses the copy for an infringing purpose, the client and not the librarian or archivist is liable. There are *no* fair-dealing concessions in relation to copyright in sound recordings and films. A repository may therefore supply copies of recordings to researchers where the repository itself owns the copyright, but must obtain permission, or ensure that permission has been obtained, from copyright holders if copies of any other recordings are to be supplied. Literary, dramatic, musical or artistic works may be copied, with appropriate acknowledgement, for the purpose of criticism or review, and spoken words may be recorded or written down and used for reporting current events or included in a broadcast, without infringement.

Libraries and archives

Playback There is nothing in the Copyright Act to prevent the playback of sound recordings held by libraries and archives for the purpose of private study and research. Playback to groups may be more of a problem, however. This is permitted in educational establishments (see below), but the archive or library may well not qualify as such. There is also a provision in the Act that a 'club, society or other organisation . . . not established or conducted for profit [whose] main objects are charitable or otherwise concerned with the advancement of religion, education or social welfare' may play recordings as part of its activities, provided the proceeds from any admission charge are 'applied solely for the purposes of the organisation', but this only covers copyright in the recordings, not in any literary, dramatic or musical works they may contain. Playback of recordings of copyright works in a repository to, say, a school party, might therefore be seen as an infringement; and the use of such recordings in the repository for public entertainment or even as illustrative material in a public lecture probably would infringe copyright in the works, unless of course the prior permission of the copyright owner(s) had been obtained. In practice such activities are covered by the various licensing schemes whose role is somewhat strengthened under the Act (see 'Copying' below).

Broadcasts Once the new Act is in force, libraries and archives designated by the Secretary of State may make or hold recordings of any broadcast or cable recording without infringing any copyright or performance right in it. This will not apply however to large-scale recordings of broadcasts made during the currency of the 1956 Act, under which off-air recording infringed copyright except in a few cases (such as the NSA) where permission had been negotiated.

Preservation copying Archives and libraries may also make a copy of 'any item in the permanent collection of the library or archive in order to preserve or replace that item . . . or in order to replace in the permanent collection of another prescribed library or archive an item which has been lost, destroyed or damaged, without thereby infringing the copyright in any literary, dramatic or musical work . . .' The Act does not state that preservation copies may be made without infringing the copyright in a recording or film, but since this copying does not affect the status of copyright owners in practical terms, repositories should not be inhibited by the lack of formal sanction in the Act.

Educational use

Copying Literary, dramatic, musical and artistic works may be copied in the course of, or in preparation for, instruction by the person giving or receiving the instruction, provided a 'reprographic process' (i.e. a process for making multiple or facsimile copies such as photocopying) is not used. Multiple 'reprographic' copies may, however, be made of published literary, dramatic or musical (not artistic) works for instructional purposes, as long as not more than one per cent of a work is copied in any quarter of the year. In practice, photocopying for educational use is covered by a licensing scheme (see 'Licensing schemes' below). Subject to some restrictions, short passages from copyright literary or dramatic works may be included in anthologies intended for educational use which are made up mainly of non-copyright material.

Performance Literary, dramatic or musical works may be performed, and recordings, films, broadcasts and cable programmes played or shown in educational establishments for instructional purposes without infringing copyright. However, the participation of any outsiders (even parents) in such activities may constitute an infringement.

Broadcasts Recordings of broadcasts or cable programmes may be made by, or on behalf of, an educational establishment for its educational purposes without infringing any of the copyrights in them, provided a licensing scheme relating to this activity (see below) is not in operation.

All this means that, subject to any licensing scheme introduced under the new Act, copies of recordings of broadcasts held by sound and film archives may be provided for use in educational establishments without permission from copyright owners.

Off-air recording

The concessions for libraries and archives and for educational use under the new Act have already been covered. In addition broadcasts and cable programmes may be recorded for private and domestic use without infringing copyright or performers' rights, provided this is solely to enable listening at a more convenient time. There appears to be no reason why such recordings made after the Act comes into force should not be acquired and used by libraries and archives.

Performers' rights

Under the Performers' Protection Acts 1958 and 1972, the consent of performers was required before live or broadcast performances could be recorded or filmed, except for private or domestic use. Offenders faced criminal prosecution, and the *Rickless v. United Artists* case in 1987 also established that performers were entitled to damages if their consent was not obtained. These performers' rights are incorporated in the new Act. Dramatic, musical and variety act performances are protected, together with readings and recitations. Performers' rights are infringed if live performances, broadcasts or cable programmes, or existing recordings are recorded, filmed or copied without consent. It is also an infringement to show or play in public, or to import, sell, hire or distribute illicit copies.

Performers' consent is often embodied in a recording contract; the new Act is infringed if a recording is made of a performance subject to such a contract, unless consent has been obtained from both the performer(s) and the person(s) with whom the contract has been signed. Performers' and recording rights are also infringed if the illicit recording is shown or played in public, broadcast, imported, sold etc.

Under the new Act performers' and recording rights expire fifty years from the end of the year in which the performance took place, but the expiry date of rights in performances executed under the earlier Acts does not appear to be stated. This may therefore mean that rights in performances will continue to be subject to indefinite restriction, as under the earlier Acts, rather than to a cut-off fifty years from the coming into force of the new Act as might have been expected. Performers' and recording rights cannot be assigned, but performers' rights may be bequeathed.

In practice the new Act reinforces the existing position which largely prevents small-scale recordists, even on behalf of archives and research bodies, from recording live performances by professional musicians, singers and actors. Such performers are normally members of the Musicians' Union or British Actors' Equity, both of which are usually very reluctant to negotiate consents outside the familiar sphere of commercial entertainment and recording, since they see the protection of performers' rights (and incomes) as one of their main tasks (see 'Performances' below).

Licensing schemes

Various rights conferred by existing copyright legislation have been administered for many years by licensing bodies which act on behalf of copyright owners. These bodies, which to a greater or lesser extent also collect and distribute fees (or 'royalties') to their members when licences are issued and are therefore often called 'collecting societies', will continue to operate under the new Act, some under rather different conditions, and further new licensing schemes may be set up.

All these bodies issue their own brochures (which have just been frantically updated) and welcome enquiries. Further useful information is also available from the National Council for Educational Technology (educational use of recordings, broadcasts and video) and the Library Association (photocopying).

Sound archivists may find they need to deal with three organizations in particular.

The Mechanical Copyright Protection Society (MCPS)

This body is owned by the Music Publishers Association whose members own or administer copyright in published music. It issues licences to, and collects royalties from, record companies, broadcasters, and anyone else who wishes to record or re-record copyright music. Repositories which record or make copies of recordings of copyright music for any purpose not permitted under the Copyright Act (see above), should obtain an annual licence from MCPS. Unless commercial use is envisaged the charge should be small.

The Performing Right Society (PRS)

The PRS issues licences to those who wish to perform copyright musical works (including lyrics and words set to music) in public, whether 'live', recorded, or through a broadcast or cable transmission. Its members are composers, lyricists and publishers. Owners or administrators of venues, radio stations and cable services are the usual licensees rather than performers themselves. The society only deals with 'non-theatric' performances: permission to perform whole plays, operas, ballets etc. in theatres is negotiated individually with copyright owners or agents.

Repositories which put on lectures, recitals, exhibitions or any other kinds of events which include the public performance of copyright music, even if purely for educational purposes, should seek a licence (again normally for a nominal amount) from the PRS.

Phonographic Performance Ltd (PPL)

Sound archive repositories will also need a licence from PPL if the performances, events and exhibitions they put on include published recordings of music. PPL operates on behalf of record companies and collects royalties in return for permission to play copyright recordings in public or on the air. It is not normally able to license the copying of copyright recordings. This must be done directly with the record company concerned, and is technically necessary even for the transfer of copyright recordings to tape for use in an internal exhibition, for which a PPL licence may already have been obtained. Under the Act as it stands there are very few concessions in relation to copyright in recordings.

The 1988 Act attempts to introduce a new basis for licensing which should be more efficient and serviceable. In a number of circumstances under the old Act copyright owners could choose to remain outside licensing schemes and possibly refuse permission to copy, record etc. A well-known case was the Dylan Thomas estate which remained outside the Copyright Licensing Agency (which licenses photocopying on behalf of copyright owners) and refused to allow any photocopying of Thomas's works. Under the new Act the fair-dealing concessions for photocopying are quite generous, and will apply *unless* a licensing scheme is set up. The Thomas estate and others will thus no longer be able to act individually. A similar arrangement provides for the recording of broadcasts off the air for educational use: it is allowed unless a scheme is set up, so the position of the Guild of Sound and Vision which used to license some aspects of educational recording should be strengthened, since non-participants will have no right to negotiate separately.

New provisions in the 1988 Act control the hire or rental of copyright recordings, but copyright owners will not be able to negotiate royalties individually; they must join a licensing scheme.

In order to regulate the operations of the new or revamped licensing bodies, and the fair operation of copyright in general, a Copyright Tribunal is being established. It will deal, for example, with complaints that a licensing body has used its new monopoly to make unfair deals with users.

These developments will be confirmed by order of the Secretary of State when negotiations are complete, which as this is being written they are not.

International copyright

The 1988 Copyright Act appears to state only that the owner of copyright in a work shall be the author, or the person to whom copyright has been assigned or bequeathed by the author, without indicating any further qualifications needed by owners (e.g. as to nationality) to enjoy protection under the Act in the UK. This may be because virtually every country is now a signatory of the Berne Convention or the Universal Copyright Convention or both. These agreements provide international protection to owners of copyright in literary, dramatic, musical and artistic works.

Under the Berne Convention (as revised in Paris in 1972) the minimum duration of copyright is the life of the author plus fifty years. Under the UCC the minimum term is the life of the author plus twenty-five years. In addition, to secure protection in UCC countries, works must show the copyright symbol, date and name of the copyright owner. The USA and USSR are signatories of the UCC alone and not of the Berne Convention. The initial term of copyright in the USA at the time of the 1972 revision was the life of the author plus twenty-eight years, but is now life plus fifty years.

International protection of copyright in sound recordings is provided by the Rome Convention of 1961 and the Phonograms Convention of 1973, but only a small number of countries are parties to either (twenty-three for the former and thirty-two for the latter). The Rome Convention affords protection by copyright in all signatory countries, but the Phonograms Convention only protects by whatever provision is made for nationals of each country. Neither the USSR nor any Eastern European country is a signatory of either, so sound recordings from these countries enjoy no copyright protection in the UK. As with the UCC, recordings must bear the phonograms' copyright symbol in order to qualify for protection in Phonograms Convention countries.

COPYRIGHT AND ACCESS IN PRACTICE

Introduction

In order not to infringe the rights of copyright owners and performers, signed agreements must be made with the parties involved and where necessary fees paid before a recording takes place. This is unlikely to be the direct responsibility of sound archivists who work in the record industry or in broadcasting, where they will not be concerned with recording and where the clearance of rights is such a major concern that specialists are employed to negotiate with performers' organizations and obtain licences from the collecting societies. But in many other contexts sound archivists also make or commission sound recordings and need to negotiate with rights' owners direct. For this purpose preprinted forms may be useful.

Care and imagination should be applied when designing forms of this kind. The aim should be to obtain the consent of the speaker, performer and/or copyright owner for the use of recordings by the repository in its normal activities, so that separate permission will not have to be sought except on rare occasions. These 'normal activities' should include:

- playback to individuals and groups on the premises
- educational use by repository staff on or off the premises
- use of extracts in illustrative matter and in lectures and talks given by repository staff
- conservation copying.

Rights' owners will also normally want assurance that copies of recordings will not be made or supplied without their consent, though it is obviously advantageous if permission to copy without consent can be negotiated in appropriate cases. Forms are quick and efficient, but much depends on personalities and attitudes; some people may not respond well to the prospect of filling in a form, no matter how simple and unofficial it looks. Agreements with them are best reached by exchange of letters; verbal agreement is not sufficient.

Performances

It is essential to get the consent of performers and copyright holders before recording takes place. Orchestras, bands, theatrical companies etc. made up of professionals will normally be approached via the local representative of the relevant trade union. In the UK the Musicians' Union tends to be suspicious of 'archival' recording proposals and permission may be refused for a 'one-off' recording. The only way round this is probably to negotiate well in advance in order to build up confidence in the work of the repository. In the minds of many musicians the concept of a recorded performance with no payment does not exist. Individual union members will sometimes consent to being recorded for archival purposes if working away from their usual context.

The British Actors' Equity may be a little more sympathetic, but (at least at the NSA) a widespread dislike of live recording has been encountered: many actors feel that if they are to be recorded, they would prefer to adjust their performances and do it in a studio, which of course is just what the 'archival' recordist does not want. The sound archivist's strongest card here is to emphasize the needs of researchers who will wish to hear works in production rather than studio reconstructions. Such 'fly on the wall' recordings will give an adequate impression but will be quite unsuitable for commercial release, so there will be little possibility of illegal exploitation.

Some erosion of this prejudice against live recording has occurred recently with the great increase in small-scale, low-budget experimental theatre. Companies are aware that their achievements are ephemeral and are therefore more interested in cooperating to produce a permanent record. In many situations actors or companies will expect the sound archivist to negotiate permission to record with their agents, and this may save a lot of time and trouble.

In the end the attitude of professional performers will also be strongly influenced by the conduct of the recordists: punctuality, unobtrusive and efficient work, adequate technical knowledge and experience when talking to the sound men on the production and so on will help to build trust; but these considerations are beyond the scope of this chapter and this book.

In practice more 'archival' recordings will probably be made of performers who are not professionals or union members, such as 'traditional' singers and musicians, or overseas performers on tour. Here the signature of the performer or his representative (e.g. his agent or the leader of the group he performs with) should be obtained in advance if at all possible. An exception might be made only if verbal consent has been given but insistence on immediate paperwork would jeopardize the recording. Most recordings of this sort will not be part of a series, and typically the recordist will be unknown to the performer and will only have a short time to complete the formalities, just at a time when the performer is preoccupied with the forthcoming performance. All the same, performers will normally agree to being recorded as long as they are convinced (by the appearance and wording of an agreement form, for instance) that their work will not be 'ripped-off' by hidden commercial interests. A condition of consent is often that a copy of the recording is supplied to the performer.

Recordings without clear consent should never be made by sound archivists or their operatives, and no privately-made recordings should be accepted when there is any chance that consent has not been obtained.

Where performers are also the copyright owners in the works which are to be recorded, their permission as such will be obtained if the agreement they sign is worded to include all rights. In a small minority of cases performers or agents may still insist that permission to record such works be obtained from MCPS or individual publishers or composers (music) or the publisher (literature and drama). This permission must in any case be sought where other copyright owners' works are being performed. It may be possible for the repository to negotiate a general annual licence from MCPS which includes live recording. Time must be allowed for these processes to take place.

A recording agreement used by the NSA jazz section to obtain recording consent is illustrated in Figure 3.1, but it may be unnecessary or counterproductive to include such detailed information and instead the form regularly used by the NSA literature and drama section may be better (Figure 3.2).

Oral history

Aspects of copyright in oral history recordings are normally covered in a recording agreement or 'clearance form' signed by the participants. It is best also to record the uses to which recordings will be put, and any restrictions on access to them, on the same form, and so this section deals with these matters as well as copyright. Chapter 2, 'Terms of deposit', p. 23 should also be referred to.

Copyright

While interviewees, speakers and lecturers are not regarded as 'performers' under the new Copyright Act, they certainly are 'authors' and therefore owners of the literary copyright in their words once they have been recorded. Many oral history practitioners imagined that their informants enjoyed copyright in their recorded words even under the 1956 Act, but broadcasters never assumed this, and the BBC for instance was not obliged to seek the permission of interviewees for the inclusion of their speech in programmes.

Under the new Act it is essential to reach written agreement on copyright ownership with speakers and informants. Most repositories which carry out oral history projects require their informants' literary copyright to be assigned to the repository, and this is stated in many of the agreement forms currently used. If copyright is assigned, this obviously gives greater freedom to use the recordings as illustrative matter and in publications. However, the increasing use of interviews in social history documentaries on television and radio means that the copyright in such interviews is now seen as having some financial value, so some informants may be unwilling to assign copyright.

Where justified by the importance of the interview, sound archivists could get round this by arranging an assignment on condition that any fee payable for commercial use should be passed on to the informant, on the same kind of basis as an author or composer might

COPYRIGHT AND PUBLIC ACCESS

THE BRITISH LIBRARY

NATIONAL SOUND ARCHIVE

29 EXHIBITION ROAD
LONDON SW7 2AS
Telephone 01-589 6603

NATIONAL SOUND ARCHIVE Recording agreement

The National Sound Archive (NSA) requests your permission to make a recording of your performance/interview

at:

on:

This recording is part of our programme to preserve in the Archive, for reference purposes only, good quality sound recordings of live performances/interviews and events.

The Archive will acknowledge your full rights in the recording and guarantees that NO COPIES will be made (except purely for conservation purposes) without your written permission. As with all other NSA holdings, this recording will remain on British Library premises at all times under close supervision. The NSA will be entitled to use the recording for any educational purposes within these premises or organised under it's auspices. The public will be able to listen to it through our Listening Service but otherwise have no other access to the recording itself. In due course details of the recording will be entered into the NSA's Catalogue.

If you agree to this request, please sign below and retain a copy:

I HEREBY AUTHORISE THE BRITISH LIBRARY NATIONAL SOUND ARCHIVE TO RECORD MY/OUR PERFORMANCE/INTERVIEW AS SPECIFIED ABOVE. I understand that my performer/author/composer rights in the recording will be strictly observed and that no copies of the recording will be made without my written permission.

Signed: Date:

Name (block letters):

Permanent address:

Signed on behalf of the National Sound Archive:

NB: If you wish to make commercial use of this recording please write to the NSA for conditions and agreement.

Figure 3.1

THE BRITISH LIBRARY

NATIONAL SOUND ARCHIVE

29 EXHIBITION ROAD
LONDON SW7 2AS
Telephone 01-589 6603

PERMISSION TO RECORD

Insofar as I have rights in the following production

....

I hereby authorise the National Sound Archive to make
a recording of it on the understanding that the
recording so made or any copy thereof, is to be used
within the archive only and is not to be passed to
any other party, performed in public, or published
without my further permission in writing.

usual signature.....................................

              date.....................

Figure 3.2

assign copyright to his publisher; and when the opportunity does
arise archivists should stick out for realistic commercial fees on
behalf of their informants, and of course as a separate issue on
behalf of the repository as owner of copyright in the recording. In
fact, however, original interviews conducted as part of oral history
projects are rarely used in programmes: suitable informants may be
identified by listening to project interviews, but then new recordings
will normally be made which can be arranged to suit the producer's
needs. Payment for copyright in these new interviews may be
inadequate, but this is not directly the concern of the repository. In
cases where the informant will not assign copyright, agreement
should at least be made that copyright will pass to the repository on
his or her death.

Copyrights in subject matter assigned to the repository and in
recordings made or arranged by the sound archivist are owned by
the employer, who in many cases will be a local authority or the

Crown. In the UK many oral history projects have been run or assisted by Community Programme schemes financed by the government's Manpower Services Commission, and some continue under the more recent Employment Training scheme which is also government-run. Recordings made by these projects are Crown copyright, which has led to problems, particularly in the use of recordings on political subjects in publications or in the deployment of resulting income. Further difficulties might arise when CP project recordings are deposited in a local authority library or record office (as many have been) which then wishes to publish them in order to finance continuing oral history work.

Ethics

As 'authors', interviewees retain moral rights in their speech under the new Act, whether copyright is assigned or not, so sound archivists must clearly avoid uses which might distort the original meaning or intention of the words, or cast the informant in a bad light by, say, using short gobbets out of context. However the establishment of goodwill and trust between interviewers and informants has always been essential and virtually all oral history recording agreements include a description of the repository or project and (either explicitly or by implication) the uses to which the recordings will be put. Without a signed indication that the inform-ant understands and agrees to these uses the sound archivist may be open to accusations of, and possibly even proceedings for, breach of confidence, and his credibility will suffer whatever the outcome.

Access

Interviewees may only agree to talk if access to the recordings is restricted for a period, and the repository may decide in any case to impose an embargo if confidential or controversial information about living people is included. For instance in an untypical but rather sinister case, Bradford Heritage Recording Unit substituted numerical references for all personal names in its cataloguing data, and placed restrictions on a number of recordings, after researchers employed by the War Crimes Commission (unsuccessfully) sought access to tapes during investigations into ethnic communities. Access only with the approval of the informant is preferable to a complete embargo, though it will mean extra work for the repository if, say, a particular set of restricted recordings becomes popular with teachers. Speakers at conferences may only sign a recording agreement if access is restricted until after the book to which their speech relates has been published.

Access restrictions are a nuisance to administer and should be avoided unless really necessary. Periods of restriction should be kept as short as possible up to a maximum of perhaps thirty years. Restrictions extending beyond the death of the informant should rarely be necessary.

Recording agreement forms

Many oral history interviews are conducted with the elderly or those mistrustful of officialdom, with whom a bureaucratic-looking form may not be the best conversation-opener. Mention of copyright and access restrictions in black and white may suggest possibilities to informants which would not otherwise have occurred to them. If the issue is fudged, however, the recorded material will be difficult if not impossible to use later, so a suitable approach must be found. Similarly recordings made by others on behalf of the repository must be covered by recording agreements, and agreements and clearances with depositors of privately recorded material should be made at the time of deposit. Preprinted forms do not have to be used: an exchange of letters is just as good, so long as the required information and permission are recorded and signed. A third method is the time-saving strategy adopted by the pioneer Oral History Research Office at the Columbia University, New York. A range of preprinted letters is prepared, each expressing a different level of restriction on access and use. Having ascertained which letter is likely to be appropriate, the interviewer presents this for signature without displaying a range of other unnecessary options to the informant. 'Form A' (the least restrictive) from this series is illustrated in Figure 3.3. Figure 3.4 shows a more typical form which lists a number of specific uses over which the informant is given a choice.

Another approach is seen in the form used by the National Life Story Collection at the NSA, Figure 3.5. The work of the collection is described but the options are kept to a minimum.

The form used by the London History Workshop Centre Sound and Video Archive, Figure 3.6, combines the two approaches and also brings in the question of commercial use.

An unusual case where a repository would not receive much of its material without imposing or at least ungrudgingly offering access restrictions is seen in the Australian Institute of Aboriginal Studies, where the background of exploitation and insensitivity by colonials has created suspicion of all research and recording among many

```
                              Form A

Dear Dr. Grele:
      This letter will confirm my understanding and agreement with
Columbia University with respect to my participation in a series of
interviews conducted by the University's Oral History Research
Office.
      1.  The interviews will be taped and a transcript made of the
tapes.  The tapes and transcript (collectively called the "Work")
will be maintained by the University and made available by the
University in accordance with University rules and general policies
for research and other scholarly purposes.
      2.  I hereby grant, assign and transfer to the University all
right, title and interest in the Work, including the literary rights
and the copyright, except that I shall retain the right to copy, use
and publish the Work in part or in full until the earlier of my death
or _____ 19   .
      3.  This letter contains our entire and complete understanding.

                                    Very truly yours,


                                    _____

                                    Date_____

ACCEPTED AND AGREED:
THE TRUSTEES OF COLUMBIA UNIVERSITY
   IN THE CITY OF NEW YORK

By_____
```

Figure 3.3

Aboriginal groups. The 'deposit of materials' form used by the Institute is illustrated in Figure 3.7. The form is appropriate for agreements with informants, recordists and depositors.

A form similar to the literature and drama form (see Figure 3.2) will probably be most suitable for obtaining agreement from individual speakers and lecturers. Ideally, however, it may be possible to persuade conference organizers to include permission to record in their correspondence or agreements with speakers.

BRADFORD HERITAGE RECORDING UNIT
140-148 Manningham Lane, Bradford, West Yorkshire BD8 7JL
Telephone (0274) 752311/752312/752301

Our Ref:
Your Ref:

CLEARANCE NOTE AND DEPOSIT INSTRUCTIONS

The purpose of this deposit agreement is to ensure that your
contribution is added to the collections of B.H.R.U. in
accordance with your wishes.

1)   Can the B.H.R.U. use your contribution:

    (a)   for public reference purposes,
      (Libraries/Museums)   ...   YES/NO

    (b)   For educational use (schools, etc.) ...   YES/NO

    (c)   for broadcasting (radio/T.V.)   ...   YES/NO

    (d)   as a source that may be published   ...   YES/NO

    (e)   in public performance (e.g. talk)   ...   YES/NO

2)   Can we mention your name?   ...   YES/NO

3)   Are you prepared to vest your copyright
      in the information in the recording to
      B.H.R.U.?   YES/NO

If you wish to apply a time restriction before your contribution
is released, please state how long.

SIGNED: (Interviewee)   ....   DATE:

ADDRESS:

SIGNED: (B.H.R.U.)   ....   DATE:

(B.H.R.U. is a collecting body for Bradford Libraries and Museums)

City of Bradford Metropolitan Council and The Manpower Services Commission MSC

Figure 3.4

THE NATIONAL LIFE STORY COLLECTION

47 Princes Gate, London SW7 2QA
01 823 7760/0865 510840

CLEARANCE NOTE AND DEPOSIT INSTRUCTIONS

The purpose of this deposit agreement is to ensure that your contribution is
added to the National Life Story Collection (NLSC) in strict accordance with
your wishes. All NLSC material will be preserved within The British Library
National Sound Archive as a permanent public reference resource for use in
research, publication, education, lectures and broadcasting.

If you wish to limit public access to any part of your contribution for a
period of years (up to a maximum of 30 years) please state these conditions
below:

I hereby assign the copyright in my contribution to the National Life Story
Collection and thereby to the National Sound Archive.

Signed .... Date: ....

Address ....

Signed (NLSC) .... Date: ....

Office use only

Full name:

Acc. no:

Playback no:

Series title:

Figure 3.5

**London History
Workshop Centre**
42 Queen Square
London WC1N 3AJ
01-831 8871

LONDON HISTORY WORKSHOP: SOUND AND VIDEO ARCHIVE

Your contribution of   will form part of the Sound and
Video Archive's extensive and growing collection of material relating to
London and Londoners, past and present. This form has been drawn up in
order to ensure that we use your contribution only in accordance with your
wishes

1. May the Archive use your contribution:

   a. for public reference   YES/NO

   b. for research purposes?   YES/NO

   c. for educational use by the Archive
       (in seminars, workshops, schools, colleges, universities)?YES/NO

   d. for broadcasting purposes (radio or tv)   YES/NO

   e. as a source of information that may be published?   YES/NO

   f. in a public performance: display or exhibition   YES/NO

2. May we mention your name?   YES/NO

LHWC is an educational charity and will use your contribution to further
public understanding of Londoners and their history.   Access to your
contribution will be at the discretion of Archive staff and then only for
the purposes of non commercial research carried out under their supervision.

 Should there be a request from outside commercial organisations to use your
material the Archive staff will endeavour, where possible, to contact you and
negotiate on your behalf an appropriate fee.   Should we be unable to contact
you the Centre undertakes to preserve your anonymity.
Are there any further restrictions you wish to place on this material?
please specify]

Signature of interviewee...........................date......

Signature of Interviewer...........................date......
===

Figure 3.6

COPYRIGHT AND PUBLIC ACCESS

AUSTRALIAN INSTITUTE OF ABORIGINAL STUDIES
_____

DEPOSIT OF MATERIAL
_____

The Institute will protect and preserve all material lodged with it in the best conditions available to the Institute both from a technical point of view (temperature and humidity control) and with regard to accessibility. The Institute has a professional staff to ensure that material will be classified and catalogued so that it is retrievable by all those authorised to consult it. Where specifically justified, the Institute retains the right to impose more stringent conditions of access and use than stipulated below. Depositors are reminded of ownership rights of consultants and performers under copyright and should refer to the relevant provisions of the Copyright Act.

1. Name of depositor _____

2. Address _____

   _____

3. Title and/or description of material _____

   _____

   _____

4. Access to this material by AIAS Library users will enable those users to use the materials in accordance with the provisions of the Australian Copyright Act. These permit limited copying for the purposes of research and study.

   Do you agree to allow access to this material by AIAS Library users?　　　　　YES/NO

   If NO, please specify restrictions on access _____

   _____

   _____

   _____

   Please name persons exempt from access restrictions _____

   _____

   _____

   _____

5. In addition to the copying permitted by the Copyright Act do you agree to allow copying of whole or part in order to return data to appropriate Aboriginal individuals or organisations?　　　YES/NO

   Do you agree to allow copying of photographs or sound recordings for any other purpose, including publication or broadcasting, with acknowledgement?　　　YES/NO

   If NO, please specify restrictions on use _____

   _____

   _____

   _____

   _____

Figure 3.7

6. Please state period of time restrictions should be maintained _____

7. Do you know whether any other person, group or community holds rights in this material?e.g performers, interviewers, funding bodies.   YES/NO

8. If YES, please specify _____

   _____

   _____

   _____

   Do you have their consent to nominate conditions for deposit of this material?   YES/NO

9. If you can no longer be contacted after a period of two years concerning restrictions on your material do you delegate to the Principal or Library Director discretion in granting access and use, according to the intention of your conditions of deposit?   YES/NO

10. Are there any special conditions attached to the handling of this material which are not mentioned above?   **YES/NO**

   _____

   _____

   _____

   _____

11. I, _____ hereby deposit the material described
   above in the Australian Institute of Aboriginal Studies under the terms and conditions set
   out herein.

   _____   _____
   Signature of depositor   for the Institute

   _____   Please return to -
   Date   The Library Director
                                              Australian Institute of Aboriginal Studies
                                              G.P.O. Box 553
                                              Canberra   A.C.T.   2601

Figure 3.7   (reverse side).

Chapter 4

DOCUMENTATION

Introduction

Documentation occupies a high proportion of staff time and intellectual effort in all libraries, museums and archives: ultimately there is no point in retaining reference materials if they cannot be traced, if their origin and contents are unknown, or if they fall apart because their age and condition have not been monitored and recorded. Written or computer-derived documentation is especially necessary for the management and use of sound archives since the nature and contents of recordings are not self-evident and the process of listening is too laborious and time-consuming to be undertaken repeatedly.

Conventionally the documentation of archives has been roughly divided into 'administrative' and 'descriptive' paperwork. Administrative documentation covers three main routines: accessioning, when the provenance of the material is recorded and it is given a general description and reference number (see Chapter 2); storage, which may require quite involved documentation if items are stored for economy of space rather than ease of retrieval[1], and conservation. Descriptive documentation (usually called 'listing' in record offices and 'cataloguing' in libraries and sound archive repositories) serves to identify the material for the user and provide an analysis and summary of its contents. However, as discussed earlier, the nature of archives, including sound archives, is dictated by the circumstances of their creation. The 'administrative' background of the material, including arrangements made in the repository, forms part of its 'description'. Recent codes aimed at standardizing documentation practice for archives and sound archives have therefore tended to amalgamate all aspects of documentation in a single sequence of data elements, a trend aided and encouraged by the requirement that these codes should form the basis for data entry on computer.[2]

Before the publications resulting from the Society of Archivists' Archival Description Project (see below) the most seminal and significant compilation for textual archives was 'MARC-AMC' (Machine readable cataloguing – archival and manuscripts control).[3] It is essentially a list of standardized data elements for use when mounting archival descriptions in the MARC format used by major libraries for the online networking of cataloguing information (though the format can profitably be used as the basis for computerized descriptions which are not intended for networking). Earlier attempts to enter archival descriptions via the existing bibliographic MARC format, based on the second edition of the *Anglo-American cataloguing rules* – 'AACRII' – had proved unsatisfactory because the range of data elements included reflected the needs of librarians of books and other published materials rather than the more flexible and wide-ranging requirements of archivists (and sound archivists).[4] In 1987 there were plans to use an adaptation of MARC-AMC as the basis for computerized cataloguing of sound recordings at the Department of Folk Culture, Library of Congress. For sound archives the unpublished code by Diana D. Hull of the NSA, and the AACRII-based code published by AAA/ARSC (currently out of print) are worthy of attention.[5] The latter states that it is 'based upon . . . AACRII' and serves to bring together general rules applicable to all library materials (AACRII chapter 1) and those devised specifically for sound recordings (chapter 6). The various rules in the AAA/ARSC code which have *no* AACRII citation serve to indicate AACRII's now widely acknowledged inadequacies for dealing with all aspects of sound recordings, let alone sound archives. Hull's compilation has a similar general arrangement, though based on the premise that the AACRII range of data elements is too limited to form a satisfactory starting point. All these codes are worthy of study if only as examples of the nit-picking detail which must be specified in descriptive schemes, particularly if they are to form the basis for data entry on computer.

Most recent and relevant to UK practitioners is the work of the Archival Description Project resulting in the *Manual of Archival Description*, whose new second edition ('MAD2') includes various special formats including one for sound archives.[6] The MAD2 sound archives format is reproduced here as Appendix II. MAD2's general recommendations derive ultimately from the 'Jenkinson' approach discussed in Chapter 1, and include many examples drawn from current practice in UK repositories. Documentation needs to reflect the original function of the material described, and the order in which it was created. Descriptions may be drawn up on several levels, reflecting the hierarchical structure of archives (and of organizations). General aspects of this 'multi-level rule' are conveniently summarized in the *MAD User Guide*[7], and the limited (though necessary) application of multi-level descriptions to sound archives is given in section 3 of the MAD2 sound archives format (Appendix II p.208). Access to subject content should be achieved as a secondary operaton through indexing. All the MAD2 formats also make provision for detailed technical descriptions and for conservation data such as the creation of copies, storage conditions, and conservation priority. The aim of the author and sponsors of MAD2 is that it should be adopted as the UK descriptive standard for archives as AACRII has been for books, although because of the very wide range of materials covered by MAD2, and the requirement for 'free text' elements in archival descriptions, no attempt is made to prescribe detailed rules on syntax, punctuation etc. of the kind typical of AACRII and MARC-AMC.

The format for sound recordings was 'designed for use in a general repository, and is concerned with descriptions of sound materials which are to be included in general finding aids'. Such a general repository might wish to contribute to and benefit from an online documentation network, and one of the purposes of the Archival Description Project, based on the original list of data elements drawn up by the Society of Archivists' Specialist Repositories Group, has been to establish a standard resulting in compatible data from numerous sources which could be mounted on a UK version of MARC-AMC or equivalent. Obviously not all data elements will be appropriate to all repositories: the point is that the elements included in local codes should result from the same analysis as performed by MAD2 so that they will be comparable in function to similar elements compiled elsewhere.

But the application of the MAD2 format need not be confined to general repositories interested in networking. It is perfectly suitable for use in repositories which hold only sound archives, and could with benefit be used as the standard for the (re)construction of documentation practices, particularly when working towards the introduction of a computer system, even if cheap and of limited capability. At the very least MAD2 provides a good introduction to the analysis of descriptions into data elements, and an *aide-memoire* to which elements may be required.

Notes on the MAD2 Sound Archives Format

The methodology and rules on which the MAD2 formats are based are explained in the main work and summarized in the *MAD User Guide*. Detailed explanations and examples relating to the sound archives format are given in section 5 of this format (Appendix II p.208). The following supplementary notes on certain data elements in the format may also be of assistance.

Arrangement and numbering

The 'reference code' element in section 5A of the sound archives format can only be applied after the recordings have been arranged in order and numbered. The amount of investigation and arrangement needed to establish a satisfactory order for numbering will depend on the type of acquisition process, the degree of care with which the recordings have been treated in the past, the stage at which the archivist became involved and so on (see Chapter 2 pp. 16–28). On the one hand the task is straightforward compared with textual archives because the administrative background is unlikely to be complex or of great age, on the other it can be much more tortuous if recordings cannot be readily assessed and identified from written markings or accompanying documentation.

Essential rules to be followed in arranging and numbering sound archives are:

i   Keep archival and non-archival (e.g. commercially published) recordings separate.

ii   Keep recordings from different organizational backgrounds separate. 'Inherited' recordings produced by the organization which employs the archivist should not be arranged and numbered with recordings deposited from outside. Each series of deposited recordings should be kept separate, even if this results in 'collections' consisting of only a few tapes or perhaps only one tape. It may also be most efficient to arrange and number its preservation, listening and other copies in a separate sequence, linked with the originals through cross-references (section 5F of the sound archives format) and below under 'Elements of conservation policy – arrangement and numbering' (p.112).

iii   If necessary, subdivide 'groups' (*MAD User Guide* pp. 5–16) of recordings into 'classes' and arrange and number individual items in chronological order within each class. New recordings recently generated should be added in order to the end of the sequence to which they belong.

iv Sequences which require no subdivision, or whose background is not clear, should (at least provisionally) be arranged and numbered in chronological order. Where no dates are apparent recordings should be arranged so as to reflect provenance as closely as possible on the basis of contents, box markings, physical appearance etc.

v Numbers applied to inherited or deposited recordings by creators or previous custodians should generally be retained unless they are erroneous or seriously confusing. New numbers usually need to be cross-referenced with the old ones, and confusion is difficult to avoid.

The following hypothetical example of the arrangement and numbering of permanently preserved radio station recordings illustrates the approach to sound archives produced by an organization:

Reference	Description
R5	Radio Rutland
	(Note: If the archivist works for Radio Rutland and deals only with recordings from this source, a reference and description at this level may not be needed. Where Radio Rutland recordings are being transferred to an outside repository which also receives recordings from other radio stations, the prefix R might denote radio station recordings, as distinct from, say, O for oral history projects, D for deposited collections etc.)
R5/1	News and current affairs department
R5/2	Music Department
R5/3	Farming and gardening department
R5/1/1	News and current affairs: live outside recordings
R5/1/2	News and current affairs: edited tapes, outtakes
	etc.

R5/1/3　　　　　News and current affairs: programmes as transmitted

　　　　　　　　etc.

R5/1/3/1–　　　　News and current affairs: individual transmitted programmes in date order

R5/1/3/1/1–3　　Three individual tapes making up one transmitted programme

This process of subnumbering may seem over-elaborate but it has the great advantage that problems (especially items known to be missing from the sequence or which turn up after numbers have been assigned and used in documentation) can be confined to one area without affecting the overall reference structure. Deposited recordings from a less structured source need only be given an overall reference number for the collection and individual numbers for the recordings in chronological order.

Content descriptions

The 'content sub-area' elements appear in section 23.5C of the MAD2 sound archives format. Two common categories requiring specialized ranges of data elements for content description are oral history and 'performance' recordings.

Oral history　The chapter on cataloguing and indexing by Roger Smither and Laura Kamel in David Lance's *An archive approach to oral history*[8] provides a good easily obtainable introduction to oral history documentation. The Imperial War Museum's 'full cataloguing' code (not the later augmented accessions format illustrated below) is discussed, and there are useful comments on indexing problems and the need for consistency which assumes crucial importance in computerized systems. A fiche page from the computer version of the IWM system is reproduced by Smither on page 38 of Lance's *Sound Archives.*[9] Following MAD2's 'Rule of information retrieval', full descriptions of oral history interviews must include a synopsis (usually based on a full transcript prepared earlier) and indexing should reflect all aspects of the interview in order that a full and balanced impression of the subject coverage is conveyed by the description.

Indexing oral history and other speech recordings needs to be done on the basis of a standard list of index terms or thesaurus, with built-in cross references. One recent approach by the National Library of Australia is described in *Oral History* vol. 15 no. 1.[10] Another approach might be by means of a numerical subject classification scheme along the lines of the Social History and Industrial Classification (SHIC) being developed by UK museums; so far no comparable scheme has been produced for oral history. An important consideration is the indexing of concepts such as 'racial discrimination', 'household budgeting', 'marriage customs' 'adolescence' etc. which are unlikely to appear (at least in a standardized form) in ordinary speech or in written transcripts.

Performance recordings There is a clear requirement for standardized terminology in describing and indexing performance recordings. All references to a particular performer, author or composer, or to a distinct work, need to be identifiable so that they will appear together in indexes. In all but the smallest collection served by manual systems this presents a considerable problem: names have variant spellings, titles may appear in the original language or in a variety of translations, etc. The conventional professional approach is to index on the basis of an authority file of standard spellings, incorporating cross references to variants. In its simplest form this involves maintaining a separate authority file on cards which are checked when each name or title is entered. Until recently all but the most powerful mainframe-based computer cataloguing systems relied on the maintenance of manual authority files. Using the latest generation of relational database packages for microcomputers, however, the authority checking routine can be built into the file structure and input routines of the system, and much time saved. There is still the requirement to establish standard forms and here sound archivists are best guided by professional library practice. The most widely accepted and compatible standards appear in chapters 22–25 of AACRII, but the procedures for establishing spellings of new names and titles can be laborious and require access to the necessary documentation and reference works. For music names and titles the 'Grove plus common sense' approach to the establishment of standards is still widespread in the UK.[11]

A less time-consuming alternative is the use of a free text indexing approach, providing access via a word-search facility which will bring together variant spellings if they have certain short combinations of letters in common. This has been found adequate, for example, by the Mechanical Copyright Protection Society for searching their massive files of works, composers etc.

Management considerations

Unfortunately, because sound recordings are compact and efficient information carriers, the work of documenting them, and particularly of describing their contents, is time-consuming and expensive. Against a desirable documentation scheme worked out theoretically (with the aid of such as MAD2) needs to be set the capacity of the repository to undertake the work. It is the rule rather than the exception that documentation systems adopted by sound archive repositories in their early days are found to be too time-consuming when the volume of acquisitions increases. For instance even in 1982 Roger Smither was commenting 'The number of cataloguers [at the Imperial War Museum Department of Sound Records] has not proved enough to keep pace with the oral history acquisitions generated by the three interviewers on the Museum staff, and the freelance interviewers who are also employed'.[12] More recently the backlog had become so unmanageable that a less time-consuming system covering less of the subject content of the recordings was adopted in order to create a usable finding-aid to the uncatalogued material (see below). However experiences at the NSA over the past dozen years provide perhaps the classic case.

Under a socialist administration in the mid-1970s a cataloguing system based on a format designed to cater for the wide range of the Archive's existing and potential holdings was devised and a group of three library-trained cataloguers ultimately recruited. The format and rules were professionally designed by the chief cataloguer and remain a model of their type.

Resources would not stretch to computerization so work began on 6″ by 4″ index cards; it was anticipated, however, that funding would be made available for a suitable system, and for a much larger cataloguing staff, as time went on. Neither of these assumptions proved correct. Some 'computerization' was achieved, enabling some catalogue records to be input onto floppy discs intended for subsequent batch processing onto microfiche, but with the changing economic circumstances of the 1980s the large body of cataloguers ceased to be a realistic possibility, and in any case management decisions placed more emphasis on the recruitment of subject curators whose main work consisted of negotiating acquisitions and answering enquiries, both of which served to point up the 'inadequacy' of the cataloguing operation and suggest that funds directed towards it would not yield a sufficient return. Meanwhile the NSA's range of acquisitions was increasing and a need to keep track of incoming collections and field recordings led to the adoption of a manual accessions and initial documentation procedure based on form-filling and unrelated to the existing cataloguing procedure. Several subject curators adapted this system for use as a crude subject finding-aid, and gradually two quite separate sources of documentation, one scientifically planned, the other much more *ad hoc*, came to exist side-by-side. As it has turned out, the two approaches have been capable of integration via a more modern flexible database system being adopted in several areas of the British Library.

With copious hindsight, most of the 'rules' applicable to decisions on documentation strategy are illustrated in the above much abbreviated cautionary tale:

i   Since documentation is central to the repository's operation, policy decisions must be made centrally and with the involvement and support of the head of the repository and all staff concerned.

ii   Ideally all the documentation compiled by the repository relating to its recordings should be held in a single system based on a single comprehensive code such as the MAD2 sound archives format. This recommendation is much easier to make in the light of the increased availability of relatively inexpensive database packages for use on microcomputers. If more than one system is to be operated (e.g. a separation of 'accessions', 'cataloguing' and 'conservation' paperwork or databases) these should be based on a single code, should be capable of eventual integration, and should not involve duplication of effort.

iii   The ideal must be weighed against the practical. Those with relevant experience within and outside the repository should be consulted so that the best prediction of performance in the long and short term can be obtained.

iv   Systems should serve immediate needs even if this means limiting their scope so that eventual overall usefulness is reduced. The time-honoured argument as to what degree of help the repository should be providing to all types of users should be rehearsed in the light of 'market research' among present and potential clientèle, but in the end the decision must always favour the immediately practicable, subject to (vii) below.

v   In most repositories the most important 'immediate need' is that documentation should keep pace with acquisitions. In a new set-up operations should be self-regulating. Where a large backlog is inherited or created by bulk transfer, the implication is that to 'keep pace' documentation will initially be very superficial.

vi   If only a proportion of holdings can be documented in depth, all staff with an interest in the selection should be involved in making it.

vii   Systems should be as adaptable and flexible as possible so that changes in resources or requirements can be accommodated. This implies that a computer-based system must be considered and probably adopted. Modern packages can provide great potential for the future reorganization of data if they are properly used.

viii   As a general rule all repository staff concerned with the acquisition and processing of recordings should participate in the work of documentation. This implies either that staff from a relevant library, archive or museum background should be recruited, or that existing staff should be given adequate training, or that the system should not be beyond the capabilities of existing or available staff to operate. The establishment of a separate, specialist 'cataloguing section' is not recommended under any circumstances, though there may be a case for employing a consultant periodically to carry out limited specialist operations, and there is certainly no problem in taking on a group of keyboarding staff to carry out routine work under supervision.

Computers

The use of computer-based documentation systems is strongly recommended. Any repository with the resources to pay staff and accommodation costs should have no difficulty in justifying the relatively low initial investment in computerization. To state only some of the most obvious advantages:

- The various ordering and indexing functions of computer systems enable tasks to be performed and information produced beyond manual capabilities yet with minimal extra staff time.
- By automating repetitive processes, further staff time is saved.

- Computer-held data is capable of rearrangement as new requirements arise; 'hard copy' is inflexible.
- If systems are set up and data is input correctly, computers do not make mistakes, and many systems will assist the correct inputting of data.
- Computerized data may be electronically transmitted or networked.

As with many other aspects of the administration of sound archives, computerized documentation requirements have much in common with those of textual archive repositories; and it is certainly possible for sound and textual archive documentation to be mounted on the same system by repositories which hold both. For newcomers to the field the terminology and groundwork are covered in *Computerising archives: some guidelines* by Phillips and Woolgar, and in the second edition of Michael Cook's *Archives and the computer.* [13] Information given here is intended to supplement these very useful works or to relate to special requirements for sound archives.

Developments in computer hard- and software are rapid: most of the specific allusions or recommendations made today will be out of date in a couple of years. By the same token, strategies which seemed sensible only two years ago are not emphasized here because they no longer appear to represent the best use of resources. For instance, several local government archive repositories in the UK elected or were 'persuaded' in recent years to adopt systems based on existing mainframe computers. At the time, the advantage of this over the use of independent microcomputers was that greater data storage capacity was available and more versatile, and powerful systems could be operated. Today there are database and free text retrieval systems for use on microcomputers powerful enough to suit the needs of even the larger local government record offices and libraries, and those tied to mainframes are in some cases regretting their dependence on central provision and possibly on 'in-house' analysts and programmers whose experience may not have been sufficient to cater for all the repository's complex requirements. Again until very recently a number of repositories (including the NSA, the Imperial War Museum Department of Sound Records, and many UK museums) opted for offline data inputting onto discs which were batch processed by a central bureau onto COM-fiche as the only affordable computerized cataloguing and indexing. The widespread use of the Museum Documentation Association's GOS package and bureau facilities is described at length in the 1986 edition of *Archives and the Computer*, but the strategy already seems old fashioned.

For the independent sound archive repository, or for custodians working in libraries or museums whose systems are found to be incompatible with requirements, a free-standing microcomputer system currently appears to be the best choice. Much greater data storage capacity is now available at relatively low cost, which means that a number of well-tried, versatile and sophisticated systems, which could only be used on mainframes or mini computers in the past, are now available as packages for micros. Direct online inputting of complex and extensive documentation may be carried out within the repository by staff responsible for data compilation; two- or three-stage inputting using data capture forms and off-site bureaux can be avoided; and users have the benefit of flexible and efficient online searching.

A number of 'home-made' microcomputer-based systems have been written by or for archivists, but the effort and time no longer seem justified in view of the wide range of commercial software packages now available. The rest of this chapter is therefore concerned with aspects of microcomputer system selection.

Sound archivists who already operate manual documentation systems will be conscious of requirements and shortcomings. Others will be using a computer from the outset. For both the standard advice is to construct a list of desirable data elements, functions and facilities and then find a suitable package. The fact is, however, that computer capabilities are so varied and complex that there seems little point in making plans before gaining familiarity with the range of packages on offer – after all, manual systems are not designed without an intimate knowledge of human capabilities. Computer application should be seen as a means of increasing possibilities, not limiting them. Many archivists and several sound archivists appear to have opted for one widely-used package, perhaps following the example of colleagues or advice from 'experts', without examining others which are clearly superior and little more expensive. The analysis given below may help to focus expectations, and a number of publications carry lists, descriptions and reviews of what is on offer.[14] Armed with some knowledge of the field, sound archivists will be better placed to fight off attempts by administration sections and senior managers to force the acceptance of unsuitable computers and software, and to achieve documentation systems which make the best use of resources available.

Hardware and software requirements are generally interdependent. If compatibility and standardization are important, and most assessors think they are, if only to ensure longevity and ease of technical assistance, packages based around the IBM PC-DOS operating system (or MS-DOS for compatibles) are preferable to others. This may immediately narrow down the choice before any detailed requirements have been considered. Consideration should continue by a process of elimination, the main aspects of which are listed and illustrated below:

Number of users If a multi-user system is required, this will have a fundamental influence on selection and costs. Requirements and resources will also affect the architecture of the system: the best multi-user option at present appears to be the use of several networked processors rather than a central processing unit since this gives greater flexibility and speed of operation for relatively little extra cost.

General approach There are currently two contrasting 'schools of thought' on computerized documentation practice. Those who need to input descriptive information at length and provide an 'automatic' index to it may prefer the *free text retrieval* approach.

An admired free text system used by several repositories for archival description is STATUS, originally devised by the Atomic Energy Authority at Harwell. A detailed description and recommendation for it, as applied to the documentation of the Duke of Wellington's Papers at Southampton University, is available.[15] This application was based on the university's mainframe computer, but a version of the software for microcomputers has now appeared.[16] Systems of this kind can cater for fields of considerable length and have a sophisticated indexing capability enabling searches on a number of character combinations to be carried out automatically without prior inputting of index terms.

Free text systems are certainly a tempting prospect for oral history collections wishing to catalogue and index long series of transcribed interviews, which may even be possible without key-boarding, using optical character recognition. But they are uneconomical on computer storage capacity, and relatively high on inputting time (in the absence of OCR) since there is no facility for avoiding the repetition of identical information. The free text index does not establish cross references between variant spellings: unless considerable care and skill are used in data preparation and input, the index will be more or less 'dirty', and complicated character string searching will be needed to locate information. Search times can be reduced by carrying out separate indexing on chosen fields, and subject keywords which do not appear in the text can be added; but the suitability of the free text approach should be questioned if this additional indexing seems likely to be needed frequently.

File structure is rigid: data from separate files cannot be combined and re-combined in various on-screen formats to suit new requirements as they arise. But if the sound archivist has inherited or wishes to computerize and index a large body of consistently spelt, carefully compiled descriptive data which he prefers to keep more or less in its original layout, the attractions of a free text system may prove conclusive.

Database systems require more analysis and structuring of documentation, and perhaps more flexibility, not to say compromise, in order to make the best use of the computer's strengths. Some packages enable fields of free text to be compiled and indexed, but more typically descriptions and other information are broken down and input as data elements, with indexing as an additional or linked task, enabling rapid economical access and manipulation. This 'professional' strategy is particularly appropriate where existing manually compiled documentation of varying style and standard is being computerized; where extensive indexing by keywords is required; or where there is a need for rigid standardization of indexed names and titles (as with many performance recordings). But although systems with validation and defaulting facilities (see below) can speed up data capture, inputting has to be relatively painstaking and time-consuming. The sound archivist and his staff in effect anticipate and facilitate the work and requirements of researchers and other users (including themselves of course), but some would argue that, where applicable, free text indexing is as much as researchers are entitled to expect, and the onus should be on them to put the time into online string searches. However at present the database model is the more common in UK archive and sound archive repositories, mainly one suspects because of the widespread marketing and proliferation of the dBase series of packages.[17]

Storage capacity Is the maximum storage capacity adequate for present and future needs? Are the data fields of fixed or variable length? A characteristic of dBase is its fixed length fields which are quite inadequate for many archival data elements. (dBase is used at the North West Sound Archive in conjunction with a system of mnemonics and abbreviations to keep field lengths within limits, at the Bradford Heritage Recording Unit, and at the London History Workshop Centre Sound and Video Archive).

Data structure This consideration applies primarily to database systems, where the choice is between *flat file* and *relational* structures. Flat systems resemble free text systems in certain respects. They may have fixed or variable length fields and may incorporate both free text and keyword indexing. They may accommodate numerous files but unlike relational systems do not permit economies on storage space: each data element in each field in each file is input and held within the confines of that file. Files are indexed separately and must be searched separately. Contrasting uses of one of the more attractive flat file systems – *Inmagic* – are seen in applications by the Imperial War Museum Department of Sound Records, and by the Irish Traditional Music Archive in Dublin.[18] The IWM application features only one file into which accessions and other readily available information about recordings are entered without time-consuming synopses. The data elements/ field names are:

AC.   Accession number
SE.   Project/series title
TI.   Name of interviewee
G.   Descriptive title of interviewee
PD.   Date of production
PC.   Production company
NAT.   Nationality of interviewee
D.   Name of donor
FA.   Form of acquisition: recording, transfer etc.
TA.   Type of acquisition: music, oral history, speech etc.
REC.   Name of interviewer
AX.   Access rating code
R.   Number of tape reels
M.   Duration in minutes
DA.   Date of accession
DP.   Date tapes processed
DC.   Date of cataloguing
CAT.   Name of cataloguer
TS.   Typescript available?
IP.   Index: people
IU.   units/organizations
IL.   locations

IE.	events
IS.	start date
IF.	finish date
IC.	concepts (e.g. anti-semitism etc.)
IO.	objects (e.g. song titles, weapons, etc.)
OL.	Original language(s)
N.	Notes about recordings
I.	Name of inputter
ID.	Input date
SF1–4.	Spare fields

In the IWM application most of the disadvantages of flat file systems are immaterial. Inmagic was adopted in Dublin because of its unlimited field lengths, dBase having been rejected on these grounds, but the system's drawbacks are also in evidence. There are eleven separate files for sound recordings, still and moving pictures, artefacts, manuscript materials, printed materials, melodies, songs, dances, biographies, ensembles, and institutions and companies, each of which has an individual data structure reflecting the character of the material described. Clearly many names and titles will appear over and over again across the files, but there is no means of indexing out these occurrences into a single sequence or of avoiding the repetition of information at the inputting stage. As in free text systems, the repetition of data also takes up valuable storage space.

Relational systems work on a different basis. The file structure reflects the main data elements common to each description. This structure need bear no relation to the screen format(s) used for data capture or display: for these purposes data destined for or derived from more than one file may be displayed on the screen simultaneously, and in a variety of combinations serving different purposes. For example an input format might marshal data elements destined for various files in an order reflecting earlier manual documentation or some other logical sequence. The more advanced the system, the wider the scope for juxtaposing file contents. Relational systems economize on storage space by storing data elements such as keywords, names and titles only once and linking them to occurrences in particular recordings or documents. The system thus depends on the compilation of standard versions of names and titles, and thereby provides a built-in authority list which simplifies the work of 'clean' indexing and cross referencing.

If fields of adequate length are catered for, relational systems appear to be potentially more efficient for the documentation of sound archives, particularly if these include performance recordings and if there is a need for 'clean', rapidly accessed indexes. A reservation might be that their data structure diverts attention from the essential uniqueness of individual archival recordings, and places more emphasis on the fact that the contents of many recordings have features which can be lumped together. In this respect free text systems enable the documentation process to reflect more closely the physical character of sound archives, largely by requiring few digressions from orthodox manual listing procedures.

After years of slow progress towards 'computerization' the NSA along with some other departments of the British Library has begun to adapt the *Advanced Revelation* relational database package as the basis for its documentation system, with the intention of running it on networked micros.[19] The package offers most of the desirable features listed below and is not significantly more expensive than more limited rival systems. A file structure such as that illustrated in Figure 4.1, incorporating both administrative and descriptive data, is the eventual aim. The Advanced Revelation package also forms the basis of the documentation system under development at Somerset Record Office.

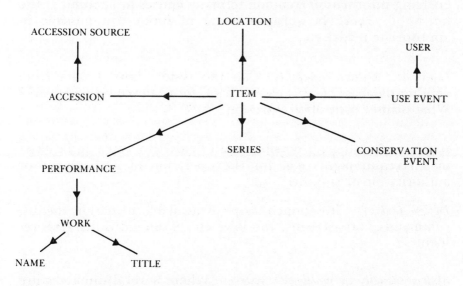

Figure 4.1 Relational database file structure incorporating administrative and descriptive data.

Method and design Software packages require adaptation for use in the documentation of sound archives: many will have been aimed primarily at business applications. Most packages are *programme driven* and require additional software to be written for particular applications, which takes time and skill. Some sound archivists may have or be able to develop an aptitude but others will be dependent on programmers who will need to be paid for their services. Supplementary programmes written by laymen are often only just adequate for the task and tend to cause problems for succeeding users. These problems are reduced in *parameter-driven* systems in which existing software within the package, backed by a data dictionary, enables specialist screen layouts, routines and links to be established without recourse to programming. Less computer skill is needed and much time and expense can be saved.

In addition to these major structural and operational aspects, choice among software packages may also depend on other features such as:

Data input facilities Is there an input validation capability, i.e. can the system be programmed to accept entries which are valid according to predetermined criteria (such as spelling) and reject others? Can a defaulting facility be brought into operation, enabling information common to many entries to be input at the touch of a key? Is wordprocessing of input text possible in appropriate fields? etc.

Input and output capability Can the system import data from another database? Can it export data, for example via a network? What printer controls are present?

Indexing Is indexing possible in all fields? Do available facilities match requirements e.g. for the operation of a thesaurus or authority file or stoplist?

Design features How much scope is available to design menus, commands, entry screens, 'windows' etc. to suit individual requirements.

System security in multi-user systems Where several inputters are likely to be working simultaneously, 'file locking' prevents data from being entered in a file which is already receiving data from another input source. This may result in data loss since the locked-off source may be unaware that input is prevented. 'Record locking' is preferable as it protects only the part of the file actually being worked on, leaving more of the system open for data entry.

Support Packages are 'supported' in several ways; quality and style vary considerably. It is obviously essential that technical support should remain available for a period of years. Is a reasonably priced service contract available? Are the instruction manuals which accompany the package easy to follow? Do the suppliers or concessionaires run a training programme? Do they provide free advice initially? Do they provide an online help service to which one can subscribe?

Practical questions of this sort are best answered by existing users. Probably the most relevant range of experience for sound archivists is available through the Society of Archivists' Computer group.[20] A number of BASC members, including those referred to in this chapter, are computer users and can be contacted via the secretary.

References

1. The use of bar-coding is becoming fashionable in computer-based storage documentation systems; its only application in sound archives appears to be at the National Archives in Washington DC.
2. In addition to the codes discussed below, see also Bureau of Canadian Archivists, *Toward descriptive standards*, Ottawa, 1985.
3. See M. J. Evans and L. B. Weber, *MARC for archives and manuscripts: a compendium of practice*, State Historical Society of Wisconsin, Madison, 1985. MARC-AMC is based on the descriptive code for archives in S. L. Hensen, *Archives, personal papers, and manuscripts: a cataloguing manual . . .*, Library of Congress, Washington DC, 1983.
4. M. Gorman and P. Winkler, *Anglo-American cataloguing rules*, 2nd ed., The Library Association, London, 1978. See also M. G. Cook, *Archives and manuscripts control: a MARC format for use with a cooperative online database* (British Library R&D Report 5945, British Library, London, 1987.
5. *Rules for the archival cataloguing of sound recordings*, Association of Recorded Sound Collections/Associated Audio Archives, 1980; the only readily available reference copy in the UK appears to be in the BLISS department of the British Library.
6. M. G. Cook and M. Procter, *A manual of archival description*, 2nd ed., Gower, Aldershot, 1990.

7. M. G. Cook and M. Procter, *A MAD user guide*, Gower, Aldershot, 1989, pp. 3–16.

8. D. Lance, *An archive approach to oral history*, Imperial War Museum/IASA, 1978, pp. 24–35.

9. D. Lance (ed.) *Sound Archives: a guide to their establishment and development*, IASA, 1983.

10. J. Fitzpatrick and S. Reid, 'Indexing a large scale oral history project' in *Oral History*, vol. 15, no. 1.

11. I.e. spellings and usages in S. Sadie (ed.), *The New Grove Dictionary of Music and Musicians*, Macmillan, London, 1980.

12. R. Smither, 'Documentation' in D. Lance (ed.), *Sound Archives: a guide to their establishment and development*, IASA 1983, p. 37.

13. C. M. Phillips and C. M. Woolgar, *Computerising archives: some guidelines*, Society of Archivists Computer Applications Committee, 1985 (obtainable from Hampshire Record Office, 20 Southgate Street, Winchester SO23 9EF); M. G. Cook, *Archives and the computer*, 2nd ed., Butterworths, London, 1986.

14. For example H. Dyer and A. Gunson, *A directory of library and information retrieval software for microcomputers*, 3rd ed., Aldershot, Gower, 1988; M. Collier (ed.), *Microcomputer software for information management: case studies*, Aldershot, Gower, 1986. Periodicals: *Vine* and *Library Micromation News* published by The Library and Information Technology Centre, Polytechnic of Central London, 235 High Holborn, London WC1V 7DN; *Program* (ASLIB, 20–24 Old Street, London EC1V 9AP); *Computers in Libraries* (Meckler UK Ltd., Grosvenor Gardens House, Grosvenor Gardens, London SW1W 0BS). A *National Inventory of Software* has been compiled on computer at Southampton University Library and may be accessed on line via the UK universities network JANET in the British Library reading room and elsewhere.

15. C. M. Woolgar, 'The Wellington Papers database: an interim report' in *Journal of the Society of Archivists*, vol. 9, no. 1 (Jan. 1988), pp. 1–29.

16. Marketed by Harwell Computerpower Ltd., Curie Avenue, Harwell, Oxfordshire, OX11 0QW.

17. dBase II, III+ and IV marketed by Ashton Tate Ltd., Oakland, 1 Bath Road, Maidenhead, Berkshire.

18. Inmagic is marketed in the UK by Head Computers Ltd., Oxted Mill, Spring Lane, Oxted, Surrey RH8 9PB.

19. Marketed by ICS Sales Ltd., Tempus Business Centre, 57 Kingsclere Road, Basingstoke, Hampshire, RG21 2XG.

20. The group distributes an informative newsletter among members of the Society of Archivists and runs training courses. Five user groups for dBase, STATUS, MODES (a data entry and management system sold by the MDA), CAIRS and STAIRS (text retrieval systems sharing some features with STATUS) have been formed.

DOCUMENTATION

The current secretary is Keith Sweetmore, West Yorkshire Archives Service, Registry of Deeds, Newstead Road, Wakefield, WF1 2DE.

Chapter 5

ACCOMMODATION, EQUIPMENT AND FACILITIES

Introduction

Few sound archivists will enjoy the luxury of designing purpose-built accommodation, but all should be aware of the essential requirements of any premises, and should press for the best possible standards whenever their recommendations are sought. Although sound archivists need to be familiar with the basic range of requirements and to keep up with recent developments (which can be rapid in the case of fire precautions for example), the critical time for the establishment or improvement of accommodation standards is at the foundation or relocation of the repository. When this opportunity arises, it is wiser in the long run, though not always possible, to reject unsuitable areas at the outset rather than accept them as a temporary solution to a pressing problem in the hope that improvements can be effected later. It is reasonable to expect the organization which has decided to take on or relocate the sound archivist to have anticipated at least some of the resource consequences. Requests for suitable working and storage areas, plant and equipment may therefore stand a better chance of sympathetic consideration at the beginning rather than later when interest and resources have been diverted to other matters.

How can future requirements be predicted, and how can funding bodies be persuaded to provide for needs which are not currently demonstrable? The information given below and in the other books and articles referred to may be helpful in indicating what can reasonably be expected, even by a small organization. Also, at least some impression of future requirements can be projected from previous performance or the experience of other similar repositories. In the UK those starting out could contact the secretary of BASC (currently c/o the NSA) or consult the *Directory of Recorded Sound Resources* for information on comparable organizations.

Every effort should be made to anticipate changes in patterns of use as the organization develops, and to influence planners accordingly. For example, problems created by remotely-sited storage areas may not be serious during the infancy of an organization, but may subsequently have a significant effect on its efficiency as 'business' grows. On the other hand, increased use by outsiders may pose insoluble security problems in cases where storage areas are too close to listening or study facilities. Funding bodies may take more notice of specifications based on precedent rather than on imaginative schemes; either way an uphill struggle can be expected.

Accommodation planning is a heavy responsibility. If facilities are being purpose-built or created by alteration to existing buildings, they should suit the currently stated specialist needs but will not be easily adaptable for other purposes, either within the repository or by others. It is essential to think big, even if the funding body rules out any provision beyond immediate requirements. As the time-lapse between initial specification and final availability of accommodation is invariably longer than promised by planners and managers, provision frequently turns out to be inadequate from the start. So think ahead and get it right – you'll be stuck with it!

Laws, bylaws and standards

All buildings where people work or study must comply with national and local legislation. In the UK the main relevant Acts are the Offices, Shops and Railway Premises Act 1963 and the Health and Safety at Work Act 1974. The Health and Safety Executive is probably the most useful government body to contact if guidance is needed. Plans must also conform to building, planning and fire regulations, which may prove to be irksome when adapting existing premises. Previously unmodified buildings will need to be brought up to the required standard when alterations are made (e.g. with regard to fireproof doors, means of escape etc.); floor loadings will have to remain within the safety limits dictated by structural surveyors (which often appear unbelievably low to the layman), and what seemed a workable and economical use of space may be declared unacceptable by the authorities. It is at this stage that the pressure for compromise may begin, and when the archivist needs to stick out as far as possible for what he really needs.

Detailed specifications for many aspects of repository accommodation and equipment are published by the various national standards organizations. Most general works on archives also include guidance on accommodation, and there are a number of more specific books and articles which may be found useful.[1] There is no British Standard covering all aspects of repository accommodation. The nearest to it is BS 5454 which covers the storage and exhibition of archives. It is used below as the basis for the section on storage accommodation.

Formulating requirements

The sound archivist should make his accommodation requirements clearly known. Someone competent to exercise the function of architect should then translate the requirements into a scheme which will be more or less acceptable to the archivist. A period of discussion and compromise is then likely, after which building or adaptation and occupation will proceed unless one or other party finds the situation unacceptable. This process may be very formal in the case of large new projects of which the sound archives are to form a part, or much more informal when only a few people are involved in accommodating a small local operation. Either way the 'architect' must be given a 'brief', or his own experience and ideas will dictate the scheme and the results, as many examples show, can be expected to be remarkably inappropriate. The more information he is given at the outset, the better the chances of achieving satisfactory premises. Accommodation for sound archives should offer the following features. Proposals which do not include these may be said with confidence to be unsuitable:

- security for holdings
- satisfactory climatic conditions
- storage accommodation separate from work and study areas
- straightforward access for visitors
- sufficient space for current activities and holdings
- some potential for expansion.

There are several ways of preparing a shopping list of accommodation and equipment requirements. One is to envisage a typical period of work and to note down every operation undertaken and facility needed in the course of it. Another is to hold a brainstorming session with colleagues at which any and every conceivable requirement may be stated and recorded, to be rationalized later. These processes, and examination of others' experience, are likely to come up with at least the following basic accommodation requirements:

- staff working area or office
- storage accommodation
- listening and study area for users
- technical preparation area
- lavatory, washroom, cloakroom, refreshment area
- cleaning facilities
- goods loading point
- parking.

Most sound archivists will have many if not all of these facilities provided for them in shared premises or as part of a larger library, museum or record office. Nothing more needs to be said here about the sanitary and cleaning facilities, and little seems worthy of special mention in relation to staff areas and offices, except to indicate that these should if at all possible be separate from storage and public areas because the requirements of these various functions are generally incompatible: working areas are noisy with telephone conversations, work in transit, briefing sessions etc. while users, particularly listeners, require silence; storage areas should for conservation (and economic) reasons be kept rather cooler than areas continuously occupied by people, and so on. Apart from the usual range of office equipment, staff responsible for transcribing, cataloguing or selecting extracts from recordings will require suitable playback equipment, normally in the form of a cassette and/or reel-to-reel player. For security and conservation reasons the number of recordings kept out of storage in working areas should be minimized and a secure cupboard or cabinet should be available to house recordings which have to be retained. Correct security and handling procedures should be codified at an early stage (see 'General security' below and NSA storage and handling code in Appendix I).

Listening and study facilities for users

Location

For most purposes, facilities for visitors are best sited near the entrance to the building, since this should provide easy access to all, including the disabled, and an easily identifiable location. Perhaps the only advantage of a characterless door down a corridor several floors up is that escape with stolen property might take a little longer. Where accommodation has to be above or below ground level the existence of a lift is an enormous advantage from many points of view.

General security

Within the study area the archivist will wish to provide good service, but his first responsibility is to the security of the holdings. Most sound archive media are easy to conceal so attention should be paid to deterring thieves. Where playback arrangements allow no contact with recordings in any form, attempts may be made by visitors to make illicit recordings on concealed 'Walkman'-type cassette recorders. In order to minimize these risks the entrance and exit (preferably the same door for both) should always be supervised when visitors are present. Visitors should not be allowed to take in bags and containers except where these are needed to carry materials for study, in which case there should be a policy of examining them on entry and exit. A notice indicating that this will be done should be posted at the entrance and no exceptions made. Lockers should be provided for bags left on entry.

If the study area has additional exits which are difficult to supervise, especially if these lead directly to a means of escape or to storage areas, it may be worth fitting or arranging a specific alarm system confined to these doors, since any intruder alarm system on the overall building will doubtless be switched off during the day. Advice could be sought from security officers or the police. Larger organizations may consider installing alarms activated by metallic tags attached to recordings. All access and egress is routed via a sensing device and unauthorized removal thus detected. Closed-circuit television scrutiny of study areas and their exits may also be thought worthwhile (though in the UK public service and local government unions are opposed to the use of CCTV and may prevent its installation). All these forms of security are fairly easy to circumvent, and their main value will be as a deterrent – cameras can be seen in operation and alarms will occasionally be set off accidentally by staff, indicating that the system does actually work.

Playback of recordings

There should be two fundamental playback rules in the repository. Firstly, original or single-copy recordings should be handled by staff only. If a user has a good reason for wishing to see the original (for example to examine the label on a disc) this should only be allowed under close staff supervision. Playback facilities should be arranged so that users are never required to play original recordings themselves. The type of arrangement will be related to the repository's conservation policy and the level of resources available.

Secondly, originals or single copies should not be used for playback, even by staff. As is stressed in Chapter 6, all sound archive media are more or less fragile and relatively short-lived. Copies should be made in case originals are damaged in use or prone to rapid deterioration. Ideally these copies should be on a reliable medium with good keeping characteristics, and at present the nearest approach to this is good quality quarter-inch standard play reel-to-reel tape. Copies on this medium will be suitable for use as security copies stored separately from the originals, and *can* also be used by staff for cataloguing, transcribing and other listening, although ideally a third copy should be run off (normally on cassette) for these purposes and the second copy kept purely for security and for use as a master from which all subsequent copies are run off.

In the Department of Sound Records at the Imperial War Museum this is in fact done and in addition to the reel-to-reel security copy a number of cassette copies are produced, one of which is kept in a sequence produced purely for listening by visitors. Cassette machines are available in the listening room and user copies are issued under supervision for headphone listening, to be returned on leaving. There is a possible danger of theft in this system, but no instance has been noted in over ten years' operation. Once all the copying has been done the operation of the playback service is economical as staff are able to get on with other routine work while supervising listeners. Recordings can be produced for listening virtually without notice so an appointment system is only needed to control the flow of visitors. Most users will be familiar with cassettes and their equipment, so copies in this format can be handled and played by users where reel-to-reel copies cannot.

Although this arrangement is excellent it is really only suitable for a well-funded organization which holds a fairly homogeneous series of recordings. At present the IWM has a staff of eight in the sound records department, two of whom are technicians. Its recordings number around 5,000 yet even here a serious backlog in copying work has begun to develop, emphasizing that the copying programme is expensive in time and materials. Various options for reducing the costs of this system while maintaining the same type of provision for listeners are given below. They get progressively cheaper but less satisfactory.

i   Reduce the number of cassette copies for internal use to one. This will only save the cost of the additional cassettes if, as is most cost effective, all the copies are made in one operation.

ii   Abandon production of reel-to-reel copies and produce cassette copies only which can be used for all purposes and serve as security copies. This may be as good as many organizations can afford. Tape costs are much reduced but cassettes are unsatisfactory for security copies. If the same copying time is needed, it might be argued that all this effort would be better devoted to producing good quality copies, since the extra cost of reel-to-reel tape is only a small proportion of overall costs. On the other hand the workload can be spread by enabling non-technical staff such as cataloguers or transcribers to make cassette copies from straightforward reel-to-reel or cassette originals as their work progresses. Where originals are cassettes an option is to buy a high-speed cassette duplicator which might at least enable a security copy of all recordings to be made, in theory as a temporary measure. The recording quality of the copies will be rather poor, but it may not be significantly worse than that of the originals in the case of oral history recordings.

iii   Produce cassette copies only on demand. This is the rock-bottom standard. If no routine copying is done, conservation and security duplication will depend entirely on current patterns of use and large areas will remain uncopied and at risk.

All the above options imply minimal playback costs by enabling users to handle recordings and use equipment themselves. The other basic approach is to entrust all handling and playback to staff, which will immediately imply higher running costs. Examples are found in both the playback facilities run by the Library of Congress, the Rodgers and Hammerstein Archives at New York Public Library, and the NSA. These are all comparatively large bodies which deal with a wide range of users listening to recordings on a variety of media. In particular their playback services need to be able to find and play a short extract which comprises only a fraction of the contents of one tape or disc which itself is one of hundreds of thousands. The production of individual listening copies on cassettes is beyond the means even of these relatively well-off organizations.

Instead, the NSA (for example) devotes such resources as it can to producing good quality reel-to-reel copies, which serve both as security copies and, as they are only handled by staff, for playback.

Original or single copies of archival recordings are never played to listeners, though in order to reduce the enormous copying burden limited categories of commercially published recordings may be played up to three times (see section III.7 of the NSA Handling Rules in Appendix I. The equivalent rule at the Library of Congress allows two plays). An appointment system is needed both to control numbers and to enable copies to be made in the many areas so far not covered by routine copying programmes.

Minimal supervision is required in the listening room but staff need to be continually involved with the playback equipment while listening is in progress. This equipment is sited remotely from the listening room in the three organizations mentioned above, though at the NSA playback staff used to operate machines mounted on a counter in the listening room, and communicated directly with users. The system was successful though noisy conversations could be difficult to avoid. Now, the playback operator may initially discuss the listener's requirements in person, but thereafter communication is usually via an intercom. Tape and disc players in the playback area are wired up via a switching console so that any set of headphones in the listening room can be connected to any machine. The listening points are equipped with tone and volume controls, and in an arrangement apparently unique to the NSA but worthy of wider use, several points are also equipped with cassette recorders in which a cassette is placed and the lid of the loading tray bolted shut from inside the machine.[2] The cassette cannot then be removed. If repeat listening is required, the recording is re-recorded onto the cassette on the first time through and can then be replayed by the listener any number of times without further involvement by the playback operator. The cassette remains in the machine ready for the next user to record over.

In the Rodgers and Hammerstein Archives the playback area is sited adjacent to storage areas several floors below the listening room. This has advantages for rapid retrieval of recordings but creates difficulties for listeners who wish to examine documentation stored with recordings (particularly in this case liner notes with discs). A solution has been to enable listeners to view the documentation via closed circuit television.

Listening accommodation and equipment

Most users wish to listen to recordings, study documentation, and make notes simultaneously, so furniture provided needs to suit these requirements. In the performing arts reading room at the Library of

Congress individual listening booths are built in, but the expense involved in installing and running such a system will be beyond virtually everyone else. Almost all individual listening will therefore be done through headphones so that several listeners can work in the same room together without disturbing one another. At the NSA individual carrells are provided, which give some privacy within one listening room. Each has a working surface about 2 feet 6 inches (76 cm.) by 18 inches (46 cm.) with a shelf above on which listening controls, headphone socket etc. are mounted. They seem to be generally satisfactory but are too small when used by music students who wish to follow bulky scores while listening (see Figure 5.1).

Figure 5.1   NSA listening facilities.

Sound archive users are normally allowed to handle written reference material relating to recordings, such as oral history transcripts, tape containers where these are the only source of information, documents which accompanied a collection of recordings at the time of deposit, commercial disc sleeves etc. Because this material is often unique and valuable it should be treated with the same care as textual archives are treated in a record office, a requirement which is often overlooked by sound archivists. Guidance is available in the standard works on archive administration. Standard recommendations would include the display of signs forbidding the use of ink while studying documents and the provision of special bookrests or supports when consulting bulky or fragile material.

Group listening

The provision of a room in which a group can listen together is often a high priority for the sound archivist. Many of his potential customers may be teachers with school parties or societies interested in subject areas served by recordings such as the performing arts, local history and traditional culture. Remotely-sited playback facilities are generally unsuitable for this form of use: recordings should be prepared on cassette and a cassette player, amplifier and speakers set up which the sound archivist or the leader of the group can use on the spot. Good quality domestic hi-fi equipment is perfectly suitable for this and wide-ranging recommendations catering for various room sizes and budgets appear regularly in such magazines as *The Gramophone* and *Hi-Fi News*, and in particular *Hi-Fi Choice*.

The room designated for group listening should be acoustically satisfactory. If it is being incorporated in new premises the recommendations of an acoustics specialist or studio designer should be sought as the general-purpose architect is most unlikely to have relevant experience. Where existing accommodation is being adapted, choice of an appropriate room will be the main consideration, since alterations to unsuitable rooms with large windows opening onto noisy roads, hard echoey surfaces, high ceilings, T- or L-shaped floor plans and so on will be costly. The presence of sound-absorbing wallcoverings or static furniture such as bookshelves or curtains is normally an advantage. Where space is limited consideration could be given to dual usage. The room used by individual listeners could be rearranged as a small auditorium during the evening, or where group listening during the day is required, individual listening could be temporarily suspended. Group listening should be arranged in compliance with copyright legislation.

Technical facilities

Sound archivists must have access to some technical facilities in order to make copies. Equipment requirements will relate to the nature of the recordings held and the type of work to be carried out.

In-house facilities are essential though they need not be very elaborate. There seems little point in setting up a sound archive if resources are not available to equip and staff a modest technical operation which will carry out most of the routine work. Some large-scale straightforward copying jobs and certain very specialized tasks might be appropriate for outside contractors to undertake, but there will always be problems over security and handling. Basic equipment requirements are:

i   machines on which each of the formats held can be played;
ii   machines on which copies can be made;
iii   a small mixer/switching console through which several copies can be made from one original, volumes controlled, vocal announcements made at the start of copies etc. according to requirements;
iv   a microphone for recording announcements;
v   an audio oscillator;
vi   playback equipment: preamplifier, amplifier and speakers;
vii   wiring and sundries including headphones, editing block (for attaching coloured leaders), a mains stabilizer to cut out electrical noise and interference etc.
viii lineup and service equipment (test tapes and discs, degaussing equipment, bulk eraser, disc cleaning materials etc.).

Minimal provision is likely to consist of one disc player, two reel-to-reel machines, two cassette machines, a very simple four-channel mixer, and the items under iv–vii above. For reliability and quality, 'professional' or 'semi-professional' reel-to-reel machines and mixer should be used. The rest can be made up of good quality hi-fi equipment. The total cost of this basic outfit at 1989 prices is likely to be about £5000. The more expensive items such as the reel-to-reel machines, microphone and speakers are fairly easy to acquire secondhand, and this is a better way of saving money than reducing standards.

If anything other than straight 'back-to-back' copying is envisaged, a more sophisticated mixer with built-in equalization facilities, and possibly also one or other of the available specialist equalization units, will also be required. In addition, the area where technical work is done should be very quiet so that results can be assessed aurally. This implies a separate room in the centre of the building, away from traffic and aircraft noise, and from other noisy work such as typing and switchboard operation. Where new premises are being built or a major adaptation made, specialist advice must be sought; effects quite contrary to requirements can be produced through the use of inappropriate designs and materials. Remember that a small acoustically sealed technical area or studio will require ventilation: the provision of a system which is quiet enough will be very expensive; and the presence of numerous items of electrical equipment will require special attention to fire and safety requirements.

It is an important though little-acknowledged part of the sound archivist's job to acquire and maintain equipment suitable for playing back all the recordings in his care. This is a major problem which is getting worse, even in relation to commonplace media such as 78 rpm discs, where the provision of styluses has been in the hands of a few specialist firms for many years, and the manufacture of suitable turntables is a minority pursuit. Those who have indulged in the use of domestic videocassettes as a cheap form of digital audio recording, or who now have custody of such recordings, are already finding a similar problem with the obsolescent PCM adaptors essential to the process.

Within the repository therefore sound archivists must stick to tried and tested media and equipment, which means in 1990 and for probably the next five to ten years, quarter-inch standard play tape and Philips-type compact cassettes, both of which have been in use for at least twenty years and are so common that they are unlikely to become difficult to obtain in the foreseeable future. Related equipment and spare parts can be expected to remain easily available for at least ten years after these media cease to be current. Sound archivists should as a matter of principle only recommend the use of well-established, reliable media and equipment if their opinions are sought on long-term preservation.

All the pressure will, of course, be against this advice. Newer media such as DAT cassettes and optical discs rely on digital recording techniques which, if of good specification, will produce recordings with a better signal-to-noise ratio, a wider frequency range, and the capability of being copied without signal deterioration. They are already comparatively cheap and will get cheaper. However, these media have no track record and there is at present little independent experimental evidence by which their longevity can be assessed. Though this may seem unlikely at present, there is no certainty that they will not be superseded by better formats and equipment within a few years. There is currently no national or international digital recording standard which industry, broadcasting and archival interests can all follow. Most crucially, modern electronic equipment is increasingly dependent on very complex miniature circuitry and precision-made parts, neither of which can be reproduced or even repaired by individual engineers at the workbench. If any of the newer formats does become as widespread as quarter-inch tape, archivists ought to be able to rely on a similarly widespread service and parts network well into the future. We are nowhere near that situation yet.

Archivists who cannot avoid receiving, say, DAT cassettes, or, where they are involved with recording, elect to use DAT, should make copies on the older formats for preservation and security. For this they will need DAT equipment which may become obsolete just as the video PCM adaptors have. Large repositories should investigate and plan the acquisition of enough equipment and spare parts to serve all future needs, just as stockholders of military equipment (to quote an example where this problem has had to be tackled systematically) must devise means of preserving obsolete rocket parts which cannot be reproduced. Those who cannot afford or do not wish to involve themselves in these matters should steer clear of new digital formats for the present.

Storage of sound archives

As a general statement, conditions suitable for the storage of textual archives are also suitable for sound archives. Guidance on this is provided in general works on documentary conservation[3] and in the lists of desiderata published by the various national standards organizations. The relevant British Standard is no. 5454: *Recommendations for the storage and exhibition of archival documents*. It has been under revision for several years and the new version is about to appear.

The Standard begins with information on general aspects of buildings and proceeds to cover storage provision for textual archives in some detail. 'Archival materials other than paper and parchment' are then covered in a short section, followed by recommendations on exhibition and reproduction facilities for textual archives. The Standard is, or will shortly be, readily available and it seems unnecessary to repeat either its general and sometimes rather self-evident recommendations, or its detailed guidelines on fire precautions, gangway widths etc. However, the brief paragraphs on 'gramophone records' and 'magnetic tape' leave much to be said, so this section concentrates on the special requirements of sound archives, while following the general layout of the Standard. No apology is offered for the use of the British Standard as a basis: despite comment that its requirements are beyond the resources of all but the richest organizations,[4] BS 5454 is actually pitched at a fairly modest level compared with similar recommendations for the storage of computer magnetic tape;[5] and in any case if first class recommendations can only produce second class provision, the outcome of second class recommendations seems unlikely to be better.

Structure and material of building

The recommendations given in clause 4 of BS 5454 provide a useful general background, particularly if new accommodation is being designed and erected. In adapting existing buildings for the storage of sound archives, safe floor loading capacities should be established before any further plans are made. Steel shelving of average density and height loaded with sound archives can be expected to exceed the capacity of virtually any conventional floor supported on timber joists.

It is often for this reason that, where storerooms of any size are needed and existing buildings are being adapted, basements below ground with strong floors are favoured. Basements can also be cool, stable, dark, and in any case unsuitable for other purposes, but their walls are often affected by damp, and pipework, wiring, drains and other services tend to be sited in them. Rooms affected by heating boilers are quite unsuitable. Hot pipes may drastically interfere with climatic control and encourage the deposit of dust. Above all the threat of flooding is always present. Basements may seem satisfactory from the point of view of security, but because they are off the beaten track, intruders may be able to penetrate them unobserved; and the ever-present services will attract maintenance men, meter readers etc. who will require supervision.

Custody and security

Collections of sound recordings worthy of permanent retention must be housed separately from working areas, primarily to prevent unauthorized removals, but also to enable handling rules to be enforced and environmental conditions to be controlled. In addition, duplicate copies should be housed in a separate storage area from the originals. Without this provision their function in security and conservation cannot be performed. In a small set-up the best arrangement may be to store 'access copies' (i.e. duplicates made for use by researchers, cataloguers etc.) in a locked room adjacent to the working or research area. The door to it can then be kept under scrutiny at all times. Logistic problems in some form are always created by storing access copies remotely, perhaps several floors below the working area in the basement of the building, or in a separate building. For larger organizations such arrangements will probably become inevitable since storage space of sufficient size will not be available in prime office areas, and it will be economically worthwhile to employ staff to fetch and carry from stores whose rental value is low. But it should be remembered that most sound archives are liable to suffer in transit: discs may be broken and the windings on tape reels disturbed. Once access copies have been made the originals or the 'archive' copies made from them should rarely be needed for reference and can with advantage be housed a long distance from headquarters. Small organizations can achieve this by making reciprocal arrangements among themselves, or by negotiating deposit in larger archives. Larger bodies may consider accommodation out-of-town where rents are low.

Access to stores should be restricted to staff (or even to 'designated staff' where appropriate), and no others allowed in unaccompanied. Many organizations now use identity card or badge systems for quick recognition of staff, authorized visitors and others. Appropriate intruder alarms should protect all vulnerable access and exit routes.

Unfortunately a significant proportion of 'unauthorized removals' from archive and library storage areas are 'inside jobs' by dishonest staff or temporary workers such as contract cleaners, student assistants and repairmen. Theft may escape detection even if the repository is successful in introducing bag searches for staff (again unlikely in the UK owing to union opposition). Permanent staff at least may be constrained by the knowledge that their movements are traceable and their personal details on record. The credentials of temporaries (i.e. recently arrived short-term workers) must be established before they enter storage areas; archivists are fully justified in refusing to admit strangers claiming to be service engineers or contractor's staff, even if this results in higher costs or uncompleted work. Temporary staff should not be allowed to work alone for long periods in areas from which recordings may be removed, and ideally all temporary staff should be supervised by a member of the permanent staff.

Within a repository a 'secure' area may be designated (normally everywhere outside the entrance and study areas) within which strangers should be challenged. Within storage areas it may be thought wise to designate a 'high security' section, perhaps consisting of shelving fitted with a lockable grille, for the storage of especially vulnerable or attractive items. Alternatively the anonymity of open runs of shelving may be regarded as sufficient or better protection.

Fire precautions

The recommendations in clause 6 of BS 5454 serve as a useful source of basic information, particularly on structural matters. In the UK implementation of laws and bye-laws relating to fire safety in buildings is the responsibility of local authority fire officers. These officials should be consulted whenever new accommodation or changed shelving layouts are planned, since long experience indicates that the requirements of one individual fire officer may differ from those of his predecessor or successor.

If fire breaks out in a sound archive store, the risk of serious loss is very great because recordings are easily damaged beyond rescue by heat, even if they do not catch fire. Particular care should therefore be taken to remove potential hazards such as any form of exposed heating or redundant wiring, and any unnecessary combustible material such as furniture, unshelved recordings or paperwork. Smoking and naked lights must obviously be banned. Points vulnerable to arson attack should be considered and for this reason among several others, stores with windows should be avoided. Especially valuable recordings, or those most vulnerable to damage by heat such as cylinders and 'acetate' discs could be given extra protection in cupboards with metal doors or behind brick or concrete partitions. All holdings should be closely shelved as this in itself provides some protection. Nothing should be left lying around in the open.

The range of fire-fighting equipment installed by most archive repositories follows well-established lines. Larger, richer organizations tend to have fixed systems which are automatically set off by an electronic detector. This is particularly valuable as a line of defence when the premises are unoccupied. The fixed system may be supplemented by hand held appliances for *ad hoc* use by staff in dealing with a small outbreak of fire which is easily contained. In smaller organizations, or where storage areas have been converted from general purpose rooms, provision is usually limited to hand-operated extinguishers. The four principal means of fire extinction are by water, gas, foam and powder.

Water Fixed sprinkler systems are often found in basements and other open areas adapted for storage use. They are cheap and effective, but can cause considerable unnecessary damage if set off as a result of a small fire triggering a detector, or worse still by a malfunctioning detector. Nevertheless sound archives are normally damaged irreversibly by any significant heat while water damaged recordings can often be successfully rescued. Zoned arrangements in which sprinklers only operate in the area near where smoke or heat have been detected are readily available and should be insisted on. 'Deluge' systems where all the sprinkler heads are triggered at once whether needed or not are unsuitable. Similarly it is essential to ensure that detectors and circuits designed to set off sprinklers are working properly. In larger storerooms hoses on reels are sometimes installed, and they provide a quick and easy way of controlling a small non-electrical fire without making too much mess. Hand-held water appliances are also effective and can only inflict a limited soaking, so they may be a wise alternative where no electrical equipment is nearby. Gas systems are probably preferable to water overall, but although water makes a mess this is far preferable to the total distortion or destruction which sound archives are certain to suffer if exposed to a fire for any period.

Gas Where a new fixed system is being installed gas is likely to be preferred. Carbon dioxide is effective but liable to suffocate anyone unfortunate enough to be trapped in the store. 'Halon' (specifically Halon 1301, a Dupont trademark), the other common alternative, appears to be effective in smaller concentrations, less of a health hazard, and therefore preferable. Hand-held gas extinguishers are also available.[6] The niceties of gas will of course be cancelled out if firemen in attendance at an outbreak decide to deploy their hoses.

Foam Though evidently not widely employed or documented the use of systems which will smother a fire outbreak by filling all airspaces with high-expansion foam may be appropriate in some repositories. A suitable type of foam must be chosen which will not harm the media in storage.

Powder Dry chemical systems designed for use on electrical, chemical and industrial fires are not suitable for use in archival stores.

The above systems have wide currency and are designed to extinguish a fire as quickly as possible. Recently another approach has been tried (e.g. in the new 'Corn Store' bookstack at the British Library's Document Supply Centre, Boston Spa), aimed at reducing some of the harmful incidental effects of the existing methods. In a CO_2 gas system, for instance, ventilation to the storage area is shut off and a lethal gas is introduced which mixes with the already toxic smoke produced by the fire. Anyone caught in the area is in danger of suffocation and firefighters need breathing apparatus if they are to gain access. The new system, relying on the fact that densely packed materials will not ignite easily, encourages the fire to burn cleanly (and possibly to burn itself out rapidly) by automatically opening vents in the walls and ceiling to create a current of clean air if a fire is detected. Doors may be left open to assist escapers, and firemen can get to the source of the fire and put it out quickly, so that overall less damage may be caused. Sound archivists should reserve judgement on this technique, since any fire, whether 'clean burning' or not, will ruin any recordings in the vicinity; but it does avoid the overkill aspects of sprinklers and gas.

Storage equipment

Although Pickett and Lemcoe[7] recommended the use of wooden shelving for magnetic tape in order to prevent damage by strong magnetic fields which may be conducted by metal, in practice the risk is very slight,[8] and in any case non-magnetic carriers are not subject to this hazard. Metal shelving is stronger and will not catch fire, so on balance it is the better option.

The recommendations in BS 5454 regarding shelving layouts seem generally reasonable: as well as making good use of space and meeting the needs of the organization, layouts must fulfil the requirements of the fire officer and of health and safety legislation. It will rarely be satisfactory to provide gangways less than 2 feet 6 inches (770 mm.) wide, but in rooms with high ceilings, it may be possible to erect shelving ten feet (3m.) high or more if the floor is strong enough. Stepladders will be needed for the higher shelves, but infrequently used material can be placed there and as the store fills up the extra capacity will justify the inconvenience. Funds for shelving and other equipment are usually more easy to obtain when facilities are being established than later, so think ahead!

It is not wise to economize on shelfspace by fixing the bottom shelves lower than six inches (150mm.) from the ground. Recordings are easily damaged by passing trolleys and feet, and no safety margin will be available in case of flooding. A top shelf acting as a 'lid' on each bay should also be provided in order to prevent the contents of the exposed shelf below from acquiring a coating of dust.

Shelving of sufficient strength should be supplied: most discs are considerably heavier by volume than books or written documents. As a rough guide, one foot run of

12-inch acetate discs (aluminium cores)		
in sleeves weighs	42 pounds	(19.2 kg)
12-inch shellac discs in sleeves	66 pounds	(30 kg)
10-inch shellac discs in sleeves	39.5 pounds	(18 kg)
12-inch vinyl discs in sleeves	46 pounds	(20.8 kg)
7-inch vinyl discs in sleeves	13 pounds	(6 kg)
quarter-inch tape on full 10-inch		
NAB alloy spools in boxes	25 pounds	(11.5 kg)
quarter-inch tape on full 7-inch plastic		
spools in boxes	12.5 pounds	(5.7 kg)
cassettes in library cases	2.85 pounds	(1.3 kg)
Beta video cassettes in boxes	5.5 pounds	(2.5 kg)
VHS video cassettes in boxes	6 pounds	(2.8 kg)

Wherever possible individual recordings should be housed in larger containers, but where this is incompatible with the need for rapid access, the shelving, especially for discs, should be very carefully specified so that adequate lateral support is provided. Shelving with box-section uprights on which the vertical distances between shelves can be adjusted is likely to be preferable. 'L' section uprights with shelves bolted in position should be avoided as the insertion and withdrawal of recordings at the ends of each shelf will be fouled by the front upright, and any lateral pressure which forces recordings against the uprights (when a shelf is full this is almost unavoidable) can cause serious damage. Even with box section systems, a means of in-filling the gap between the front and rear upright at the ends of each shelf should be provided so that a flush, even surface is presented to the adjacent recording. Discs require intermediate lateral support along each shelf: a minimum of one divider every nine inches (23 cm.) is needed; one every six inches (15 cm) is better. These dividers should be rigid and firmly fixed top and bottom to maintain discs in an upright position, but completely satisfactory commercially manufactured metal dividers do not appear to be available, at least in the UK.

Most companies can supply dividers which clip into holes at standard distances along the shelves, but the clips are made of sharp springy steel which can scratch sleeves and other soft containers. Other systems involve dividers with protruding lugs which fit into holes along the shelves, and these are better, although they share with other types a 'rolled edge' at front and rear, which keeps them rigid but can damage discs adjacent to them. A solution is to stick infill panels of sufficient thickness to each side of the dividers, but a completely satisfactory and economic method of doing this is hard to devise. Purpose-built systems are likely to be very expensive, so the best solution seems to be to create or commission a modest system of pigeonholes made of plywood, glue and nails, which will stand on the shelves and present no uneven surfaces to the recordings (see Figure 5.2). Each pigeonhole should be filled so that discs are subject

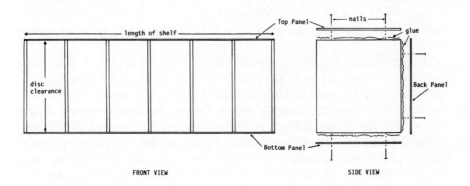

Figure 5.2   Do-it-yourself shelf support for discs.

Note: This should be placed on a steel shelf strong enough to carry the discs, and should be constructed so that end panels rest closely on the steel shelving uprights. Rough edges should be smoothed down. It is not intended for use unsupported or as a transit case.

to sufficient lateral pressure to keep them upright, but not so tightly that discs are difficult to insert or withdraw. Each pigeonhole should contain discs of only one size.

Tapes are always stored upright on edge. The larger sizes in particular tend to slip and slide around on metal shelves, so it may be worth installing dividers as for discs. The individual storage of cassettes on any form of conventional shelving is usually inconvenient and wasteful of space.

In most situations shelving of a standard depth should be specified for the whole store. This standard will relate to the size of the largest medium (e.g. 12-inch/30 cm. discs) to be held in any quantity. If there are a few items which are individually larger, these can be separately catered for, but the adaptability of shelving will be seriously limited if an attempt is made to match the existing distribution of sizes in the collection. The smaller sizes are best boxed up in larger containers anyway.

Shelving should be adequately cross-braced, but not fully enclosed by steel panelling as this restricts air circulation. Where recordings are shelved individually some barrier should be provided at the rear of each shelf or items can easily slip through, at best interfering with material on adjacent shelving, at worst falling to the ground with a crash.

Mobile shelving is *not* recommended for sound archives. The most common systems are not equipped with brakes so there is nothing to prevent one run from jarring against the next whenever it is moved. Even careful operation usually results in an appreciable bump which causes individual recordings to slide forward and eventually off the shelves. Individually shelved shellac and 'acetate' discs are particularly at risk from this tendency, and in any case, lengthy mobile runs of such discs are likely to be too heavy for easy handling. Even if prevented from sliding, wax cylinders and 'acetates' may still be damaged by jarring, and windings on tape spools may be dislodged. Despite all this, economic factors may dictate the installation of a mobile system, in which case the guidelines in BS 5454 should be followed. Breakable discs are almost certain to be damaged sooner or later if shelved individually so they must be boxed up, and operators must be clearly and regularly instructed to move the shelving with extreme care.

Climate

BS 5454 recommends that temperatures between 13 and 18 degrees C, and a relative humidity level between 55 and 65 per cent should be maintained in storage areas for textual archives. These levels are also broadly appropriate for sound archives. (Under the section 'Archival materials other than paper and parchment' later in the Standard, somewhat lower temperature and RH ranges are recommended for magnetic tape.) Pickett and Lemcoe recommend 21 degrees C and 50 per cent relative humidity for all forms of discs, and there does not appear to have been a more authoritative research-based statement since. Because elements of magnetic tape are hygroscopic, it is more sensitive to unsuitable or rapidly changing climatic conditions. There is general agreement among recent researchers that dry storage conditions are advisable. Forty per cent RH at 18–20 degrees C is generally recommended.[9]

Climate must be kept stable. If less-than-ideal conditions cannot be avoided, it is far preferable for these to remain constant than for frequent minor alterations to be made in an attempt to achieve a 'better average'. Magnetic tape is the most susceptible to changes, which can lead to more rapid physical deterioration and increased 'print through'. Proposed storage areas where rapid temperature and RH cycling (e.g. between day and night) is endemic should be ruled out. Rooms with windows should be avoided. Central heating systems operated by time clocks should be shut off, drained, and preferably disconnected.

General advice on climatic control standards is given in BS 5454, but equipment should not be acquired without specialist advice. Small-scale dehumidification and temperature control systems can often be installed without much disruption and at comparatively low cost, but they can only be specified and designed after a period spent monitoring the existing conditions. Simply setting up a dehumidifier or putting in an extractor fan may produce results quite different from requirements, for example by allowing cold wet air directly into the store, or creating pockets of very moist or very dry air in remote corners. Most storage areas will be situated in towns subject to air pollution which is harmful to archival media and their containers. More elaborate air conditioning will be required if pollutants such as sulphur dioxide are to be reduced to a harmless level (the British Standard recommends the exclusion of particles larger than $10\mu g/m^3$). Systems which use an electrostatic dust filter should not be installed as these generate harmful levels of ozone.

A useful brief introduction to the problems involved with air conditioning has recently been provided by Clifford Harkness of the Ulster Folk and Transport Museum.[10] Difficulties can be expected since most manufacturers do not supply equipment suitable for archival storage areas as part of their normal range. Great emphasis should be placed on the reliability of electronic control systems, and the provision of some back-up should a failure occur.

Even where air conditioning is available, it is still a good idea to store magnetic tape spools in individual polyethylene bags as indicated in Chapter 6. These provide a cheap and convenient defence against disaster or system failure.

Lightning conductors

Although the danger to magnetic recordings from magnets in electrical and audio equipment is very slight, currents induced by lightning are powerful enough to wipe or distort large numbers of tapes in the vicinity. This possibility should be countered by routing the lightning conductor away from storage areas.

Monitoring

The maintenance of satisfactory RH and temperature levels depends on information from monitoring devices. If funds are very limited, frequent readings can be taken using a whirling hygrometer in conjunction with published tables (more accurate than a wall-mounted hair hygrometer), or a hand-held electronic meter with digital display which can now be had for as little as £50. But there is really no substitute for a thermohygrograph which will automatically indicate temperature and RH variation on a chart. Versions are available which can be set for various timespans from one day to one month. The use of a thermohygrograph is really the only way of monitoring conditions at night or in remote and infrequently visited stores. Electronic meters which produce a periodic printout could be used instead, but they are more expensive. Their readings may be more reliable but will not be continuous.

Automatic smoke detection as specified in BS 5454 is the other essential form of monitoring with which all stores (not to mention other parts of the premises) should be equipped. Detectors will be linked to an alarm system and if required to the local fire station. In many locations flood detectors which monitor the presence of moisture at floor level are a worthwhile precaution, and should be an essential requirement in basement stores.

Containers

Many repositories store their recordings individually on open shelves like library books, but unless the rate of use or need for interfiling is very great there seems little point in this. Many shelving problems can be avoided by storing individual recordings in larger containers, which will also give additional protection against dust and rough handling, and will greatly simplify bulk moving operations. Discs and tapes should remain in their individual containers or sleeves within the larger boxes. For those who can afford it, 'archival' boxes made of acid-free board are best for long-term storage, although they can be very stiff and unwieldy; information about manufacturers is available from the Society of Archivists' Conservation Group or from adverts in the Society's Journal. Otherwise corrugated cardboard boxes will be quite adequate in the short term and should be stored flat, to be folded up into shape when needed. Boxes should be close fitting; those for 10-inch, 12-inch or larger discs should hold about 20 items each and should be placed upright, not flat, on shelves. Discs of different sizes should not be placed in the same box. Boxes for 10-inch tape spools should hold about 10 or 12 in each so that four boxes will fit upright on a standard yard or metre-wide shelf. Smaller-sized tapes and cassettes are relatively lightweight so containers should be designed to hold a manageable number, which will be partly dictated by the rate of use. Cassette boxes are best confined to 30 or 40 items and stacked three or four high on standard shelving. This avoids the need for uneconomical narrow shelving which is of no use for other purposes. Suitable individual containers for the various media are covered under the relevant sections below.

Disaster planning

Since the Florence flood disaster in 1966 more attention has been paid by large libraries and archive repositories to the systematic salvage, damage limitation and rehabilitation of library and archive materials in the event of disaster. Research and action have concentrated on the development of management strategies, and on perfecting methods of rescuing large numbers of damaged materials. Inevitably the main emphasis has been on fire and flood damage to books and textual archives. A useful summary of recent thinking, supplemented by an excellent bibliography, has appeared in Sally Buchanan's recent RAMP study on disaster planning.[11] There is now so much specialist literature on the subject, including the principal recent British contribution by Anderson and McIntyre for the National Library of Scotland,[12] that only an outline needs to be given here. In addition the Buchanan study, and many of the works listed in its bibliography, provide a wide range of specialist information on firefighting, floodproofing, monitoring equipment and other matters dealt with in earlier sections of this chapter.

There is general agreement that disaster management should centre on the compilation of a written plan. Potential hazards should be assessed and preventative measures taken, but there must also be a recognition that no premises can be made completely disaster-proof. The disaster plan should indicate who is to assess the situation and take control, what the chain of command will be and which order of priority will be applied to threatened or damaged materials. It should describe the procedure for rescuing and rehabilitating damaged materials, and should include clearly written 'what to do' information for immediate guidance when fire, flood etc. is discovered, and the names and telephone numbers of outside contractors or specialists who may be needed.

Once the plan has been drawn up, staff should be trained to play their part safely and systematically. Equipment likely to be needed in immediate rescue work, such as supplies of plastic bags, absorbent cloths and sponges, and protective clothing, should be assembled and kept readily available nearby. Preprinted forms may be useful for the clerical work needed when damaged items are transferred to temporary storage or removed from the repository altogether.

As for specialist measures, there appears to be comparatively little in print on the bulk rescue of sound archives. There is useful guidance on tape rehabilitation in Geller's study.[13] J.-M. Fontaine announced an investigation of the effects of fire on the various sound archive media at the 1987 Joint Technical Symposium in Berlin; the results will be published by the Bibliothèque Nationale and may lead to more informed recommendations for storage, fire prevention, and rescue.[14] Dietrich Lotichius's solitary description of successful rescue work following a small-scale flood is repeatedly quoted.[15] IASA's *Sound archives: a guide to their establishment and development* and McWilliams's guide to the preservation and restoration of recordings both ignore the question.[16]

Almost all sound archive media are thermoplastic and more or less inflammable. High temperatures can distort, disfigure or melt them even if they do not catch fire. 'Blue Amberol' cylinders and 'acetate' discs are made of cellulose nitrate which is almost impossible to extinguish once it has caught fire. As emphasized above, therefore, fire prevention and extinction must be among the first points considered in storage planning. In the present state of our knowledge there is little the archivist can do with fire-damaged recordings except clear up the mess.

Water damage is relatively less serious. First, it is possible to prevent major damage by sealing recordings in waterproof containers. The main disc formats are not critically affected by water and can be successfully air dried, though their containers may be worse affected. Tape is more of a problem. If polyester-based magnetic tape is soaked and left untreated it is liable to disintegrate as the oxide binder is hygroscopic. The layers of tape on a spool are likely to stick together as a result. The normally suggested drying process (see Geller, p. 35) involves spooling through affected tapes and wiping them with absorbent tissue or other lint-free material. This is straightforward with computer tapes for which cleaning machines are routinely available, but a conventional tape recorder would need to be adapted for drying quarter-inch tape, and cassette formats may prove impossible to dry in this way – another argument against the archival use of cassettes!

If a large number of tapes are affected this type of drying process will take many days, during which untreated tapes will deteriorate. At worst these should be kept cool to prevent the growth of mould. On present limited evidence a better alternative is to freeze wet tapes until they can be dealt with. This will arrest binder deterioration and mould growth, though the expansion of the water as it freezes may cause stretching. In the absence of anything better a domestic food freezer can be used to hold tapes (and other media), at least until better provision can be made. At the NSA a preliminary experiment indicates that the full freeze/vacuum-dry rescue process developed for books and paper documents will also work with tapes.[17] In the UK more information about this technique, including the names of companies which offer a service, is available from the British Library's National Preservation Office.

The NSA also has recent unwanted experience of the speed with which mould can grow on tapes and containers if humid storage conditions are maintained for more than a few days. In this case climatic conditions in a remote store were altered without warning and were found to be warm and damp during a routine inspection. About 5000 tapes in cardboard boxes were more or less covered in mildew within ten days. Bulk rescue measures were needed because the mould spores had to be killed before the tapes could be safely brought into the repository's main premises for cleaning and reboxing. As expected, a sample test indicated that recording quality was unaffected by gamma atomic irradiation, so all the affected tapes were bagged up and sent to a bulk irradiation plant for treatment.[18] Once neutralized the affected tapes could be shelved and cleaned in an orderly manner without danger to other materials.

References

1. M. Duchein, *Les bâtiments d'archives: construction et equipment*, Paris, 1985; V. Gondos (ed.), *Reader for archives and record centre buildings*,

Washington, 1970; L. Bell, 'The archivist and his accommodation' in *Archivaria*, VIII, 1979, pp. 83–90; L. Bell, 'Archival accommodation in the United Kingdom' in *Journal of the Society of Archivists*, vol. 6, no. 6, 1980, pp. 345–364; D. Thomas, 'Archive buildings: international comparisons' in *Journal of the Society of Archivists*, vol. 9, no. 1, 1988, pp. 38–44; T. Walch, *Archives and manuscripts: security*, Society of American Archivists, Chicago, 1977. See also L. W. Blair, 'A bibliography of materials on the planning and construction of library buildings' in AAA Committee of the Association for Recorded Sound Collections, *Audio preservation: a planning study* (appendix II C8 Tab. C), Rockville, MD, 1988.

2. This is a simple operation: details can be had from the Chief Engineer, NSA.

3. G. M. and D. G. Cunha, *Conservation of library materials . . .*, 2nd ed., 2 vols., Scarecrow Press, Metuchen, New Jersey, 1983; M. L. Ritzenthaler, *Archives and manuscripts: conservation* (SAA Basic Manual Series), Society of American Archivists, Chicago, 1983.

4. E. Staziker, 'Climatic control: a hopeless bewilderment?' in *Journal of the Society of Archivists*, vol. 8, no. 8, 1986, pp. 171–173.

5. S. B. Geller, *Care and handling of computer magnetic storage media* (NBS Special Publication 500–101), National Bureau of Standards, Washington, 1983.

6. D. Schüller, 'Preliminary recommendations for fire precautions and fire extinguishing methods in sound archives' in *Phonographic Bulletin* 35, March 1983, pp. 21–23.

7. A. G. Pickett and M. M. Lemcoe, *Preservation and storage of sound recordings*, Library of Congress, Washington, 1959, p. 62.

8. Geller, *op. cit.*, pp. 37–51.

9. J. Wheeler, 'Long-term storage of videotape' in *Journal of the society of motion picture and TV engineers*, June 1983, pp. 650–654, and in A. Hanford (ed.), *Panorama of audiovisual archives*, ƆBC Data Publications, London, 1986; J. Wheeler, 'Archiving the various audio and video tape formats' in E. Orbanz (ed.), *Archiving the audio-visual heritage*, Stiftung Deutsche Kinemathek, West Berlin, 1988; H. N. Bertram and E. F. Cuddihy, 'Kinetics of humid aging of magnetic recording tape' in *IEEE Transactions on Magnetics*, vol. MAG-18, no. 5, September 1982, pp. 993–999; Tape Head Interface Committee, 'A care and handling manual for magnetic tape recording' in F. Kalil (ed.), *Magnetic tape recording for the eighties*, NASA reference publication no. 1075, NASA, Greenbelt, Maryland, 1982, p. 147; Geller, *op. cit.*, pp. 115–119.

10. C. Harkness, 'Criteria for air conditioning in audio visual archives' in Orbanz, *op. cit.*, pp. 37–41.

11. S. A. Buchanan, *Disaster planning: preparedness and recovery for libraries and archives* (ref. PGI–88/WS/6), UNESCO, Paris, 1988.

12. H. Anderson and J. E. McIntyre, *Planning manual for disaster control in*

Scottish libraries and record offices, National Library of Scotland, Edinburgh, 1985.

13. Geller, *op. cit.*, pp. 28–36.
14. J.-M. Fontaine, 'Effects of fire on sound and audiovisual recording supports', in Orbanz, *op. cit.*, pp. 43–46.
15. D. Lotichius, 'Measures for the preservation and for the protection of archived program property on sound archives' in *Phonographic Bulletin* 31, November 1981, pp. 37–39.
16. D. Lance (ed.), *Sound archives: a guide to their establishment and development*, IASA, Milton Keynes, 1983; J. McWilliams, *The preservation and restoration of sound recordings*, American Association for State and Local History, Nashville TN, 1979.
17. A selection of quarter-inch tapes on 10-inch spools were modulated with standard test tones at 7½ ips, partially soaked for 24 hours then placed in the British Library's blast freezer at −28 degrees C. Two days later they were moved to a heat controlled shelf in a vacuum drying chamber and dried for two days. No physical damage was found on any tape and no measurable signal deterioration was observed except on two long-play tapes where a drop in volume in the 10 khz tone of between −1 and −2 dBs was noted in the sections of tape which had been in the water. The effect was inaudible and in any case thin-backed tape of this kind is not recommended for archival use. See A. Ward, A. Barker and P. Copeland, 'Freeze-drying magnetic tapes after flood damage' in *BASC News*, no. 5, 1989. Subsequently the drying service run by the UK Atomic Energy Authority at Harwell, Oxfordshire, announced that they had successfully rescued some flood damaged tapes by vacuum drying.
18. See Geller, *op. cit.*, p. 43. As it happened the affected tapes were covered by a virtually complete set of reel-to-reel duplicates, most of which had been produced from the now mouldy tapes or in parallel with them. Signal levels were therefore easy to monitor by comparison with the copies.

Chapter 6

CONSERVATION OF SOUND ARCHIVES

GENERAL METHODOLOGY

Characteristics of sound archives

Much of the value of sound archives lies in their capacity to convey an accurate and complete record.

Where a recording of speech is being used as an audio notebook, the loss of a small portion of it may be of no more significance than, say, the obliteration of a small area of a written document: the sense may easily be reconstructed. But the quality and usefulness of most other types of sound recording are seriously affected even by minor damage, particularly where recordings of artistic performances are concerned. The need for special care in the custody and handling of recording media is well accepted in the computer world – mainframe computer installations invariably incorporate secure, air conditioned storage for data tapes – but provision for sound archives held on similar media is usually less appropriate even though the risk of damage or loss may be greater.[1] Recordings are subject both to 'internal' and 'external' damage. Most sound carriers gradually disintegrate. Some, like 'acetate' discs, have a very short reliable life because their chemical constituents decompose. Others like wax cylinders and many shellac formulations will remain playable over long periods while gradually deteriorating. The rate of disintegration of sound recording media is often influenced by the conditions in which they are kept. All carriers, except perhaps compact discs, are easily damaged during playback. Tape gets tangled in machines; discs and cylinders are scratched or worn by needles or styluses. All are easy to damage if handled inappropriately or carelessly.

In addition, magnetic recordings are susceptible to obliteration by exposure to strong magnetic fields.

A further characteristic of sound archives serves to twist the knife in the archivist's back: they are dependent on complex technology whose rate of obsolescence has been rapidly increasing in the 1970s and 1980s. Technical developments and improvements occur in the commercial environment of the recording, broadcasting, video and hi-fi industries and are not influenced by archivists. Recordings may be received by an archivist for which playback equipment is no longer available, and cannot be reconstructed because the complex electronic circuitry is impossible to reproduce.

These facts have two main implications for the sound archivist: first, in addition to the already elaborate measures required in the custody and handling of textual archives, further more fastidious provision needs to be made for sound archives; second, sooner or later all sound archives will need to be copied. In this way the sonic content of short-lived or obsolescent carriers can be preserved, and the risk of damage to original recordings minimized. These implications are inescapable and should form the basis of all conservation policy and planning in sound archives.

Elements of conservation policy

Preservation of originals

Because of the fragility and tendency to obsolescence of sound carriers, the principle that 'the sound is more important than the medium' has gained general acceptance throughout the sound archives profession. This attitude reflects a major difference between sound and textual archives: although custodians of written archives frequently arrange for fragile, valuable, or heavily used originals to be photocopied, microfilmed or otherwise reproduced as a conservation measure, few would claim that these originals may then be destroyed. This is essentially because (i) from both the legal and research viewpoints the evidential value of written documents is at best only partially transferred to copies because (ii) the complete nature of most written documents is impossible to copy. In addition (iii) microfilm, at present the most commonly used medium for conservation copying of documents, has poorer long-term keeping properties than much of the material being copied.

Point (i) also applies to sound recordings. Before sanctioning the disposal of originals the sound archivist must consider whether the value of the recordings as evidence will be reduced if the originals are lost. The answer, unfortunately, must always be more or less emphatically affirmative, if only because original carriers, or at least their containers, usually bear contemporary markings, numbers, labels, handwriting and so on which are essential to their identification. The date of recording is normally a vital piece of information which may not be clear from the recording itself or its labelling. It can normally be deduced fairly accurately from the detailed appearance of the original, but as with written documents, a copy may be of very limited use for this sort of investigation. Long experience also indicates that today's new wonder technique for copying old recordings onto new media is certain to be improved on tomorrow. If the originals have been destroyed, all scope for recopying by improved methods is lost.

To take the most obvious example, copying wax cylinders onto acetate discs and destroying the cylinders does not appear today as the attractive space-saving option it did 40 years ago. Besides, as Velson Horie has argued,[2] the assumption that short-lived sound carriers such as cellulose acetate tape have embarked on a one-way journey to the scrap heap may be altogether too cavalier. Research has enabled us to deacidify paper, and work on the stablization of cellulose acetate film is making good progress, so there seems no reason in principle why deterioration in audio carriers should not be reversible. The patient should be kept alive as long as possible in case a cure is discovered.

However the textual archivist's second and third problems already bear less heavily on the sound archivist, and will carry still less weight once an archivally satisfactory form of digital recording has been achieved. Even with good quality analogue recording a very faithful reproduction of virtually the entire sound content of an original recording can be produced; and in any case, sound archivists at present have no choice: if they are to ensure the preservation of their holdings they *must* copy them sooner or later. Originals may be bulky, crumbling and of little intrinsic value. When the storage space runs out, the sound archivist can dispose of these with fewer misgivings than the textual archivist in the same situation faced with the architect's department's long series of plans which were copied on 35mm roll film ten years ago.

Copying

Copying (also referred to as 'rerecording', 'dubbing', 'duplicating' or 'transcribing') of sound archives is an essential routine aimed at

- preventing damage to originals through handling and playing;

- providing security copies in case originals are damaged or stolen;
- ensuring the permanent preservation of recordings as original carriers deteriorate.

As previously indicated, the same copy may have to serve all three purposes, though ideally at least two copies should be made including one 'duplicate master' on an archivally suitable medium, from which any further copies can be run off, and one copy for general reference and playback. As there is currently no permanent recording medium, copies for conservation purposes should be made on the nearest approach to it, which at present and for the next few years will mean good quality polyester-based ferric oxide-coated quarter-inch 'standard play' (i.e. 0.002 inch or 0.005 cm. thickness) magnetic tape, recorded in the analogue mode. Tape which has been spliced should not be used, as all splicing tapes, including 'good quality' makes, are flimsy and rely on relatively short-lived pressure sensitive adhesives which will fail sooner than the tape. Obviously no editing and splicing should be carried out on tapes intended for long-term retention. Other media, for the reasons indicated in Chapter 5, do not offer sufficient reliability for widespread and long-term use at present, though digital recordings are in principle superior to analogue recordings in terms of quality and longevity, and certain types of optical discs promise most of what the sound archivist could wish for. The characteristics of the newer formats and their archival potential are discussed in the later parts of this chapter.

A standard procedure for conservation copying should be decided and written up so that all copies will have uniform and predictable characteristics. The following aspects should be considered for inclusion in this code of practice.

Configuration of copies The relationship between originals and copies should be kept simple. Ideally one original should be copied onto one playback carrier. In cases where the repository holds many recordings of short duration, e.g. on cylinder or 10-inch acetates, several may have to be included on one tape reel in order to make economical use of space, in which case the items should be arranged as far as possible in 'archival' order as decided by the sound archivist, and not spread at random over several reels in order to use every inch of tape. Conservation tapes recorded at 7½ ips holding several items should not exceed the 7-inch reel size. 10-inch reels will hold too many short items for easy documentation and retrieval.

Arrangement and numbering   In cases where all conservation copies are simply 'back-to-back' versions of the originals on the same type and size of carrier, they are best numbered by the same system as the originals with a prefix or suffix to distinguish them. But where the repository holds a varied range of original carriers this system can cause confusion and is wasteful of tape and space, so it is better to arrange copies in series unrelated to originals, numbered and shelved by reel size, in which each additional copy simply gets the next available number in the appropriate series. The latter system is used at the NSA, where the various reel sizes are distinguishd by a letter prefix (T = 10-inch, M = 5¾-inch, 0 = 5-inch etc.). It works well as long as clear rules for cross-referencing the original and copy numbers are laid down and religiously observed.

Recording speed   7½ inches per second (ips), (19cm/s) is normally the minimum acceptable speed for good quality recordings on quarter-inch tape and is very widely adopted for conservation copies. There will be some quality loss if originals were recorded at a higher speed – most radio recordings are made at 15 ips (38cm/s) for instance – and no quality improvement if originals were recorded at 3¾ ips (9.5cm/s) or slower speeds. The sound archivist will have to decide whether to keep to the original speed or maintain total uniformity at 7½. Adequate recording quality for speech can be achieved at 3¾ ips if professional standard equipment which plays at this speed can be found. 3¾ is not however adequate for music or other types of sound, and is not recommended. Slow speed recording on expensive high-specification tape and equipment seems rather pointless. Archivists thinking in these terms are probably better off standardizing on cassettes.

Tones and announcements   As a safeguard against physical damage the first six feet (two metres) of each copy tape should be left blank. Where the repository has the use of suitable equipment and a competent operator, lineup tones should be recorded onto each tape before recordings appear. The use of tones (and the term 'lineup') have their origin in broadcasting, where a tone of known frequency (conventionally 1 khz) is recorded at a set volume in relation to the peak volume of the programme recorded, as measured on a peak programme meter (PPM). When the tape is replayed the tone is lined up with the meter on the replay machine so that it reads at the set volume. The programme can then be replayed or broadcast without danger of its volume exceeding acceptable limits. This information is also useful when the repository's copies are being used for playback, but the time and effort involved would hardly be justified if this were its only purpose. However, lineup tones can also be used to provide an objective indication of signal strength in analogue tape recordings, and thus a means of assessing the condition of recordings over a period. If *all* the factors affecting the volume of the tone when recorded remain constant at the playback stage, the PPM reading should always be the same unless some deterioration has occurred. If the meter reading is low under these circumstances the most likely cause will be some technical defect such as a dirty playback head on the tape machine, but if this can be ruled out then signal deterioration should be suspected and steps taken to inspect other contemporary tapes, and isolate the cause.

A single tone is not much use for the objective measurement of signal strength if the rules which applied when it was recorded are not known or cannot be applied at playback. This problem can be overcome without much extra effort by recording two or three tones at different frequencies but the same volume at the beginning of the tape. Subsequently all the tones should play back at the same volume, but if one or other is low then, other factors having been eliminated, something must have affected the tape since it was recorded. At the NSA, in addition to the 1 khz tone, tones at 6 khz and 10 khz are recorded since these are also used by engineering staff to check that the equalization characteristic and azimuth setting of the replay machine are compatible with the tape. Tones should be recorded direct from an oscillator and not from a prerecorded lineup tape or disc. They are not essential and are best avoided unless the repository has the necessary technical facilities.[3]

It is more important that each separate item on the copy tape should be preceded by a clearly spoken announcement giving the numerical reference of the original, the numerical reference of the copy and a brief description of the item and the series from which it comes as appropriate. This serves to link the recording with related written documentation, and provides an invaluable means of identification if this documentation is lost or destroyed.

As an aid to locating the starts of individual items on a copy tape a five-second burst of low frequency tone can be recorded before the announcement. This will be heard as a 'blip' during fast-wind monitoring, enabling the starts of individual items to be located.

Leaders As a further physical protection about six feet (2 metres) of leader may be attached to each end of the tape using a type of splicing tape from which the adhesive does not ooze, and a make of leader tape with permanent colour which will not wipe off. Reels of tape are supplied by some manufacturers with leaders already attached. Colours used by the NSA are given in section V1.4 (*e*) of its handling rules (see Appendix I). According to loose UK convention, white leader indicates the start or 'head' of a standard play reel, green the start of a long play (i.e. 0.0015 inch or 0.0038cm thickness) reel, and red the end (or 'tail') of both. At the NSA leader colours are used more to indicate recording mode and track configuration. Tape thickness (nearly always standard play) is documented on a label fixed to the spool. Leaders are not essential if blank tape is left at each end of the reel, and some repositories deliberately avoid them because they quite rightly consider even the better makes of pressure sensitive splicing tape to be inadequate in the long term. On balance it is probably best to attach leaders to frequently used tapes: these can be replaced if they wear out.

Recording standards Information of general relevance is given here. All sound archivists require some knowledge of tape copying procedures and standards, and many need to know how to copy discs. Basic equipment required for copying work is described in Chapter 5, under 'Technical facilities'. The more specialized equipment and methods applicable to unusual media such as wax cylinders are covered later in this chapter. Tape recorders and disc players used to produce conservation copies need to be of 'professional' or near professional standard (i.e. the sort of machines a small professional recording studio might use). As a rule in the field of analogue recording, cheaper or less sophisticated tape machines do not provide the range of adjustment necessary for satisfactory recording and playback, and are not designed to withstand the continuous use which a repository is likely to make of its copying equipment.[4] Professional reel-to-reel machines are built to withstand continuous heavy use. When vulnerable parts such as tape heads wear out they can be replaced. Current or recent models may therefore be bought secondhand with some confidence.

If a lot of disc playing is anticipated, turntables and pickups of recent specification but robust character from well-established manufacturers are generally preferable to newer designs with the latest gimmicks. A turntable which plays at + or − 78 rpm as well as the more modern speeds will probably be essential, and few of these are in current production. It may therefore be necessary to track down secondhand equipment which will also be cheaper, but wear and damage to turntables and pickup assemblies are not always easy to spot, so there is some risk involved.

The distinction between professional and 'amateur' cassette

machines is less clear-cut than with other equipment, and most repositories use standard good quality hi-fi machines for copying work. Some makes have a better reputation than others for internal robustness and reliability, which rarely relates to their outward appearance. Machines should be capable of playing all types of cassettes (e.g. among coatings: ferric, chrome-dioxide, 'metal'; Dolby, DBX noise reduction etc.) handled by the repository. Cassette machines are relatively cheap and should be acquired new; old models may have an inadequate range of settings and their previous use and service history may be difficult to ascertain.

Equipment should be regularly serviced according to a schedule. On tape and cassette machines this must include cleaning and demagnetizing the heads, and on all machines playing speed should be checked with a stroboscopic monitoring device or frequency counter.

The tape recorder on which the conservation copies are made should be set up with the aid of a standard calibration tape (a collection of prerecorded line-up tones) to produce recordings which conform to the appropriate international standards for the tape specification and speeds to be used.[5] Readjustment is required if tape of a different specification is used, so it is best to choose a well-proven good performance tape and stick to it. Periodically an improved tape specification may have to be adopted, at which point machine settings can be changed, but this is unlikely to be more than once every five years unless a supplier goes out of business.

Machines on which the originals are to be played will need more piecemeal adjustment to suit the carrier. For tapes known to have been recorded to a particular standard, the machine can be lined up to that standard using an appropriate calibration tape, or tones on the tapes themselves. Otherwise the age and type of the tape will have to be guessed at and optimal settings arrived at by experiment. The alignment of the playback head or 'azimuth' can be finely adjusted by trial and error. If the azimuth of the recording machine was different from that of the playback machine, the recording may sound more or less muted until a compensating adjustment has been made. This is a simple operation which can effect a significant improvement, and is essential if any noise reduction system in use is to function correctly. For more detailed information see below, 'Conservation of tape – copying'.

The equalization standards currently used by manufacturers of commercial discs, and frequency response test discs relating to them, are available, and disc players can be set up in relation to these. Unpublished disc recordings from small cutting studios, or older

115

commercial discs, may require more research and experiment, though since 1955 most disc recording has conformed to an international standard.[6]

Discs and cylinders should only be replayed with a stylus of appropriate tip diameter and profile. Unless specific information is available, these specifications are normally determined by trial and error. Any repository intending to replay or copy discs should lay in a stock of the more common stylus sizes. Correct replay speeds should be ascertained by research or in the absence of hard facts, by listening and guesswork. Speeds adopted must be included in technical documentation. Episodic changes in pitch caused by recording defects can be corrected by connecting up a varispeed control to the machine on which copies are being played. For further information of playback of direct cut discs see below under 'Conservation of discs – copying'.

There are two general approaches to the copying of recordings from earlier eras. The *conservation* approach aims to reproduce every element of sound detectable by a playback device, whether produced by the original subject or introduced in the form of mechanical or electronic noise or distortion by the recording process or subsequent (mis)use of the carrier. In doing this the consensus appears to sanction forms of equalization which reflect recording standards in use when the original recording was made (e.g. as outlined above in connection with lining up machines), and the use of devices such as the groove wall selector stage of the Packburn noise reduction system which will reduce as far as possible the introduction of further unwanted noise during the copying process, insofar as this can be done without affecting the wanted recording.[7] No attempt is made to 'correct' existing faults by the subjective application of additional filtering or equalization.

The *restoration* approach seeks to reduce the elements introduced by the original recording process and later use so that only the sounds produced by the original subject are left. In its most common form this involves 'cutting down the noise' by electronic and mechanical means of varying subtlety and complexity, but the result may still sound unrealistic, especially if recording was carried out originally by 'acoustic' means. Further steps beyond the basic matching-up routines described above may therefore be needed to 'unscramble' the inherent harmonic distortions and limitations and give as true an impression of the original sound as possible.[8] Reliable computer-based techniques for removing unwanted noise without greatly distorting or attenuating the original recording are only just appearing in 1989. Hitherto conventional restoration methods have to some extent also affected the original recording for example by filtering higher frequencies in order to cut down hiss and crackle, which can also remove much of the clarity of the wanted recording unless very skilfully done.

The two approaches are analogues with 'conservation' and 'restoration' attitudes to the treatment of deterioration in textual archives. Conservation is aimed at preventing further deterioration but not at carrying out any work which cannot be reversed or identified. Restoration involves returning the material to its original appearance so that repairs are 'invisible' and new is indistinguishable from old. The problem with restoration, both of documents and recordings, is that even when technical problems have been overcome standards remain more or less subjective and tend to change over the years along with fashion and the latest research. Conservation is therefore the appropriate technique for the archivist in both cases. William Storm of the Belfer Audio Laboratory and Archive at Syracuse University has campaigned over many years for the adoption of international re-recording standards in sound archives, based on an analysis of all the acoustic elements, technologies and commercial forces which contribute to the sound of recordings.[9]

Unrestored 'flat' conservation copies provide an essential safeguard and an objective point of reference. Their existence enables repeated restoration attempts to be made as improved methods are developed. Where fragile or short-lived originals are being copied it is always wise to make two copies in any case. The flat copy should serve as the new master while a 'restored' copy can also be made for listening.

Handling

The sound archivist should produce guidelines on the handling of recordings in his care. Basically recordings should not be withdrawn from storage and kept in work areas more than necessary, and should always be treated with the care appropriate to fragile objects. Staff should receive training in the handling of recordings; others should not be allowed to handle them except under close supervision. The National Sound Archive's *General code of practice on the storage, handling and playback of recordings* is reproduced in Appendix I. It is more elaborate than most organizations will require and includes a number of references to technical and storage matters. Readers may find it useful as a basis for the creation of their own guidelines.

Managing and documenting conservation work

Small, recently established repositories dealing with a limited range of media need to decide the level of conservation activity they can afford and then put this into practice as part of their regular operations. As recordings come in they should go through copying or other appropriate routines so that all items in storage can be assumed to have been processed to a set standard. Documentation will reflect the completion of this operation.

Larger repositories, which cannot afford to carry out conservation measures on all incoming material as it arrives, face a more complex administrative problem. Many sound archivists will need to assess large accumulations of recordings whose provenance and custodial history are not fully recorded. For this purpose provision needs to be made for the conservation status of the material to be recorded at the accessioning stage. This status will relate to the characteristics and condition of recordings as analysed later in this chapter. For instance carriers such as 'acetate' discs will probably be placed in an 'immediate treatment' category; standard-play polyester tape may be considered sufficiently stable to require immediate duplication only for playback; other categories may be subject to regular monitoring. A programme of conservation work (in practice this will amount largely to a programme of cleaning or mending originals and copying them) can then be drawn up. When scheduled recordings come through for treatment a record will be kept of the work carried out and the specifications adopted. An indication of this should also be attached to the original and copy recordings themselves.

Routine monitoring of most analogue recordings in storage is a very difficult exercise. Effective monitoring must depend on a known standard, but such a basis cannot be established by visual inspection unless something obvious is amiss such as peeling laminates on discs or deformed tape packs. Very few repositories will be able to afford routine aural assessment, but even where this is possible, its results are difficult to measure and document if based on subjective impressions – again unless obvious defects such as dropouts or serious print-through are evident. The only reliable means of assessing gradual deterioration is to measure variations in test tones if these are available.

Nevertheless, if resources allow, routine periodic inspections, at least of samples from each storage area and type of recording, should be carried out. Partly (I gather) as a theoretical exercise the US National Archives drew up inspection report forms on which the constant and variable characteristics of recordings could be reported (see Figure 6.1). The forms are reproduced here as an indication of what a fairly detailed assessment might entail. At the very least all repository staff should be enjoined to report any faults encountered while using recordings, so that other materials obtained from the same source or stored nearby can also be checked on.

Digital recordings are more easily monitored. Dropouts in the recording, which are normally inaudible, are indicated by the rate at which error correction digits are used. In the most commonly used monitoring technique, this 'bit error rate' can be measured using equipment at present costing around the same price as a DAT recorder.

Repositories at least have some control over the characteristics of their own recordings and conservation copies. Test tones should be applied where appropriate; recording specifications should be to a standard and any variations carefully noted; a limited range of tape whose specifications have been established by independent testing (e.g. by a broadcasting organization) should be used exclusively. Some repositories go so far as to record the manufacturing dates and batch numbers of new tape in order to identify other potentially faulty tapes if one is found to be defective.

Except where conservation routines are standardized and invariable, in which case a general statement covering all recordings might suffice, provision must be made in the repository's documentation system for recording the results of initial assessments, monitoring inspections, and conservation work. Categories of information to be considered will be found in sections 5D- 5G of the *Manual of Archival Description*'s special format for sound recordings (see Appendix II). In manual systems based on registers or forms, conservation information will typically be kept separately from the main descriptive records produced by the repository, though some elements such as reference numbers of conservation copies will probably be incorporated. Where a computer with separately located terminals is in use a central record of all information relating to a particular recording has obvious advantages and is likely to be favoured. In either case it is normal for conservation staff themselves to be responsible for creating records of the work they have done. In addition, where a wide range of work is undertaken by conservators, some at short notice and not necessarily concerned with routine conservation, each should maintain a brief log of work undertaken day by day. Apart from the usefulness of this in assessing efficiency, it provides a safeguard should other forms of documentation fail.

			GENERAL SERVICES ADMINISTRATION NATIONAL ARCHIVES AND RECORDS SERVICE **INSPECTION REPORT** TAPE RECORDINGS		RECORD GROUP NO.	

VAULT NO.

TITLE

CONSTANT FACTORS				MATERIAL		ORIGINAL CONDITION	
REEL SIZE		FULL TRACK		POLYESTER		EXCELLENT	
FOOTAGE		HALF TRACK		ACETATE		GOOD	
ORIGINAL		DUAL TRACK		PAPER		FAIR	
MASTER						POOR	
DUPLICATE		COMPLETE				VERY POOR	
SPEED I.P.S.		EDITED				PARTS BAD	
MONAURAL						UNPLAYABLE	
STEREO		RUNNING TIME *(Min.)*				OTHER	
THICKNESS							
TAPE WIDTH							
REMARKS						MANUFACTURER	

NAR FORM MAR 67 **165A**

VARIABLE FACTORS										
INSPECTION DATES										
NORMAL										
OVER-RECORDED										
UNDER-RECORDED										
PRINT THRU										
MUTILATED										
OXIDE PEELING										
WARPED										
DETERIORATED										
POOR SPLICES										
MANY SPLICES										
SOILED										
WORN										
LEADERS										
UNREPAIRABLE										
OTHER										
CURRENT CONDITION										
SPECIAL HANDLING										
INSPECTED BY										

Figure 6.1

120

CONSERVATION OF SOUND ARCHIVES

121

CONSERVATION OF SOUND ARCHIVE MEDIA: AN HISTORICAL AND TECHNICAL SURVEY

Cylinders

Historical background

The original phonograph invented in 1877 by Thomas Edison (1847-1931) consisted of a mouthpiece connected to a diaphragm, to the centre of which a stylus was attached. The stylus impinged on a sheet of tinfoil wrapped round a grooved brass cylinder. To make a recording the operator shouted into the mouthpiece while turning the cylinder by means of a crank. Movement of the diaphragm caused the stylus to make indentations in the tinfoil. To reproduce the sound, the stylus was placed in contact with the foil and as the crank was turned, the indentations caused the diaphragm to vibrate and produce sounds corresponding to the message shouted by the operator. During the process of reproduction, however, most of the indentations were erased; the tinfoil phonograph could not therefore produce recordings for long- or even short-term retention, and it was left to Alexander Graham Bell, his cousin Chichester Bell and an associate Charles Sumner Tainter, working in Washington DC, to develop Edison's idea.

In 1885 they announced a recording machine which used cardboard cylinders with a wax coating which fitted over a revolving mandrell. Instead of the cylinder moving sideways under the stylus, the stylus and diaphragm moved along the cylinder as it revolved. As in Edison's machine, movement of the diaphragm was translated into upward and downward movements of the stylus, resulting in vertical or 'hill-and-dale' modulation of the surface of the cylinder. Using a wax-coated cylinder, however, Bell and Tainter were able to cut the recording into the grooves whereas Edison's stylus produced much less durable indentations. This meant that wax cylinder recordings could potentially be removed from the recording machine and retained for repeated replay. In the absence of rival media these replayable cylinders were often confusingly referred to in contemporary literature as 'records'.

Edison's response was to incorporate many of Bell and Tainter's ideas in his 'New Phonograph' of 1887, closely followed by the 'Perfected Phonograph' in 1888. Both employed the same essential techniques as Bell and Tainter, though power was supplied by a battery and for the Perfected Phonograph cylinders of a solid wax compound were supplied. With minor modifications (for instance there were various other early modes of power supply such as treadles and weights, all to be superseded almost entirely by spring-driven motors), machines of this sort remained in use throughout the 'cylinder era' (1880s until World War I) for both recording and playback. Initially they were expensive and were used to give recitals to large audiences. Later they became common in many households in the US and Europe, and were used both for domestic amusement and entertainment, and for some research purposes (see Figure 6.2).

Figure 6.2   An Edison 'Home' phonograph of c. 1905, a typical spring-driven good quality general purpose machine.

It was in the fields of ethnomusicology and linguistics that the 'serious' potential of the phonograph was soon realized, since no form of written notation or phonetics was equal to the task of conveying the music and language of 'primitive' people. The earliest ethnomusical recordings were of Passamaquoddy Indians by Jesse W. Fewkes in 1890, now held by the Archive of Folk Culture in the Library of Congress.[10]

The earliest comparable British-made recordings, both of music and speech, resulted from A.C. Haddon's expedition to the Torres Straits islands in 1898, which are now at the NSA.[11] Many of those involved in 'collecting' folksong in England, Scotland and Ireland before World War I used the phonograph as an *aide-memoire* rather than a permanent record. Using a shaving machine or the shaving attachment which could be fitted to the phonograph, the surface of many cylinders was removed once the contents had been transcribed, and they were reused. Of those cylinders that survived journeys from foreign parts,[12] many were no doubt thrown away. And of those that do survive, many show signs of serious groove damage resulting from repeated playing during the transcription process. The Australian pianist and composer Percy Grainger appears to have been the first field recordist in England to value his recordings in their own right, though Sir James Frazer, or his wife, put some effort into assembling a collection of over 2000 field recorded cylinders from India, Africa and elsewhere during this period.

Sound recording quickly emerged as an entertainment medium, and owes most of its subsequent development to this role. Prerecorded cylinders were distributed from 1889 onwards. Initially these had to be recorded individually, then by several machines recording simultaneously. Pantographic duplicating machines (probably first used in the mid-1890s; the technique was called 'doubling', soon shortened to 'dubbing' – the term still in wide use today for the equivalent activity) helped to increase rates of production, but the quality of such copies was not highly regarded. Finally between 1900 and 1902 a method of moulding cylinders in metal shells generated from an original wax master was perfected, enabling 'mass production' to commence. Edison introduced narrow-grooved moulded cylinders in 1908, which would play for over four minutes instead of two. Meanwhile unbreakable moulded cylinders made of celluloid (notably the 'Indestructable' brand from 1907) had begun to appear; Edison brought out the definitive version with his 'Blue Amberol' cylinders in 1912.

In the UK the Edison Bell Phonograph Corporation acquired the Edison and Bell-Tainter patents, and it was through this company that most cylinders and cylinder machines were sold in Britain until around 1903, when the patents had expired and several further small companies, together with the main Edison company itself (now represented in Britain by the National Phonograph Company) entered the field.

The Edison Company, though not always the first to develop new techniques, was the 'market leader' in cylinders. This was at least partly because of Edison's own personal commitment to the superiority of cylinders over discs, but unfortunately his preference was not shared in the long run by the buying public and even he ceased publishing entertainment cylinders in 1929, well after most companies and consumers had gone over to discs.

Throughout its currency, cylinder technology underwent no fundamental changes. All recordings were made by the acoustic method, using a horn or horns of various shapes and sizes to pick up the sound and transfer it mechanically to the cutting stylus, essentially as Edison had done with the tinfoil phonograph, and all replay was through acoustic horns, shaped and mounted with increasing sophistication. Cylinders were dead before electrical recording became common. But cylinder recorders remained the only viable field recording machines until the 1930s, and so a few collections of ethnographic research cylinders survive from the interwar years.

Much longer to survive was the office application of reusable wax cylinders in dictating machines. Early and frequently illustrated versions were treadle-powered and looked like sewing machines. Between the wars they were manufactured with mains-powered electric motors. A few continued to be sold until the early 1960s, but the technology was rapidly disappearing as more convenient forms of instantaneous recording, and then magnetic tape, became common. Remarkably few dictation cylinders are encountered today (in the UK at least) considering their once wide distribution.

Recognizing cylinders

The following are general rules only. Short runs of non-standard cylinders were periodically made by various companies for special purposes, but these are rarely encountered at sales, in antique shops or in private collections today. If a cylinder is difficult to categorize from its appearance, advice can be sought from one of the large institutions which hold collections of the various types, or through the City of London Phonograph and Gramophone Society[13] or the Association of Recorded Sound Collections.[14]

Soft wax cylinders   Cylinders intended for direct cutting on recording or copying machines were made of a fairly soft wax compound and have a waxy feel and normally a strong waxy smell. Edison's original wax cylinders were a cream/white colour but by about 1890 they had been replaced by the much more common light brown cylinders. According to Frow and Sefl[15] a typical recipe for the composition from which brown wax cylinder blanks were moulded was 12lb stearic acid/1lb caustic soda/1lb ceresin or paraffin wax/1 oz aluminium oxide. Other ingredients used in Edison wax cylinders were 'burgundy pitch', frankincense, colophony, beeswax, olive oil, montan wax, petroleum jelly, carnauba wax, spermaceti and aluminium stearate.[16] The NSA has a few dark brown or black soft wax cylinders of standard size among its collections, and the later dictating cylinders from Edison's Ediphone company were black.

Most soft wax cylinders were of the 'standard' size: 4⅛ inches (10.5 cm) long by 2⅛ inches (5.5 cm) in outside diameter, designed to hold two minutes of recordings cut at 100 'threads' (i.e. grooves) per inch.[17] The normal length of dictating machine cylinders was 6⅛ inches (15.5 cm), but the diameter could be up to 2⅜ inches (6 cm) to allow repeated shaving and reuse. From 1899 Edison also began selling 'Concert' cylinders with a longer playing time, for use on a range of machines with a larger mandrel. These cylinders were approximately 4¼ inches (10.8 cm) long by 5 inches (12.7 cm) in diameter (see Figures 6.3 and 6.4).

Figure 6.3   A standard size Edison Bell blank wax cylinder.

Prerecorded soft wax cylinders are now comparatively rare. They were produced by direct-cutting or dubbing and are more likely to have a hand-written label than a printed one to identify them. In fact it requires knowledge and experience to distinguish them from locally made 'pirate' copies (see Figure 6.5). Although the distinction between 'professional' and 'amateur' recording was in its infancy, it is normally possible to identify studio recordings by their reasonably clean starts (possibly preceded by a deliberate-sounding announce-ment) and finishes, and by the content which may be identifiable from surviving catalogues; and with experience the normal studio acoustic becomes familiar. In any case successful recordings of bands and ensembles were difficult to make except in a studio. Edison continued to produce Concert-size cylinders by the original direct-cut method until they were discontinued in 1907-8.

Surviving unpublished direct-cut cylinders will have started life as blanks and are usually found in the original containers with notes by the recordist written on the box or lid and/or sometimes scratched on the rim of the cylinder. Some recordists made notes of varying detail on separate slips of paper and inserted them inside the cylinder for safekeeping. The most commonly found blanks in the UK were sold by Edison Bell and have their name on the lid-label and a label with 'Blank Cylinder' on the box. Any cylinders which appear to hold 'private' recordings could be of great interest because so few non-commercial recordings survive from the early years of the century.

Two very small collections of ethnomusical recordings made on dictating cylinders are held by the NSA, and a number were listed by the Federal Cylinder Project, including those among the well-known Frances Densmore recordings of North American Indian Music,[18] so clearly unidentified dictating cylinders should be investigated – a tiresome necessity since satisfactory working machines which will take this size need to be specially constructed or adapted for the purpose. The results are bound to be disappointing in most cases. The NSA holds one collection of Australian field recordings on Concert-size cylinders, but this format does not appear to have been widely used for private recordings.

Despite the scholarly aura surrounding non-commercial wax cylinders in the remarkable collections of various public institutions, it should not be forgotten that their most common use was for domestic amusement.

A few blanks are often found among collections of non-commercial cylinders. If they are unused and in good condition they will have a shiny surface and no grooves; if they have been shaved the helical tracings of the shaving cutter may be noticeable and the thickness of wax obviously reduced.

Other cylinders The later types of cylinders were produced by moulding and are therefore not the product of direct original recording.[19] Following the precedent of Edison's 'Gold Moulded' cylinders from 1902, all the early moulded cylinders were black in colour and made of a harder compound than brown wax. Typically the compound still had a little wax in it and smelled somewhat of wax, but it mostly contained metallic soaps and bore more resemblance to the shellac compounds used in early discs. These cylinders typically have their maker's name and the title of their contents moulded into the outer edge of one end, and they were sold in gaily coloured containers with maker's name and regalia on the box and a printed label indicating the contents on the lid.

Later improvements included the use of an even harder compound (still black) which would hold grooves of about half the width

Figure 6.4   An Ediphone 6-inch dictating machine cylinder.

Figure 6.5   A selection of locally-made copies of commercial cylinders.

of earlier cylinders and therefore play for over four minutes instead of two. The pioneering Edison version of 1908 was called the 'Amberol' cylinder but it was very brittle and was superseded in 1912 by Edison's remarkable 'Blue Amberol' cylinder, made of bright blue nitrocellulose (often referred to as celluloid) on a plaster core and very hard-wearing. At the very end Edison also put out a celluloid 'Royal Purple Amberol' series (see Figures 6.6 and 6.7). Earlier celluloid cylinders such as the 'Indestructable' are usually black in colour on a cardboard core.

Figure 6.6 **A range of Edison prerecorded published cylinders in typical containers.**

Figure 6.7 **Prerecorded published wax cylinder by Edison's competitors.**

All Edison moulded cylinders were of the standard 'four-inch' size except for a 'Kinetophone' series used for sound synchronization with Edison films in 1912-13. These were about 10 inches long with a 5-inch diameter and made of celluloid, but they were not widely distributed. There appear to have been some concert-size moulded cylinders by other makers, but the only non-standard moulded cylinders which regularly turn up were published by Pathé in France. They are the standard length but 3½ inches in diameter and made of a fairly waxy black compound. In fact French companies were responsible for producing some of the major oddities in the history of cylinders. H. J. Loiret for instance began selling the 'Merveilleux' miniature cylinder player, with its tiny celluloid cylinders, from 1893, while Pathé manufactured machines designed to play cylinders with a 5-inch diameter and 14 inches long in the early years of the century.

Conservation and handling of soft wax cylinders

Characteristics   In the unlikely event that wax cylinders have been kept under favourable conditions over the years, and rarely played or handled, they may still appear 'as good as new'. Their constituents are not subject to rapid chemical breakdown, but newly made blanks (e.g. those which the Miller-Morris Company have recently started making in the UK) appear relatively less hard and brittle than those held by the NSA, all of which are between 50 and 90 years old now, and have been subject to the very gradual migration or evaporation of softening constituents. Presumably they will go on getting harder until they are so fragile that they cannot be handled or played. The rule must be therefore that all cylinders considered worthy of permanent preservation should have their contents copied onto tape as soon as practicable. However, many cylinders will in any case be affected by other problems.

Most will have been physically damaged to some extent by repeated playback or rough handling. Warping caused by unsuitable storage environments will cause stylus tracking problems on many cylinders. In addition, because cylinder technology died out rapidly in the 1920s many will have been stored away for many years, often in damp or dirty conditions, and are thus frequently in a poor state when rediscovered. Cardboard containers may have been attacked by vermin or insects, and in particular the cylinders themselves may have been affected by mould which feeds on nutrients in the wax compound and creates white blotches of varying size on the surface. Recordings on mould-affected cylinders are usually very badly damaged: a loud roar is heard on replay about which little can be done since the grooves are physically eaten into.

Cylinders are usually found in their original containers but unfortunately these are not ideal for long-term storage. Normally within the container there is an additional inner cardboard liner, with fluffy gauze stuck to its inner side. This gauze is intended to protect the grooves from damage and to a greater or lesser extent is in contact with the surface of the cylinder. In cases where mould has grown, its incidence on the cylinder surface is often clearly related to the pattern of contact with the gauze, presumably because the gauze harbours damp (see Figure 6.8). Wax cylinders should therefore be

Figure 6.8   **A mould affected wax cylinder. The relationship between the corrugated gauze-lined insert and the mould is clearly visible.**

stored separately from boxes of this type, though not before some foolproof system has been devised through which box, lid and cylinder can all be identified. Apart from physical damage, mould is by far the most serious and widespread problem encountered with the NSA's cylinders, but others have encountered further difficulties.

The general introduction to the Federal cylinder project volumes speaks for instance of softening agent exudation: a soft compound was achieved originally by the addition of castor oil, olive oil or mineral oil to other cylinder constituents, but these oils have tended to work their way out over the years causing microscopic or even more visible damage to the cylinder surface and clogging up the grooves with an oily film. Perhaps this phenomenon is encouraged by the North American climate; it has not been clearly identified among the NSA's collections, except on some Ediphone cylinders where the migrating oil has soaked into the cardboard containers. As with mould damage, recordings tend to be irretrievably obliterated by this process.[20]

Handling   All wax cylinders are very fragile. They will break, usually into many pieces, if dropped or crushed. The handling of wax cylinders should be kept to an absolute minimum and restricted to

131

experienced personnel. Wax, especially the soft brown wax compounds, will distort and eventually melt in the presence of heat, so contact with fingers should be kept as brief as possible. Great care should be taken not to touch the grooved area. A cylinder kept in a cylindrical box should be removed by placing two fingers down the centre and applying sufficient gentle pressure on the inside surface to grip and withdraw it. It should then be carried on a rigid cardboard tube or perhaps a pencil, held at both ends.

Repair Repairing broken wax cylinders requires skill, experience and luck. Normally a repair will only be worth attempting if the cylinder is unique, and the purpose will only be to keep the pieces together long enough for a copy to be made. If there is a single clean break it is often possible to tape the two halves together top and bottom. Where there are more than two pieces attempts can be made to piece them together jigsaw fashion using a suitably shaped hollow former which will need to be slightly conical to match the shape of the inside of the cylinder and of the mandrel on the cylinder machine. There seems little future in attempting complicated repairs without a former, so provision will also have to be available to replay repaired cylinders with the former in place – a modified mandrel may be the answer. 'Welding' together cracks by melting and merging the wax on each side of a crack with a soldering iron (working on the inside surface of the cylinder of course) should only be attempted in the last resort.

Copying The Federal Cylinder Project introductory volume is also worth consulting for its detailed description of a conventional modern cylinder copying apparatus and procedure.[21]

The equipment and skills involved are specialized and there are probably fewer than half a dozen engineers in the UK who could offer a service. In-house facilities will be worth setting up if any quantity are to be copied, though in such cases the majority will probably be moulded commercial cylinders which are perhaps a little easier to cope with. Any UK sound archivist with a cylinder problem is urged to consult the conservation manager at the NSA.

Until the early 1970s the usual way of copying cylinders was to replay them on an original acoustic machine (possibly adapted for use with a mains-driven motor). An appropriate horn was connected up and the results recorded with a microphone. This method has the possible advantage that the equalization effect of the equipment, if skilfully chosen, may serve to compensate for distortions in the recording and produce a clear and balanced copy, though the more likely outcome is a copy subject to considerable distortion resulting from horn inadequacies. However, the technique is unsatisfactory since the stylus weight will erode the cylinder grooves as replay takes place, in many cases worsening an already serious problem.

Less destructive techniques are now available. A purpose-built but relatively cheap adaptor can be used on a conventional cylinder machine to replace the mechanical soundbox with an electrical pickup.[22] Or the original replay apparatus can be removed from the machine and a conventional pickup arm designed for disc replay mounted up to replace it. Since the arm pivots from a fixed point the stylus will describe a gradual arc across the cylinder instead of a straight line, but the effect of this will be relatively insignificant. Better still a parallel tracking arm can be adapted, but the expense and degree of modification required are probably not worthwhile as some of the conventional cylinder player's other faults, such as irregular playing speed and noisy bearings, will still be present. Further major adaptation or a completely new machine will be needed if a higher standard is required.

Very few modern machines are commercially available and they are expensive;[23] the dedicated may enjoy the challenge of constructing their own. One of the major problems in using modern lightweight pickups on cylinders is their tendency to bounce off course when jolted by a patch of groove wear or a bump in a warped cylinder, particularly if they rely on gravity alone, without a feed screw, to keep them on course.[24]

From 1902 the standard replay speed for Edison cylinders was 160 rpm but before that various slower speeds were used. No standardization should be expected among privately recorded cylinders. Speeds were often adjusted to suit the length of the material. Some research recordists sounded a pitch pipe or tuning fork at the start of the cylinder, but beyond this, subjective judgement is normally the only guide. Copying cylinders too fast or too slow is not a disaster – speeds can be adjusted later by copying the tape in the light of improved knowledge.

A wide range of groove profiles can also be anticipated, requiring an appropriate range of up to 10 styluses from which the most efficient can be chosen by trial and error. Attempts to 'read' cylinder grooves with laser beams have attracted some attention recently, and it seems likely that this method is capable of extracting more information than the conventional stylus, particularly from damaged or broken cylinders which present severe or insoluble tracking problems. (The same technique could be used on discs which are too badly damaged for replay by conventional means).

However no one appears to be able to focus a laser in such a way as to separate the wanted recording from the noise producing elements in the groove, with the result that unprocessed laser copies even of undamaged cylinders are very noisy.[25] Progress may result from the application of computer-based digital restoration methods.[26]

There can be few exceptions to the rule that once the copying apparatus has been finally set up and adjusted, at least two copies should be made, one flat, one filtered, one as a duplicate master, one as a copy for use.

Storage   Wax cylinders are very susceptible to mould growth so they must be kept in constant cool dry conditions.   Because the contemporary cylindrical boxes are actually unsuitable for their permanent storage, wax cylinders should be transferred to more suitable containers; but the old boxes should also be retained if they have any useful notes or markings on them, and conservation measures such as deacidification at least considered.[27]

Labelling cylinders then certainly becomes a major difficulty. The only satisfactory method seems to be to affix a prewritten paper label using some archivally suitable adhesive to the inside surface of each cylinder. Once removed from their original boxes cylinders should be stored in a way which will minimize the possibility of handling damage while maintaining free air circulation around them. Such conditions are not easy to create, and at present there appear to be no readily available replacement containers of suitable archival standard.

The most satisfactory mode of long-term storage is probably in a purpose-built drawer with rigid upright cylindrical pegs fixed to its base, all made of archivally suitable materials. The height and diameter of these pegs should roughly correspond to the inside dimensions of the type of cylinder to be stored in the drawer. They should be sufficiently spaced out to allow free air circulation round them and easy access for individual removal. Any free play between the cylinder and its support could be packed out with a layer of inert plastic packing material or archival tissue, taking care not to apply pressure to the inside of the cylinder; but it is a disadvantage of this system that cylinders are difficult to immobilize completely. No provision is made for the storage or transport of cylinders individually, but since all items should have been copied onto tape before being placed in archival storage, the need for this will be minimal. Flat boxes designed to fit existing standard shelving, with pegs fixed to their bases to hold a number of cylinders, might be an alternative, but drawers can be relied on not to drop or collapse.

An ingenious individual cylinder box has been designed and used by the Library of Congress Motion Picture and Sound Recordings Division, in which the cylinder is supported within the box at each end by a protruding pyramid which impinges only on the inner edge of each rim of the cylinder. There is no contact between the cylinder and the outer walls of the box, thus permitting free air circulation. However, the outward pressure exerted on the edge of the cylinder by the pyramids has resulted in some breakages, so caution seems advisable.[28]

Cylinders may be received in a contemporary proprietary case holding perhaps 50 or 100. The cylinders will have been removed from their original boxes and placed in the baize- or velvet-lined mould-harbouring compartments provided in the case. Clearly such cylinders should be rehoused after copying, and the characteristic scraps of paper with identifying information, often stuffed down the centre of each cylinder, should be preserved separately.

Conservation of moulded cylinders

Apart from the few very rare examples mentioned above, moulded cylinders were a mass-produced entertainment medium and do not contain archival recordings. In any case there is little to be said concerning their conservation which does not also apply to direct-cut wax cylinders.

Cylinders made of hard, fragile compounds should be handled, stored and copied in the same way as wax cylinders. They do not appear to be as susceptible to mould as their predecessors, but the safe procedure should still be to store them separately from the original gauze-lined containers. Amberol-type narrow groove cylinders will require a separate set of replay styluses.

Celluloid cylinders present less of a problem since they are considerably more robust. Mould growth, hardly ever observed, can be cleaned off with a lint-free cloth and if necessary distilled water (do not immerse these cylinders in water as the inner surface is not water-resistant). Their containers, like all the others, are made of acidic cardboard and should be deacidified, but after copying the risk of returning the cylinders to them appears to be minimal in the short term, and most repositories will no doubt consider the many problems created by reboxing to be not worth while in this case (but see below).

Yes, Blue Amberol and other 'indestructible' cylinders *are* made of nitrocellulose which *is* the same stuff as the early films which decompose and spontaneously catch fire are made of. However there are no recorded instances of similar problems with celluloid cylinders. The NSA's Blue Amberols, all 60 or more years old now, still look in better shape than many lightly used vinyl discs.

Recent research indicates that celluloid cylinders are subject to very gradual decomposition, but that even cylinders which are visibly deteriorating will not spontaneously ignite until heated to a temperature of 150 degrees C (302 degrees F) which is 60 degrees higher than the ignition temperature of nitrate film in good condition. Risks are minimized by allowing gases produced in the process of decomposition to escape, which suggests that these cylinders, like all the others for different reasons, should in due course be stored separately from their original close-fitting containers.

In practice therefore there should never be a problem unless the celluloid cylinders are set alight by a fire originating elsewhere. If this happens, they will be almost impossible to extinguish and will give off noxious fumes, so for this reason the sound archivist should inform those concerned with fire safety and perhaps arrange for separate remote storage after copying.[29]

Discs

Historical background

The essentials of the system still used for recording sound on disc were announced in September 1887 by Emile Berliner (1851-1929) working in Washington DC. His initial machine used the same basic method of sound transfer – the diaphragm-activated stylus – as cylinder recorders, but employed a revolving disc as the recording medium, into the surface of which a spiral groove was cut by the stylus. The cutting motion of the stylus was from side to side, modulating the walls of the groove rather than the base as in vertical-cut cylinder recording.

Most disc recording since has been by Berliner's 'lateral cut' method. His original discs were glass coated with lamp black. After the recording had been traced in the lamp black it was fixed with lacquer and then photo-engraved. In 1888 Berliner went over to five-inch diameter zinc discs with a wax coating. The stylus cut through the wax exposing the zinc, which was then etched to produce a permanent groove. Using this etched disc as a matrix, copies made of a thermo-plastic compound (celluloid, vulcanite, and from 1897 shellac) were produced, initially under licence by a German firm of toy makers, Kämmerer and Reinhardt, who also manufactured and sold a simple hand-cranked 'gramophone' on which the discs could be played. These discs were notable for their loud surface noise, and even the most skilled operator found it difficult to keep them rotating at a constant speed. However the ease with which discs could be duplicated by pressing was already clear (several years before the more difficult process of moulding duplicate cylinders became available), and this early association of the disc format with the commercial mass-distribution of studio-recorded material has remained to the present day.

Eldridge R. Johnson, shortly to found the Victor Talking Machine Company, collaborated with Berliner from 1897 and was mainly responsible for raising the status of disc technology to a level at which it could provide ultimately fatal competition to Edison's cylinders. He perfected the first spring-driven gramophone and then devised a method of recording onto wax discs from which metal stampers could be produced and pressings of much better quality achieved. Seven-inch (17 cm) discs emanating from this process, pressed in shellac, began to appear in 1899, ten-inch (25 cm) in 1901 and twelve-inch (30 cm) in 1903. Already by 1901 Columbia, having made a deal with Johnson, had begun to issue lateral-cut discs, and they had abandoned cylinders altogether within a few years.

An important reason for the eventual success of discs in the commercial battle with cylinders was the quality of performer with which discs rapidly became associated. An agency for importing Berliner's products was set up in London in 1897. (It was shortly to become the Gramophone Company, acquiring the British copyright on the 'His Master's Voice' trademark, and ultimately merged with Columbia and several other major labels to form EMI in 1931.) In 1898 Fred Gaisberg was sent by Berliner to set up a recording studio in London. Gaisberg set about attracting significant performers to the studio and in 1901 made a recording trip to Russia when ten-inch discs of Chaliapin and others were cut, to be issued the same year in a new 'Red Label' series. Gaisberg and others then went on to record many famous names in various European cities – most notably Enrico Caruso in Milan (1902) – and these artists became the first 'recording stars'. Their records sold in large numbers, both in Britain and as issued by Victor in America, thus spreading their popularity and increasing their status and that of the issuing companies.

Although hard-wax cutting discs were produced which could be used for immediate playback, disc-recording machines appear never to have been manufactured for domestic use and there are only a few isolated instances of their use in field recording as an aid to research. The most significant was probably the 'Wiener Archivphonograf' used by the Phonogrammarchiv to make over 3000 research recordings in many countries of the world up to 1930. It used an Edison diaphragm and stylus to produce vertical-cut recordings, but the medium was 6-inch (15 cm) wax discs, chosen because it was possible to generate metal matrices from them and press good-quality duplicates for distribution at a time (1899) when a satisfactory means of duplicating cylinders by moulding had yet to be perfected.[30]

Cutting waxes used in the studios of record companies were shaved and reused after each session, so they are unlikely to impinge on the work of many sound archivists. On the other hand the specialist archives of older-established companies (EMI is the principal example in the UK) are likely to hold long runs of the 'metal parts' produced from wax originals and used in the production of stampers, and possibly of test pressings generated in the course of disc manufacture. Pressings of this kind are also frequently encountered at sales or in private hands, and should be examined as they may contain material which was not ultimately issued: many were produced in order to enable alternate 'takes' to be evaluated, and can illustrate the development of a particular performance. Tests emanating from aborted projects or experimental work are likely to be of even greater interest and value.

Until the mid-1920s the recording technique used by all the record companies was the 'acoustic' method based essentially on Edison's original invention. Sound waves were captured by a recording horn and transmitted to a diaphragm which activated the cutting stylus. Horns of various materials, sizes and shapes were tried in conjunction with diaphragms of various materials (most usually glass) and diameters. Engineers became skilled at placing bands and soloists before the horn so that the loud instruments did not drown the voices and other quieter elements. Although clear, natural-sounding recordings could be made by these methods, the limited or selective frequency response of recording horns and diaphragms led to some distortion in most cases, and the method was never successfully used to record performances or events outside the studio such as an orchestra in a concert hall.

Improvements came with the development of electrical recording, though the record companies (especially in the US – rather like the movie moguls when faced with the possibility of talking pictures) were slow to introduce new methods. This reluctance may have been partly due to the very poor results obtained by some experimenters in the early days of electrical recording, which appear to have given the technique a bad name initially. How to do it was no secret: sound waves had to be converted by a microphone into voltages which would be amplified sufficiently to activate an electro-mechanical cutting stylus. Microphones of various sorts had been under development since the 1880s, but satisfactory amplifiers, based on a prototype patented by Lee de Forest in 1906, were not generally adopted until after World War I, and a fully adequate cutting head was not produced until 1923.

Some interesting electrical recordings made by the Admiralty in the course of wartime submarine detection work were described and played by Sir William Bragg during his series of 'juvenile' lectures at the Royal Institution in 1919. The recordings are preserved on shellac pressings at the Royal Institution, and although the subject matter (morse-code bleeps and engine noises) is hardly riveting the recordings are clear and loud, indicating the use of an amplifier, though Bragg gave few details of the recording technique beyond describing the microphone.[31] These unpublished discs may hold the first amplified electrical recordings to survive.

The first electrical recording to find its way onto a published disc was actually a 'field recording' of poor technical quality made in November 1920 by Lionel Guest and H.O. Merriman, who strung up microphones in Westminster Abbey and recorded the funeral service for 'A British Warrior', relaying the proceedings down telephone lines to the cutting equipment in a van outside.[32]

Guest and Merriman continued to work on aspects of electrical recording for Columbia, along with others such as B.F. Meissner for Brunswick in Chicago and Owens and Hewitt for Victor; but the breakthrough came in 1923 when Joseph P. Maxfield's team at the Bell Telephone Laboratories perfected the 'rubberline' recorder which effectively damped out the unwanted mechanical resonances in the recording head which had vitiated most electrical recording hitherto. It was incorporated in the Western Electric recording system which was the first to be installed by the major recording companies in Britain and the US from around 1925.[33]

Wax recording blanks continued to be used by the record companies as cutting masters until the late 1940s, but elsewhere new methods were rapidly being developed. In the US a system of recording on wax-coated aluminium discs from which cellulose acetate pressings could be generated found favour with broadcasters, while in Europe a 'direct cut' technique was sought in which the cutting 'master' disc itself could be played back without further processing. Various base materials and coatings were tried, and some recordings directly cut into soft aluminium discs have survived, together with the loud surface noise characteristic of this medium.

But the most successful discs were perfected in London by Cecil Watts, using cellulose nitrate lacquer on an aluminium core. He also developed a relatively compact disc-cutting machine, and the system was adopted and improved by the BBC from 1934.[34] Direct-cut discs rapidly became the most widespread recording medium in broadcasting, and particularly after World War II many small-scale recording concerns, of which Watts's Marguerite Sound Services was the prototype, sprang up around this relatively cheap and compact equipment (see Figure 6.9).[35] Portable battery-powered versions mounted in vans and cars enabled many classic field recordings of traditional music, wartime events, sports matches etc. to be made.

Figure 6.9.   A portable disc-cutting machine c. 1950.

Ultimately lacquer discs supplanted wax as the cutting medium used by record companies, where they have remained in continuous use to the present day, to be supplanted in some quarters by 'direct metal mastering' on copper discs only very recently.

Direct-cut discs are referred to by various names – as 'instantaneous disks' in US broadcasting and archive circles; as 'lacquers' in the UK record industry – but most people call them 'acetates'. Cellulose acetate was no doubt experimented with as a coating for discs in the early days, but cellulose nitrate has been the most widely used coating since the 1930s, so the survival of the erroneous name, too well engrained to alter now, is curious. As the carriers of unique recordings, 'acetates' were the only disc recording medium to be of serious interest to all archivists until the advent of optical discs designed for use with digital recording equipment (usually referred to as 'recordable CDs' or WORM – 'write once read many' discs).

The record industry played an important part in the development of discs before World War II, but completely took them over after the war. Major changes occurred in recording speed, groove pitch, and pressing material (all at much the same time) and a few years later in recording mode, resulting in the commercially issued discs which are still familiar today.

Since Berliner's time most commercially issued discs had been pressed with a groove pitch of around 100 per inch to be played at or around 78 revolutions per minute. Among the few significant exceptions were those issued by the French Pathé company which, in its early independent years used faster speeds and, incidentally, recorded by the vertical rather than lateral cut method. As a general rule popular music was published on 10-inch discs and 'serious' music on 12-inch, but a number of smaller sizes were quite common between the wars. Many small-scale experiments with narrower grooves and/or slower speeds designed to produce longer playing time were made in the 1920s and 1930s, notably the 16-inch discs pressed by the Vitaphone Company in the US for use as synchronized film soundtracks, which played at 33 rpm (1926), and the 450 grooves-per-inch discs issued by Edison in 1927.

The first widely adopted new standard originated in the publication of long-playing 10- and 12-inch vinyl pressings by the American Columbia Company in 1948. These had 224-300 grooves per inch and played at $33\frac{1}{3}$ rpm. Shortly afterwards RCA issued seven-inch vinyl microgroove discs played at 45 rpm. Each format became associated initially with a different repertoire and clientèle, and both became firmly established so that most significant record companies (e.g. Decca and EMI in the UK) were issuing discs on both formats by the early 1950s.

It is curious that major companies took so long to adopt flexible 'unbreakable' materials for discs. Although several types of 'plastic' records were published by smaller companies during the interwar years, and the superiority of such materials (usually cellulose nitrate-based) widely touted, all the major companies remained with shellac compounds until the first long-players came out. 'LPs' and 'singles' are still very much alive. Ten-inch LPs ceased in the early 1960s, and seven-inch, 45 rpm 'extended play' discs, first published in 1953, have been largely if not entirely superseded by '12-inch singles' in recent years.

EMI was the last major UK company to include 78s in their catalogue: they were finally withdrawn in 1962, but some 'mood music' publishers such as Boosey and Hawkes continued to issue 78s until the late 1960s. The very widespread use of 'acetates' for all kinds of recording work was roughly coterminous with 78 rpm discs, but $33\frac{1}{3}$ rpm microgroove acetates from the late 1950s and 1960s (usually ex-broadcasting or record industry) may well be encountered by sound archivists, and of course they are still used in the routine production of vinyl discs by the record industry.

The most recent modification to Berliner's technique has been the almost universal adoption of 'stereophonic' disc cutting and pressing, following its initial introduction in 1958. In order to achieve a more realistic impression of spacial distribution on replay through headphones or two suitably placed speakers, original sounds are divided laterally, either by recording through two microphones (there are various approaches to microphone placing depending on the effect required), or through several microphones and mixing the results onto two channels. The two channels could be transferred to disc using concentric grooves and two replay styluses, or by a single groove modulated by the two separate channels. By the latter method the two channels are cut at 90 degrees to each other, either in vertical-lateral (VL) configuration, with one channel in the bottom of the groove and the other on the side, or by the '45/45' system in which both channels are cut on the sides of the groove at 45 degrees to the surface of the disc. Both these methods were perfected in the UK by A.D. Blumlein and patented in 1931, but the 45/45 technique has become the industry standard for all commercially issued stereo recordings.[36]

Since World War II there have been two strands of development in disc recording which do not derive from the techniques pioneered by Edison and Berliner. In the 1950s various types of recordable magnetic discs were produced, normally for use in dictating machines for which open-reel tape was rather unwieldy. Modest recording performance was outweighed by the advantage of rapid access to different parts of the disc. The Emidicta machine used plain sheets of plastic coated with ferric oxide, the spiral track being achieved by an auxiliary spiral-grooved disc placed on top which pulled the recording head across. Another system brought out by Pye involved pre-grooved discs: the grooves were of rectangular cross-section and the recording head moved in the flat bottom of the groove. Both systems were short-lived and surviving discs (whose contents would be mostly of ephemeral value) rare.

In more recent times many experiments with digital audiorecording on magnetic computer discs have been tried. Floppy discs are not suitable as their capacity is too limited, but Winchester-type hard discs, though incapable of being removed from computer equipment once in use, have begun to play a successful role in the temporary storage and manipulation of recordings by up-to-date studios.

However, the arrival of 'optical' discs has already had a revolutionary and permanent effect on the traditional pattern of disc recording and publishing. The new methods derive from successful experiments carried out by the Dutch Philips company in the 1970s which initially resulted in the demonstration of an optically-read videodisc format in 1978. The technique was also applied to digital audiorecording, and an international standard 4.7 inch (12 cm) diameter disc known as the 'compact disc' was developed jointly by Philips and by Sony in Japan. It was launched in Japan in October 1982 and is already in very widespread use as a medium for commercially published music recordings of all kinds. The rapid commercial success of the CD encouraged the development of other digital data storage applications based on the CD-audio format. Among these is the WORM ('write once read many') disc intended primarily for computer data storage as a rival to tape and hard discs, but also capable of holding digital sound recordings and still images. The adoption of WORM discs as a permanent archival storage medium for sound recordings is widely anticipated.

Commercially published CDs are 1.2 mm thick and have several layers. The 'bottom' (i.e. the side without printed information which faces down when inserted in a CD player) is most usually a layer of transparent polycarbonate, produced by injection moulding. During this process the digitized recording is impressed onto the upper surface of the polycarbonate by a metal stamper derived from a glass matrix cut with a laser. The digits are represented by a line of microscopic pits arranged in a spiral. This surface is 'metallized' (with aluminium in the standard commercially issued CD) and covered with a transparent protective coating of acrylic lacquer which also holds printed information on disc contents. In the CD player the encoded recording is 'read' from below by a laser beam which is focused on the pits (assisted by the refractive effect of the polycarbonate) and reflected back off them into the pickup. The spiral track is on average about three miles long. The recorded area is a maximum of 3.55 cm wide, into which about 20,200 track revolutions can be squeezed.

The principles of digital recording are described in simple terms in the section on magnetic recording below. As was frequently demonstrated by imaginative apologists when CDs were first marketed, the error correction capability of the format is so large and efficient that information removed by drilling holes through discs can be completely reconstructed. The format also includes subcodes which are used to locate start points on the disc (the equivalent of scrolls between bands on an LP). Since replay involves no physical contact with the disc, wear and tear are minimal, and digital recordings may be reproduced if necessary with no reduction in quality. However, transparency and physical stability in the polycarbonate base layer are essential to the function of CDs and WORM discs. Polycarbonate is regarded as 'very stable', but it seems unlikely that the standard aluminium coating will be suitable for long-term archival use in view of its tendency to oxidization. Discs metallized with platinum are at present regarded as potentially the most reliable, subject to the results of current trials.

Recognizing discs

Older published discs Guidance given here is general and brief. Virtually all published discs bear a preprinted label from which they can be identified, and there are many sources of further information in the form of manufacturers' catalogues, published discographies, magazines for record collectors and music enthusiasts, and books about the record industry and recording artists.

After initial experiments with other materials Berliner settled on a black pigmented shellac compound for his pressings, and this material, in various formulations, remained in very widespread use until the end of the 78 rpm era in the late 1950s.

The first double-sided pressings were issued in Germany by the International Zonophone Company in 1903 and by Odeon in 1904. Columbia also issued a few 14-inch double-sided discs in America, but production quickly ceased in the face of worries over patent infringement. No other double-sided records appeared until 1907. As a general rule therefore, published single-sided pressings on which the blank side is completely plain are likely to be early acoustic recordings. The catalogue number and recording details of pre-1900 Berliner pressings were handwritten or stamped onto the matrix centre and are therefore found pressed onto the disc. Seven-inch Berliners are quite rare and the five-inch ones from the Kämmerer and Reinhardt period are seldom encountered even in the saleroom.

Preprinted disc labels were introduced by Eldridge R. Johnson in 1900, after which, as it turned out, virtually all commercially published lateral-cut discs from that day to this have borne labels with the company name, title and performer of the material recorded, catalogue number and other details such as the place of manufacture and patent dates, surrounded, surmounted or otherwise embellished by company regalia and trademarks. Two companies with major involvement in cylinder publishing – Pathé in France and Edison in the USA – perpetuated 'cylinder' practices on their discs through vertical-cutting and an embossed labelling style for at least part of their output. Pathé's non-conformity extended to issuing discs of greater diameter than the standard 10 and 12 inches, often to be played from the centre outwards, while Edison's 'Diamond' discs, pressed from a hard bakelite-like material, were about ¼ inch thick – about three times as thick as the 78s issued by other companies.

Published discs have to be in extraordinarily bad condition for the label information to be illegible, but if the label should prove to be inadequate, nearly all pressings also have some sort of number pressed into them. This is usually called the matrix number, and throughout the period when discs were produced from metal parts generated directly from waxes and acetates, the number related exclusively to a specific recording undertaken at a particular time and date.

Where the relevant company archives survive, the numbers can therefore be used to establish an exact chronology, and to distinguish one performance of a piece from another, since companies not infrequently issued two different 'takes' under the same catalogue number and label. With the advent of taperecording and editing, published discs are no longer necessarily the product of one recording session on one occasion, but they still bear a number. Vinyl pressings from larger companies with their own pressing facilities usually still bear matrix numbers, but pressings from independent plants issued by smaller companies tend to bear the catalogue number.[37] In either case it should be possible to discover the origin of a pressing from this information.

'Run in' grooves at the outer edges of records were not introduced until 1930, prior to which discs had a plain ungrooved area round the edge or, on some earlier issues, a raised edge to prevent the needle from spilling off. Partly because of this, discs from the acoustic era, particularly pre-1920, tend to be thicker in appearance than the later electrical recordings.

Published discs pressed from materials other than shellac before World War II are unusual though hardly rare. 'Flexidiscs' of one sort or another often turn up among collections of old records in junkshops and auctions. They were usually the product of some enterprise unrelated to the mainstream record companies. An early example in the UK were Goodson records pressed in a very flexible white celluloid and advertised as the 'first unbreakable discs'. The most common are perhaps those on the Durium label which originated in New York City in 1930. They were single-sided and pressed in brown celluloid laminated onto a thick paper base. Now they are usually found with a pronounced curl and often surface cracks. They were cheap to buy and not made to last. Others makes in lurid transparent celluloid were issued primarily as advertising vehicles. Publishers of these unorthodox records clearly made a point of avoiding the traditional black colouring.

Other pressings   Pressings made in the course of commercial record production and promotion are often among, or derived from, the possessions of those connected with the music industry. *Test pressings* were and are made by record-pressing plants for use in checking the quality of the metal stampers before mass production commences. 78 rpm tests often have special labels with 'test record' or somesuch printed on them, to which handwritten identification may have been added, or they may have a plain white label (see Figure 6.10). Shellac tests are normally single-sided, but examination of the matrix number usually indicates that the pressing represents one side of a disc subsequently issued in large numbers. Vinyl tests are more normally double-sided, and a plain white label is usual.

Promotional records were and are produced, perhaps before the final printed version of the label is available, in order to create advance interest in new publications among the record trade and on radio. The 78 rpm versions normally have a preprinted label with the company's name and a warning such as 'advance copy – not for sale'. Information on content may also be printed, typed or hand-written on this label. More recent 'promos' tend to be identical to the intended issue with the warning overprinted on the sleeve. Tests and promos for records which remained unissued are very rare but there are a number of celebrated examples.

Private pressings may be of more interest to the archivist. They used to be quite common in the heyday of the small recording and disc-cutting studios which recorded direct on acetates. The latter were known to deteriorate after a few playings, so if repeated use was envisaged or a number of copies required then clients might order a quantity of pressings to be run off from the acetate. These typically bear the printed label of the studio (more than likely the same as used on its acetates) with content details typed in. They were mainly used as demonstration recordings by performers, though some were clearly just souvenirs or gifts.

In the 1960s and 1970s, when vinyl record production in the UK was cheap, the recording of performances or events by clubs, colleges etc. for private issue on disc was quite common. There were still a few studios or freelance engineers around who could make the recordings and the pressing arrangements as a standard service, but quite often amateur recordings were used and sent direct to a pressing plant for processing. The results usually look like 12-inch vinyl test pressings with a plain white label; the content information normally appears on the sleeve or as an insert. Increased costs and the advent of cassette duplicating have reduced the need for private pressings to the extent that very few livings are made from them now.

On a much larger scale the BBC and many other broadcasting organizations used short runs of pressings as a means of duplicating recordings. The policy was to keep several copies in case one was

Figure 6.10.   A group of test pressings with typical labels.

damaged or wore out, or if the same recording was wanted in different places. Uniquely now, the BBC still keeps compilations of shorter items on short runs of pressings, though in recent times these will have originally been tape recordings. Radio discs are quite often found in private hands and are easily identifiable from label information (see Figure 6.11).

Figure 6.11.   A group of BBC Sound Archive pressings.

Direct-cut discs   To deal with the unusual first: direct-cut metal discs are occasionally found. Aluminium discs (which were actually embossed rather than cut) were used professionally for short periods in the 1930s, more commonly by radio stations in the US than in the UK. They are typically of 12-inch diameter with a bright metallic surface and a label without preprinted content details but with a warning not to use steel needles. They should not be confused with the metal parts used in the production of pressed discs. These have a very shiny brass- or silver-coloured metallic surface and no label or centre hole. They are noticeably heavy and are usually packed in heavyweight cardboard jackets which bear identifying information.

More common in Britain are small diameter aluminium or zinc discs, mainly emanating from coin-operated recording machines which used to be a standard feature in the amusement arcades of seaside towns. Many families have preserved one or two of these as souvenirs, and sound archivists may be asked how to transfer them onto a more modern medium. The NSA has also accumulated a few Mivoice seven-inch direct-cut copper discs on which it was clearly possible to make good quality recordings with low background noise.

Direct-cut soft plastic discs (e.g. Permarec and Calibre discs in the UK) may come to light occasionally; they appear to have been used professionally, but not in the course of commercial disc production or 'serious' recordings. Plastic direct-cut dictating machine discs of various makes, sizes, designs and colours were again more common in the US than in Britain during the 1940s and 1950s, but are now in any case rarely found since their content was entirely ephemeral.

Much more common and significant are 'acetate' discs. They were made in a variety of sizes, the most common diameters being 10-inch (25cm), 12-inch (30cm), 13-inch (33cm), and 16-inch (41cm) though larger and smaller sizes are not rare. If in good condition they have a shiny, normally black surface and superficially resemble vinyl LPs or new 78 pressings, but they are heavier and much less flexible than LPs. The metal core (aluminium or occasionally zinc) is sometimes visible round the edge, but a more reliable place to look is at the centre hole where the metal is invariably visible – the 'centre hole check' is suggested as a standard means of quickly identifying acetates. Acetates may also have an additional hole near the centre intended to locate in an additional pin on the cutting turntable to prevent slipping, but it will not be visible if there is a label. See Figure 6.12.

As a general rule acetates do not have plain white labels but normally bear a label preprinted with the name and address of the cutting studio which recorded them, or in the case of ex-broadcasting discs the name of the company or corporation. Content details are almost always in manuscript, though a typed label is occasionally found. They are never preprinted. There may be a warning to 'use trailing needles only'. The characteristic container for acetates is a flat tinplate box around 1½ inches (4 cm) deep. In the UK they are normally square and often painted black, though round ones resembling film canisters are also found. Inside a bolt is fixed in the centre and the discs threaded over it with cardboard or plastic washers to separate them and prevent damage to their fragile surfaces. When the container is full a nut is screwed onto the bolt to

Figure 6.12. 'Acetate' discs.

prevent movement. Otherwise they are housed in plain individual sleeves.

Acetates which have begun to decompose may have an oily surface as the castor oil plasticizer migrates, or the lacquer may show signs of cracking. In advanced cases the surface begins to detach itself from the core and break up into flakes leaving the metal exposed (see Figure 6.13). During wartime metal shortages some acetates were made with glass cores. Most seem to have been coated with transparent lacquer so that at least their extreme fragility is obvious; but others had the conventional black coating, and are not surprisingly broken on arrival in many cases (see Figure 6.14).

As if the above situation were not complex enough, a further problem arises in distinguishing 'acetates' from 'gelatines', which are identical in appearance except that they do not smell of castor oil. The NSA has recently found random examples interspersed among long runs of ordinary acetates, and they appear to have been used interchangeably in small numbers by British cutting studios. Their

Figure 6.13. 'Acetate' discs with surfaces in an advanced stage of decomposition.

lifespan and pattern of deterioration are also similar to those of acetates, so it is not essential that they be identified except if a wet cleaning process is proposed (see below).

Conservation of discs

Characteristics The Pickett and Lemcoe study remains the most relevant and useful source of information on disc properties and longevity.[38] The study sticks to generalizations on 'shellac' discs because there are so many different formulations. Shellac is normally present as a binding material, though a typical '78' might contain 12 per cent shellac by weight, but 15 per cent other gums and resins. Some 'shellacs' have no shellac in them at all. The major ingredients by weight are normally fillers such as whiting ($CaCO_3$) and aluminium silicate. Shellac gradually 'cures', becoming more brittle. New 78s tended therefore to be less fragile than older ones. Eventually a point is reached where the shellac is fully cured and the disc relatively brittle. In some cases this is indicated by a tendency for

Figure 6.14 'Acetate' discs. Left: conventional black lacquer on aluminium core. Right: transparent lacquer on glass core.

the grooved surface to break up even when the disc is played with a lightweight pickup. The rate of curing and embrittlement varies, and under good storage conditions may take perhaps 100 years. The curing process is accelerated by moisture.

Moisture also encourages mould, which readily grows and feeds on the organic constituents of many shellacs, causing irreversible damage to the grooved surface, though this is not normally as catastrophic as fungal damage to wax cylinders. Dry storage conditions are thus essential for 78s.

Pickett and Lemcoe carried out a more thorough investigation of 'acetate' discs and described in detail how the surface coating deteriorates through the shedding and migration of the plasticizer (normally castor oil) and the continuous decomposition of the constituents of nitrocellulose (see Figure 6.15). The products of decomposition (oxides, gases) in turn react with each other to further destructive effect. At the time of the study there were numerous 15-year-old acetates in good condition at the Library of

Figure 6.15 An 'acetate' disc whose surface has decomposed and 'dried out'.

Congress, but it was assumed that lifespan would be rather less than the c. 50-year life expectancy of nitrocellulose film. It seems fair to assume that any acetate disc over thirty years old is at risk.

Pickett and Lemcoe also carried out a detailed study and controlled tests on 12-inch 'LP' discs and 7-inch '45s'. LPs were and are produced in heated presses from 'vinyl' (polyvinyl chloride) while 45s were often made of injection-moulded polystyrene. In order to prevent the destabilization of vinyl when exposed to heat in the disc press, stabilizers are introduced by the manufacturer. This process *could* be aimed more specifically at the long-term preservation of LPs, but normally its only function is to enable the manufacturer to produce an article for sale. As a result a small minority of vinyls may become unstable. Increased surface noise on some early vinyls is attributed to this, while some may warp even when quite new. 'Stable' LPs will also warp if exposed to high or fluctuating temperatures or if stored horizontally, vertically without adequate support, or leaning at an angle. Subsequent experience has generally confirmed Pickett and Lemcoe's conclusion that most vinyl LPs will have a long shelf-life if stored under appropriate conditions (see below and under 'Storage equipment' in Chapter 5). Polystyrene discs have proved to be less stable, and spontaneous warping and cracking have been observed even in well-stored examples.

Neither acetates nor vinyls is seriously affected by damp. Mould grows on labels but does not eat into the playing surface.

Because of their widespread potential for many forms of information storage, optical discs are currently the subject of several studies primarily aimed at testing the stability of polycarbonate and the longevity of the various types of metallized coatings. Tests conducted by Sony in Japan indicate considerable likely longevity for Sony WORM discs. A more comprehensive set of tests centred on the Plasmon double-sided disc is currently under way at the NSA.

In practice the most common and serious defects encountered in all discs are the result of misuse, or at least use inconducive to long-term survival. 78s were conventionally played with steel needles mounted in heavy reproducers which wore away the groove surface. The softer surface of vinyl discs is equally vulnerable to worn styluses or maladjusted playback apparatus. Grooves harbour dirt which, unless completely removed, may be picked up by the stylus and ground into groove walls, damaging both the disc and possibly the stylus.

Handling   All types of discs are easily damaged by rough handling. They should not be left lying around, especially without protective sleeves or near sources of heat. Playing surfaces should never be touched except during cleaning operations; staff who regularly handle discs could be issued with soft fabric gloves, as deposits of perspiration attract dirt. Handling rules such as those used at the NSA should be produced and enforced by all repositories (see Appendix I). Handling should be confined to staff who have received adequate training.

Cleaning and repair   In the absence of many controlled experiments the procedures noted below have been arrived at largely by trial and error and are not universally applicable. Where possible it is always wise to try out new or unfamiliar cleaning and repair techniques on expendable discs before tackling valuable or unique material.

All discs should be cleaned before playback with a soft, clean cloth, working with a circular motion in the direction of the grooves. Even unplayed discs straight from the manufacturer usually have a coating of loose dust which should be removed in this manner. (A recent paper by Gerald Gibson of the Library of Congress recommends wiping compact discs radially, *across* the direction of playback, however.[39] Vinyl discs often develop a static charge which may attract dirt. This should be neutralized using a proprietary anti-static gun, an anti-static turntable mat and where appropriate by creating a humid microclimate around the turntable, possibly by placing dishes of water close by. 'Anti-static cleaning fluids' should be avoided. Heavier coatings of loose dust may be loosened with a soft brush working with a circular motion, or with a purpose-designed fixed brush under which the disc is rotated on the turntable.

Acetate and vinyl discs may be washed in water, possibly with the addition of a small amount of mild detergent, then rinsed in demineralized water and left to dry in clean air at a normal temperature, though discs may be replayed while wet without detriment to surface or signal. Care should be taken to keep the label dry, especially if it contains manuscript information in fugitive ink. The task of washing discs is made easier with specially designed equipment. Machines as supplied by Keith Monks or Nitty Gritty have turntables and carefully directed sprays and brushes followed by vacuum suction to remove the water and leave the disc dry for playback. Ultrasonic baths of various sizes and designs are also used: discs are suspended in a container of demineralized water so that the label remains dry, and ultrasonic waves passed through the water which dislodge ingrained dirt very effectively.

Gelatine-coated discs, which may be found among acetates, must not be washed as gelatine is water-soluble. Since gelatines and acetates are virtually indistinguishable, it is unfortunately necessary to wet a small unused area (perhaps near the centre or on the unused reverse side) in order to be certain in every case. The recommendation in the NSA's code of practice for transferring acetates (Appendix III) that all discs should be copied as a pre-caution before any cleaning is carried out will also help to avoid catastrophe.

Dirty shellac discs are often also washed using the above methods, and experience at the NSA at least has produced little if any evidence of adverse results. It should be remembered however that shellac compounds can contain a wide variety of fillers and other ingredients, some of which may absorb water. Some makes of shellac discs were laminated onto a paper core: if they *must* be washed a technique involving minimal wetting should be used; they should not be immersed. Wetting shellac appears to harden and embrittle it. Mould growth on shellacs damages their surfaces so they should be allowed to dry out thoroughly and completely in a suitable rack before return to storage.

Chemical cleaners should be avoided if possible. When all else has failed alcohol in weak solution has been quite widely used without mishap, but the procedure is risky with 78s as shellac is soluble in alcohol. Freon TF has also been widely and successfully used as a solvent on discs affected by greasy dirt, though it tends to evaporate too quickly if used at ordinary room temperatures. It is suitable for the careful cleaning of acetates which might break up if subjected to more vigorous washing.[40]

Badly smashed shellac discs are very difficult to 'reconstruct', but it is possible to rerecord the contents of discs which have broken cleanly into two or three pieces by sticking them together with adhesive tape on one side and playing the other side, then reversing the process. The cracks will produce loud clicks on the copy but these can often be edited out fairly easily if further restoration is required. The broken pieces should *not* be placed together in their original sleeve and returned to storage: this may result in further damage to the disc and possibly those shelved adjacent to it. Each piece should be separately housed in a suitably labelled sleeve and all kept away from the main collection of undamaged discs.

Acetates whose surfaces have begun to shrink, crack and flake off are at present irrecoverable. Recent successful work at Manchester Polytechnic on the stabilization of cellulose triacetate and cellulose nitrate film has led to the suggestion that similar techniques might work on acetate discs.[41] Meanwhile, if the laser beam method of 'reading' cylinder grooves is perfected, this could perhaps also be applied to acetates whose surfaces are unplayable by methods involving physical contact.

Using a frequently quoted technique, warped vinyls have been successfully flattened by placing them between two pieces of plate glass and applying mild heat in an oven or with a portable lamp until a temperature of around, but not much more than, 135 degrees Fahrenheit is reached. The 'sandwich' is then removed, placed on a flat surface, weighted down with something heavy like a large book, and left for 24 hours. The method does not always work: sometimes discs emerge more badly warped than before. This is probably because some warping is caused by internal stresses which will only be increased by heating (see above). The method should perhaps be avoided with warped discs which are known to have been carefully and correctly stored. Fortunately even quite serious warping appears to have little effect on groove dimensions: successful copying onto tape is normally possible once a suitable means of keeping the stylus in the groove has been found.

Copying Disc copying is such a commonplace conservation exercise that the main items of equipment and the normal rerecording standards have been covered in the general conservation sections above. The following guidelines relate to particular problems in transferring direct-cut discs.

In *aluminium discs* the grooves were actually embossed, not cut.

There was no removal of material from the groove; rather it was 'pushed aside' by the stylus. The result is that 'horns' or ridges occur above each groove wall. It is therefore possible to play the 'land' between the grooves rather than the grooves themselves. If a rather distorted reproduction is heard, possibly accompanied by an echo effect coinciding with the revolution-rate of the disc, this probably means that the replay stylus is on the wrong track.

The manufacturers recommended fibre replay needles, but a modern lightweight pickup with a conventional diamond stylus is perfectly satisfactory. A sapphire stylus should not be used as sapphire is a form of aluminium oxide which can form an affinity with the metal of the disc, damaging both.

The surface of *'acetate' discs* has to be soft enough to cut and will not stand repeated replay without deterioration. Every effort should therefore be made to achieve a satisfactory copy in one replay, or at worst in two if a 'safety' copy is being made before the disc is thoroughly cleaned. In order to help prevent the material cut from the grooves during recording ('swarf') from fouling the cutting stylus, many portable one-man disc cutters were designed to record from the centre outwards. The cutting process imparted consider- able drag on the turntable and so the outside edge of discs may be found to have been recorded at a slightly slower speed; and even studio machines could not always be operated at a constant speed during World War II owing to voltage fluctuations in the electricity supply. These problems do not generally affect commercial record- ings of the period, which were mostly cut in wax on weight-powered turntables.

Because of the type of cutting stylus supplied with portable equipment until the mid-1950s, recordings are likely to suffer from high-frequency losses towards the centre. Where mild 'restoration' is being attempted, for instance in order to match the end of one disc with the start of the next, some adjustment of the treble response as the pickup travels across the disc will be necessary. These deficiences principally affect the quality of recording on the side walls of the groove. Better high frequency response may often be obtained from the groove base by using a fine-tipped playback stylus.

Storage General storage conditions and suitable shelving are covered in the sections on storage above.

Pickett and Lemcoe also produced what has remained the only research-based standard for individual disc sleeves. They recom- mended a sleeve made of a specially manufactured laminate: the inner layer is of polyethylene, providing a smooth, mould-resistant surface against the disc. Polyethylene is not completely gas and moisture resistant so the next layer is soft aluminium foil to prevent all ingress of air and moisture. Outside this is stiff cardboard to help prevent wrinkling in the sleeve and warping in the disc, covered on the outside with a further layer of polyethylene. Sleeves of this design continue to be used by the Library of Congress (without the outer polyethylene layer) but do not appear to have been adopted anywhere else, at least partly on grounds of cost. At LC discs are allowed to stabilize in optimum climatic conditions before insertion in the sleeves. If playback copies have been made, the sleeves are heat sealed down the fourth side, ensuring complete insulation of the disc from air and moisture.

On a more modest level sleeves should at least be fairly stiff, dustproof and smooth on the inside. The following points may give some guidance.

Shellac pressings were originally sold in more or less stiff card sleeves, later replaced by heavy paper. Both had holes in the sides through which the label could be read and therefore provide little protection against dust. The card sleeves are now usually dirty and often crumbling through acidity. The paper ones tend to crinkle and tear. Both are best discarded and replaced. The NSA has experimented with polyethylene lined stiff paper sleeves, and with acid-free sleeves of rather stiffer light card lined with kraft paper, which were based on the specification for storage envelopes widely used for archival storage. Both have no side hole and a fold-over lid. The kraft-lined type have remained stiffer and more stable; the flaps on the plastic-lined ones attract dust and tend to curl, probably because the two materials in the laminate have different coefficients of expansion.

Envelopes like these are unpopular with people used to reading the labels on 78s without removing them from their sleeves. One solution is to enclose the disc in a polyethylene inner sleeve (preferably the kind with an outer supporting layer of stiff paper, though these have not been made as a standard line in the 10-inch size by any UK manufacturer for many years) through which the label can be read, and insert this in a card outer with side holes. Where the original sleeves are clean and tidy this is also a way of economizing by keeping them in use. As an alternative the BBC uses a specially manufactured light card sleeve with side holes and a built-in polyethylene lining. These types should always be shelved so that if there is an open edge it is facing inwards on the shelf. Plastic-lined sleeves provide a barrier between the disc and the outer layer of paper or cardboard and this may help to protect the disc if mould breaks out, since it usually attacks the sleeve first.[42]

Acetates usually arrive in tin boxes or (typically it seems) in side-hole sleeves lined with stiff cellophane which has usually shrunk, distorting the sleeve and producing a ridged effect on the inner surface. These sleeves, and any other types of inadequate standard, should be replaced with envelopes or lined sleeves as described above. Special care should be taken to prevent creases in any plastic inner sleeve used, as these can damage the soft disc surface even under the light compression required for satisfactory upright storage on shelves. Discs in tins could be repacked in modern sleeves or left in the boxes if they are clean and dust-tight.

No style of sleeve can prevent the deterioration of acetates, though discs which have been carefully and cleanly stored do last longer than those which have been left exposed to dirt and damp. As Pickett and Lemcoe pointed out, ideal conditions are hardly possible to provide, since it is desirable both to allow oozing plasticizer and the products of decomposition to escape, and to prevent exposure to air, moisture and dust.

Vinyl pressings have been supplied from the beginning with inner and outer sleeves. Many inner sleeves (particularly early ones made of waxed paper and suchlike) will be found damaged and should be replaced with modern polyethylene-lined inner sleeves. The familiar 12-inch inner sleeves made of stiff paper lined with polyethylene are the most suitable, but they are becoming less easy to obtain, and many LPs are now supplied with plain polyethylene inners, which tend to crease and crinkle, or plain paper ones which tear easily and have a rougher inner surface. These ought to be replaced.

Outer sleeves are of stiff but usually acidic card which deteriorates quite rapidly. In the 1950s and 1960s their outer surface was typically a glossy cellophane which has tended to delaminate. In appropriate cases, and where resources allow, consideration should be given to deacidification treatment for outer sleeves. They can be replaced by better quality sleeves of course, but this implies the removal of the liner notes and other information which published LP sleeves invariably carry, and which in many cases constitute the main source of information on disc contents. Within the next few years the deterioration of acidic LP sleeves will increase as a problem, though it will affect disc libraries much more heavily than sound archives. Ultimately the solution may be to record the disc and 'film' the sleeve on optical disc.

Where LPs have been supplied shrink-wrapped, the wrapping

should be removed immediately as it will continue to shrink and cause the disc to warp.

Magnetic recording

Historical background

Magnetic recording is achieved in its crudest form by connecting the electrical output from a microphone to an electromagnet and bringing a moving magnetic substance (typically steel wire or flexible tape coated with ferric oxide, less often a disc format) into contact with it in such a way that the pattern of sound pressures picked up by the microphone is conveyed in the form of variations in magnetic strength to the recording medium. The original sound is reproduced by reversing the process and replacing the microphone with a speaker or earpiece.

A process of this kind was described by Oberlin Smith (1840–1926) in the US periodical *The Electrical World* and recently rediscovered evidence suggests that he also conducted experiments on what would have been the first magnetic recorder.[43] However, the first machine to be manufactured was a wire recorder known as the Telegraphone, which was demonstrated by the Dane Valdemar Poulsen in 1898; later versions of it were used in various countries for telegraphy and dictation. The German Kurt Stille developed the idea in the early 1920s and produced a wire dictating machine, and a film sound recorder based on 6 mm (later 3 mm) steel tape. Even as developed by the film producer Ludwig Blattner the latter was never adopted by film makers, but the BBC installed two of the machines and went on to commission improved versions from the 'British Blattnerphone Company' and later Marconi, which were used for various recording operations (though not field recording – they were too big and heavy) throughout the 1930s and 1940s. Meanwhile improvements in wire recorders in the UK and US received a boost from wartime communications needs, and by the late 1940s their use in the States, particularly by the armed forces, was widespread.

A few high quality wire machines capable of good music recording were produced after the war but by then attention was switching to tape recording. All the early developments took place in Germany where the Allgemeine Elektrizitäts Gesellschaft (AEG) began work on a recording machine in 1931. It was based on a flexible tape coated with magnetic material (originally soft iron powder) devised by Fritz Pfleumer. The resulting 'Magnetophon' was first demonstrated publicly in 1935; it made use of quarter inch (6 mm) cellulose acetate tape coated with ferric oxide which the firm IG Farben (soon to become the Badische Analin und Soda Fabrik – BASF) had developed. The tape was the prototype on which all later magnetic tape was modelled. It was much cheaper than the steel tape required for Blattner-type recorders and could be cut-edited and spliced in seconds. Simple editing could be carried out on steel tape, but the ends had to be welded or soldered together, a cumbersome job which produced an audible blip on replay.

The improvement in signal-to-noise ratio produced by applying high-frequency bias to the recording head was discovered (or rediscovered) by accident in 1940 by Walter Weber of the German Broadcasting Corporation (RRG), where tape recorders had recently been introduced. Good quality music recording and broadcasting became possible, and listeners could no longer be certain whether a broadcast was live or recorded, on the basis of its sound quality or duration. These advantages were exploited by the German military during World War II, and it became clear to the allies when a number of machines were captured towards the end of the war that magnetic recording had progressed much further in Germany than elsewhere during the period. Specifications of the most recent Magnetophon (the K7), which ran at 30.31 inches per second (77 cm/sec.) with a frequency response of 50–10,000 Hz and a dynamic range of 60 dB were widely published, and studio machines based on its principles were brought out in the late 1940s by EMI in England and (among others) Ampex in the US.

These early machines recorded a single mono track on the tape. During the 1950s, more sensitive tape and better quality recording and playback heads were developed, and acceptable recordings at 15 and 7.5 ips became possible. A twin-track configuration was standardized enabling a mono recording in two directions or a stereo recording in one direction.

Magnetic tape recording spread rapidly in broadcasting (though the BBC was slow to switch from disc-based technology and storage). Among recording companies, the Deutsche Grammophon Gesellschaft (DGG, now part of Polygram) had the advantage of access to the Magnetophon and was using a K4 model in 1946. Elsewhere tape machines came into widespread use at about the same time as shellac 78s were being replaced by vinyl discs. Initially they were simply used as substitutes for disc cutting machines, though the advantages of longer uninterrupted recording time and of being able to edit out unwanted matter with a razor blade were immediately available.

By the mid-1960s tape had begun to revolutionize the conduct of studio recording through the advent of multi-tracking. Using extra-wide tape (half-inch, one-inch and two-inch reel-to-reel tape have all become common), anything up to 48 synchronous tracks can be separately recorded and then mixed together via a console to produce a two-track stereo master for record production or broadcast, the various elements of which will sound as though they were recorded simultaneously. Except for deliberate 'live' recordings, it is now very rare for a published disc or tape to result from a single unedited or unenhanced performance. Mixing and remixing recordings for commercial release has become a separate trade.

Major advances also occured in location recording of all kinds with the advent of tape. The average 1950s professional tape recorder, though bulky and heavy, was already less cumbersome than the portable disc-cutting apparatus used by broadcasters, and could with sufficient notice be transported, set up and operated by one person. In the UK in 1952 EMI brought out a genuinely portable tape recorder, the L2, which was widely adopted by BBC news interviewers. Because it relied on valves and bulky short-life batteries there was no room for a rewind mechanism, erase head or built-in speaker. Transistorized circuitry enabled more sophisticated portable machines to be made. In Europe the Uher 4000 series machines have become the most popular and widespread over the last 20 years. Recording at 7½ ips (they also work at 3¾ and 1⅞) they are capable of broadcast standard speech recording, and were until very recently the standard radio reporter's machine. The Uher's recording performance and speed control are regarded as not quite adequate for good music recording. For this, portable reel-to-reel machines, such as the Swiss-manufactured Nagra and Stellavox recorders, have set a very high standard. They are still widely used by film makers.

A few manufacturers such as Soundmirror and Simon were already aiming tape recorders at the domestic market in the late 1940s. By the early 1960s many British families had acquired a Philips, Ferguson, Grundig, Elizabethan or similar portable mains-operated valve machine. Typically these recorders were designed to economize on tape and were fitted with half-track or more often quarter-track heads. They were usually run at 3¾ ips and could accommodate 7-inch spools. They were widely used for the technically illegal copying of broadcasts off the air, for copying published discs (which was more than technically illegal), and for recording domestic events. Philips and a few others also produced smaller transistorized recorders for amateur use, but with their 3-inch

Figure 6.16   The EMI L2 recorder as illustrated in a contemporary
advertisement. By courtesy of EMI archives.

spools, 1⅞ (or thereabouts) speed and cheap microphones they were
not capable of undistorted recording.

Despite their wide distribution, tape recorders remained a hobby
for men and boys during most of the 1960s, perhaps because reel-to-
reel tape was generally thought to need some technical skill to cope
with – attempts to market prerecorded reel-to-reel tapes were a
failure.

Strategies to overcome this began with encased 'talking books' for
the blind in the early 1950s, and in 1958 RCA brought out a
'cassette' system, in which two spools of ¼-inch tape were enclosed in
a plastic case which enabled them to be taken off the machine
without touching or respooling the tape. Some were issued with
prerecorded music, and because they would not play on ordinary
tape recorders special players were designed and sold. In Britain a
similar but incompatible system was announced by Garrard in 1959.
Manufacturers then started experimenting with miniature cassette
systems using thin ⅛-inch wide tape mounted on a hub and
permanently encased in plastic. The earliest type was issued by CBS

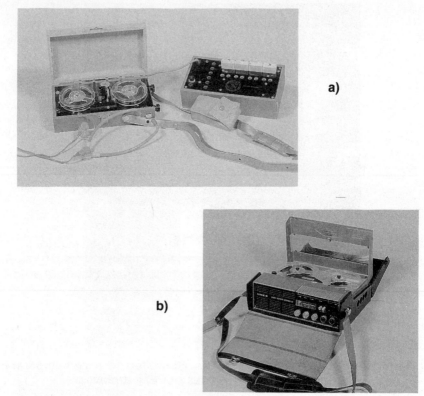

Figure 6.17   Recent portable reel-to-reel tape recorders used by professionals: a) the Ficord, with battery charger (made
under licence from Stellavox), b) Uher 4200 and c) Nagra
IVS.

Figure 6.18. **Domestic reel-to-reel tape recorders from the early 1960s. Left: a Clarion battery-operated miniature recorder made by the Trix Company, Nuremburg. Right: a Stella quarter-track mains-operated machine.**

in 1961. The cassette was $^5/_{16}$-inch thick and 3 inches square, and contained one reel of prerecorded tape which played at 1⅞ ips in one direction for 64 minutes. CBS also sold a compatible player which had no recording facilities built in.

Various other cassette designs soon appeared in the States, but the crucial development took place in Holland where Philips designed what came to be called the Compact Cassette and marketed it in 1964 together with a machine capable of recording and playback. Other very similar cassettes (e.g. an almost identical but slightly larger two-spool version by Grundig) came and went, but by the early 1970s the Philips design has been generally adopted, at least partly because Philips agreed to license the design to any manufacturer free of royalty charges as long as no variations were introduced. The only competitors to survive for a period were the prerecorded 8-track quadraphonic cartridge systems designed for use in cars. Their superior clarity, before noise reduction and 'metal' tape became common, gave them an advantage in competition with engine and road noise.

The Philips cassette runs at 1⅞ ips (4.75 cm/sec.) and the original 'C60' which played for 30 minutes per side has been augmented by longer playing versions (C90, C120 etc.) containing thinner tape. The medium was originally sold blank for domestic recording but in the 1980s a vast industry in prerecorded cassettes has grown up, greatly assisted by the vogue for integrated domestic hi-fi systems, increasing miniaturization following the Sony 'Walkman' prototype, and the almost universal use of cassettes as the medium for prerecorded music in cars. The technical performance of cassettes has been greatly assisted by the development of high sensitivity tape coatings, and in particular by developments in noise reduction systems (see Appendix IV).

The vast commercial resources marshalled behind cassettes since the late 1970s have enabled some very sophisticated portable recorders such as the Sony Walkman Professional series and the Marantz CP430 to be sold at very modest prices. Since their recording performance is comparable with all but the most expensive portable reel-to-reel machines, they have largely taken over as standard issue for radio reporters and serious oral historians.

All the developments chronicled so far are technically descended from the ideas and inventions of Smith and Poulsen, and are said to belong to the era of 'analogue' recording; the pattern of tape magnetization is analogous with the waveforms of the sounds being recorded. But just as CDs have signalled a radical change in disc development, so magnetic recording is being revolutionized by digital technology.

This borrows techniques from the world of computers: waveforms are converted into binary code and transferred to tape (or other medium such as magnetic or optical disc) as a stream of digits. The conversion is achieved by sampling the waveform at very frequent intervals, rather in the way that a cine film 'samples' the action in a series of frames; and just as the separation between frames is undetectable on replay, so the individual samples reform into recognizable sound when the digits are converted back into analogue form. High frequency sound waves carrying high pitched sounds oscillate more rapidly than low frequency waves and therefore require more frequent sampling to convey them in digital form. The 'sampling rate' therefore directly affects the frequency response capability of the system. A response range of nought to 20,000 cycles per second (or 20,000 Hertz [Hz] or 20 kiloHertz [kHz]) is regarded as sufficient for most purposes. In order to achieve this the sound must be sampled 40,000 times per second, and most digital recording systems sample at around (usually somewhat above) this rate.

Each time the sound is sampled its volume, or more correctly 'amplitude', at that instant is measured in binary code. This process is called quantization, and its quality depends on the capability of the system to record accurate values. Digital conversion enforces a certain rigidity – this is its principal weakness – but it will plot the complex patterns of sound waves more accurately if the intervals on the scale (the 'quantization intervals') are small. The task resembles that of plotting a sound wave by means of coordinates on a graph. The more accurate the coordinates the less jerky the curve will be. Sufficient accuracy for music recording can be achieved with a digital capacity of 16 bits which makes 65,535 possible quantization intervals available for each sample.

If a cheaper 14 bit system is used, quiet sounds are unacceptably affected by 'quantization noise' caused by too many quantization values falling outside the true shape of the sound wave. Ultimately some quantization will always be inaccurate which means that all digital systems introduce some audible distortion to very quiet sounds. Distortion is also inevitable if frequencies higher than the sampling rate can cope with are present in the signal. In practice therefore all digital recorders carry out specific electronic processing of the signal in order to minimize these problems. Having done this the digits are transferred to tape, most commonly by a process known as pulse code modulation.

In exchange for the (to some unacceptable) processing of sounds, digital recording offers at least two great advantages over analogue methods. Firstly, the process introduces much lower background noise during both recording or copying. Secondly every commercially available system incorporates an error correction facility consisting of a stream of check digits which run alongside the encoded recording and serve to remedy any missing information, normally by interpolation from adjacent data. Thus 'dropouts' caused by defects in tape coatings or inaccurate rerecording are automatically made good – to the extent that it is usually impossible to tell if faults are occurring without special monitoring apparatus. Recordings can be copied and recopied without any loss of quality until transfer errors have become so large that the correction circuit cannot deal with them. Digital tape recordings can therefore survive a certain amount of, say, oxide shedding which would be completely destructive to analogue recordings. Because of these advantages, digital recording is thought likely to supersede analogue recording more or less gradually over perhaps the next twenty years.

At present there are two contrasting forms of digital tape recording equipment which have been taken up by different groups of users. For those larger studios which can afford them *stationary head* systems such as 'DASH' (Digital Audio Stationary Head) and 'Pro-Digi', whose design is derived from analogue reel-to-reel recorders, offer most of the facilities (e.g. razor-blade editing, multitracking,

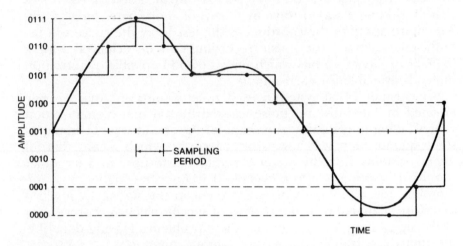

(a) **Number of quantization intervals is low, resulting in a poor approximation.**

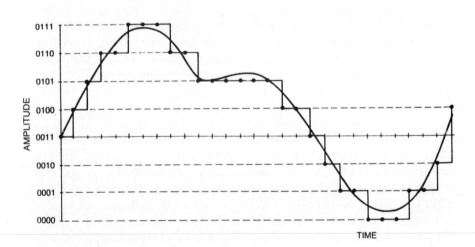

(b) **Sampling rate is doubled, but quantization approximation is still poor.**

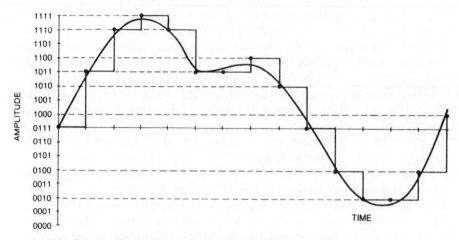

(c) With low sampling rate, but double the number of quantization intervals, quantization approximation is improved.

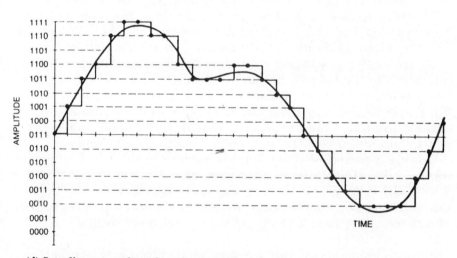

(d) Sampling rate and number of quantization intervals have both been doubled.

Source: *Principles of Digital Audio* K. C. Pohlmann.

Figure 6.19 Graphic representation of four examples of different quantization and sampling resolutions.

synchronized recording) enjoyed with professional analogue equipment, and use the same reel-to-reel tape formats.

For the less wealthy various systems based on the *rotary head* technology of video recorders are available. Initially these took the form of 'conversion kits' enabling high quality digital audio recordings to be made digitally on existing video formats. Perhaps the most common was developed by Sony and marketed in 1982 as a portable combination, consisting of a miniature Betamax video recorder and matching 'F1' PCM adaptor to convert the signal by pulse code modulation. Various Japanese manufacturers briefly included PCM adaptors in their repertoire of specialist hi-fi equipment, but the vogue for them (or sales potential) has now virtually ceased.

Adaptors for other video formats such as VHS and Sony's more recent Video-8 have also been available, while a more 'professional' kit including electronic editing facilities has been based on the U-Matic format, and is now the standard method of mastering compact discs. These cheaper forms of digital recording are often used by studios to down-load finished analogue recordings for storage, but have otherwise found limited favour owing to a general preference for physical editing.

In 1988 Sony brought out the 'DAT' (Digital Audio Tape) miniature rotary-head recorder in which the various elements in the PCM-video technique are brought together in a machine no larger than a cassette recorder and using a new-style two-hour miniature cassette. Many applications for the format, particularly in broadcasting, are under discussion and development, but its survival at present is in the balance despite the fact that, for once, much time and trouble were spent in obtaining international agreement on the format before it was released. DAT cassettes and machines are around five times more expensive than average Philips-type equivalents, and do not offer the public enormous advantages; and following a period of bitter legal wrangling in the US, hardly any prerecorded DAT cassettes have been issued and it is clear that the trade wishes to protect its investment in compact discs. The two formats have been deliberately designed to be incompatible, so that direct recording from CDs to DAT cassettes is impossible.

Tape developments provide a less exciting chronicle. Essentially the medium consists of a backing material, a magnetic substance and a binder to hold the two together. In 1934 BASF quickly abandoned Fritz Pfleumer's paper backing in favour of cellulose acetate. In 1936 carbonyl-iron particles gave way to iron oxide (Fe_2O_3) as the magnetic layer, to be replaced in 1939 by gamma-Ferric Oxide ($\gamma-Fe_2O_3$), which has remained in widespread use to the present day. Improvements in the size, shape and alignment on the tape of oxide particles have gradually improved the 'coercivity' of the tapes and increased the dynamic range which can be recorded, though the rate of improvement up to the mid-1950s was much more rapid than it has been since.[44] Most recently, particularly in response to the needs of the slow-playing-speed cassette industry, yet more sensitive coatings have been developed: 'cobalt-doped' ferric oxide, chrome dioxide, and, once again, iron (referred to as 'metal'). DAT cassettes are metal coated.

In the later years of the war and immediately after it BASF and the related company AGFA manufactured tapes on a polyvinyl chloride (PVC) base since this material was regarded as superior to cellulose acetate and cellulose triacetate as it was less fragile. Postwar imitators in Britain (primarily EMI) and the US (Ampex) produced tape on similar lines from similar materials, though the Soundmirror company manufactured paper-based tape for a short period. (Examples at the NSA have survived in better condition than much acetate-based tape, in fact). The range and character of backing materials familiar today were developed in the mid-1950s. All manufacturers shifted increasingly to the use of polyethylene terephthalate (known as polyester, mylar or PET) as the base material for their most up-to-date tape specifications. In response to demand for longer playing times from the domestic market, tapes with a thinner backing were produced, first as long-play (.0015 inch [.03 mm] as opposed to the .002 inch [.05 mm] of professional standard-play tape), then double-play (.001 inch, .025 mm). The stability of the tape pack on the spool was improved by the introduction of matt-backed tapes, but successful efforts were also made to reduce the roughness of the oxide coating on early tapes which produced head-wear and recording noise.

Recognizing tapes

This is only a brief survey of quarter-inch open-reel tape. Wider open-reel tapes are rarely found outside the recording studio (or mainframe computer installation), and will almost certainly be polyester-based. Expert knowledge of obsolete cassette types is unlikely to enjoy much application as the chance of finding a compatible machine is remote, and only a small minority were used in any quantity for other than prerecorded commercial releases. Modern cassette and videotape formats are too well-identified to require further elaboration.

The main concern here is with the quick identification of backing materials and major problems; a definitive assessment can only be obtained by chemical analysis. It is important to be able to identify older tapes as they will probably be cellulose acetate or cellulose triacetate, both of which have a limited lifespan. Most acetate tape was manufactured between the mid-1940s and the late 1950s. Any tape known to be from this period should be treated as acetate until proven otherwise. It may be possible to identify the make and type of the tape from its packaging, and many tapes have the maker's name and/or the type number printed on the non-magnetic side. A specification could then be obtained from the manufacturer (most of the early major companies are still very much in business), or by consulting contemporary professional periodicals such as the *Journal of the Audio Engineering Society* or *Studio Sound*. Some tapes have or had the nature of the base material e.g. 'mylar' or 'acetate' printed on the box, which may be all the archivist needs to know.

Tape which is shiny on the non-magnetic side is likely to be over 20 years old: most tape since the late 1960s has been coated with a matt backing to help it spool more evenly. Double-play and other thin-backed reel-to-reel tapes were much more common in the 1950s and 1960s, before the advent of cassettes, than they are today. And such tape is more susceptible to the phenomena associated with poor storage conditions such as curling, spoking, and windowing (see below), so the presence of these will also suggest (along with other appearances no doubt) that the tape is of some age. Early spools contrast noticeably with those of today. Ten-inch or larger diameter spools with solid ferrous flanges and centre holes incompatible with modern NAB standards will suggest tapes from the 1940s which will probably be acetate. Seven-inch spools from the 1950s tend to be narrower between the flanges than the standard modern transparent plastic ones. They may be of aluminium, coloured plastic, or a brown fibrous bakelite material, the latter riveted together at the centre rather than moulded in one piece.

Soundmirror paper tape is easy to identify since its backing is light blotchy brown paper quite unlike plastics in appearance. It may still be packed in the distinctive synonymous box (see Figure 6.21).

In addition to the above, and in cases where tape may have been removed from its original box or spool, other methods of identification are available.

Cellulose acetate Old acetate tape, particularly the thin type designed for amateur use, is notoriously fragile and tends to break frequently even at ordinary replay speeds. This provides the best-

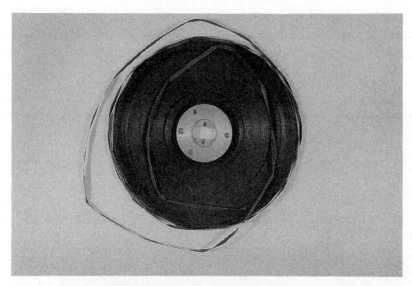

Figure 6.20. Cellulose acetate tape from the mid-1950s showing characteristic 'cupping' in the early stages of decomposition.

known test for acetate: take a short length, grasp each end firmly and tug apart. Acetate will break cleanly with little or no stretching. In the early days of taperecording when breaking mechanisms on recorders were abrupt, the fragility of acetate was seen as something of an asset: PVC tape tended to stretch rather than snap so the recording would be irrevocably distorted. Acetate might break but could be spliced together with no harm done. Tapes with wanted recordings obviously cannot be tested in this way. Another less reliable test is to hold the tape up to the light: acetate is slightly translucent.

Polyvinyl chloride PVC tape stretches before it breaks and is difficult to distinguish from polyester. One method which may work is to thrash a cleanly broken end of tape against a hard surface (or hit the tape end with something hard like a pencil or ruler). Under this treatment PVC tape tends to split into longitudinal strands 'like a brush'. This 'test' is obviously destructive and only appropriate on scrap tape. PVC was used concurrently with acetate but is far less common.

Polyester This material is in almost universal use today and has been the most common backing medium since about 1960. It is used in all

Figure 6.21. A reel of Soundmirror paper-backed tape and its original box.

the current audio and video formats. Under test it will withstand a heavier load before stretching and will then stretch for longer before breaking. Its 'tear load' is about double that of acetate. Any tape which stretches when pulled lengthwise is probably polyester. As it stretches it elongates and narrows down – the 'bootlace' effect.

Conservation of tape

Characteristics Cellulose acetate backing is unsatisfactory in the long term as its formulation includes a plasticizer, which means that it absorbs atmospheric moisture much more readily than polyester[45] and its constituents can begin to interreact and decompose if insufficiently stabilized. Acetate tape may already be difficult or impossible to replay 20 years after manufacture. Recent work on acetate film by, for instance, the team at Manchester Polytechnic[46] suggests that the longevity of acetate tape could be greatly increased

174

by chemical stabilization. This could be attractive to the few repositories with large uncopied holdings on acetate: copying will still be required, but stabilization might speed up the work by reducing the acetate's tendency to break at frequent intervals.

PVC backings also include a plasticizer and are therefore similarly unstable.

Polyester's formula does not include a potentially migrant plasticizer and it therefore has the potential for long life. Artificial aging tests recently conducted by the US National Bureau of Standards indicate no deterioration under suitable storage conditions in the first 20 years of life. Tests carried out at Manchester Polytechnic found that during the period required for acetate tape to decompose completely (perhaps 30 years), no measurable decomposition in polyester was observed while storage temperatures remained below 60 degrees F.[47] These findings indicate that deterioration in polyester might *begin* after 20-30 years, but that under suitable storage it will remain in satisfactory playable condition for perhaps 100 years or longer before needing to be copied. Greater longevity is unpredictable largely because of doubts about the binder which holds the backing and coatings together. Although widely reported as a 'trade secret' the binding material used for both the magnetic and backcoat layers on modern tape is a polyester urethane elastoplasmer. It is the least stable element of the components of polyester tape, and is prone to failure under damp or humid conditions.

All types of tape suffer under unsuitable storage conditions:

Loose or uneven winding tensions on spools can result in lateral slippage of tape layers on the reel, leaving isolated layers protruding and exposed to damage. Where tension is slack near the hub but tight towards the circumference, characteristic distortions may be produced, such as 'spoking', where crease lines radiating from the hub appear, producing a series of bumps and flats round the edge instead of a smooth round wind (older UK readers: the threepenny bit effect) or in bad cases 'windowing', where the tensions which produce spoking cause the tape pack to buckle so much that gaps appear in places between the tape layers.

Spoking and windowing may be worsened or caused by *fluctuating storage temperatures* which also produce uneven tensions across the tape pack, particularly if the coefficients of expansion of tape and spool are different. Spoking, particularly in double-play or other thinly backed tapes, is often accompanied by curling or 'cupping' along the tape length. The effect of uneven tensions and distortions on the spool can be to produce uneven stretching of tape, the result of which may be audible as episodic changes of pitch. Little can be

Figure 6.22. Tape storage problems: (top) adhesive oozing from splices, (bottom left and right) pack distortion resulting from uneven winding tensions and rough handling and storage. All three examples were over 25 years old and had been subjected to a variety of unsuitable storage environments in that period.

done to correct this distortion once it has occurred. High or fluctuating temperatures also tend to increase print-through (see below).

Tape is affected worst of all by *high relative humidity*: backing materials stretch, binders degenerate and start to ooze and migrate, adjacent layers stick together and oxide coatings start to come loose and may be shed completely when playback is attempted. Affected tapes leave gummy residues on tape transports and heads, producing audible 'squeal' or 'flutter' on playback as the tape momentarily sticks and then slips forward. Many reports also indicate that the abrasivity of tape coatings (producing increased wear on the heads of tape machines) increases considerably once the RH of the operating environment reaches 45-50 per cent. On the other hand, where the ambient RH is very low, the phenomenon known as 'brown stain', where recording heads become coated with oxide which has to be polished off with an abrasive, tends to increase.

Print-through occurs in analogue recordings when the pattern of magnetization of one layer of tape penetrates the intervening backing layer and produces a superficial and weak magnetization in the adjacent layer. The effect can be very noticeable when a quiet period in the recording is followed by loud sounds. The outline of the forthcoming sound can be heard as a pre-echo during the playback of the quiet period. Optimum conditions for audible print-through are created by the use of double-play or other tape with a thin backing which provides a poor barrier between layers on the spool; recording at professional speeds such as 7½ ips so that the printed 'echo' is heard immediately before or after the loud sound (it is often remarked the print-through on cassettes, despite the thin tape backing used, is less obvious than on reel-to-reel tapes); storage on the spool with the start of the recording at the outer edge rather than at the centre ('head out' rather than 'tail out'), so that the print produces a pre-echo rather than 'after echo' which is usually less obtrusive; and storage in high or fluctuating temperatures. Print-through does not affect the playback of digitally recorded tapes.

Handling The NSA code of practice on storage and handling (Appendix I) covers the essential requirements: tapes should not be left lying around away from their containers or exposed to the obvious hazards. Loose ends should not be allowed to trail on the floor or pick up dirt from work surfaces. Tape should be touched as little as possible; as discussed earlier, leaders attached to tape ends may help. It is particularly easy for unskilled operators to damage reel-to-reel tape in machines: no staff should be allowed near tape players without supervised instruction and practice with 'dummy' tapes. On the other hand technicians should ensure that correct servicing procedures have been carried out on machines so that tapes are not damaged by dirty or malfunctioning components.

It is pointless to take care over rewinding tapes at the correct tension (see below) if they are then banged around on the way to and from storage. If a tape is dropped or jolted it should be rewound. Tapes should be kept upright in work areas and during transit so that the risk of lateral slippage between layers is minimized.

Working environments should not be detrimental to tape, or

produce characteristics in tape which are harmful to tape recorders. In particular relative humidity should be regulated at a level below 50 per cent which is lower, for instance, than the average ambient RH in many parts of Europe. Tapes withdrawn from storage should ideally be allowed to acclimatize in the working environment for perhaps 24 hours before playback.

Conservation   (i)   *Paper, acetate and PVC tape*   Recordings on these media should be copied onto standard play polyester tape. Where storage space is at a premium, the retention of the original tapes may be difficult to defend, but the containers may be worth saving for the information written on them.

(ii)   *Polyester tape*   Polyester tape is comparatively stable but still requires careful maintenance if its potential is to be fully exploited:

Storage should conform to standards indicated below and in Chapter 5.

Cleaning should not be needed on tapes which have been recorded once and subsequently stored in dust-tight containers. Tape cleaning machines are used to remove dust particles and other contaminants from instrumentation and computer tapes as a routine exercise, since even a minute dropout can seriously distort a digital data recording. However these machines operate by scraping the tape surface with a razor blade, and unintended damage does occur, so the procedure seems far too risky to be worthwhile for digital or analogue audio tapes intended for long retention.[48] If areas of tapes or spools are dirty they can be wiped with a damp lint-free cloth or non-abrasive sponge, and dried before respooling. Solvents such as Freon TF or alcohol should not be used on tape.

Spooling and respooling. A spooling tension of around four ounces is recommended for producing an even, stressless pack of quarter-inch tape. This is best achieved by spooling from end to end at replay speed; fast-winding or rewinding induces higher tensions and can produce unevenness in the pack. The spooling tensions of machines regularly used prior to the return of tapes to storage should be checked. In some situations it may be worth installing one or more machines in the storage area which can be used by storage staff purely for routine spooling and respooling. (For no apparent reason, some individual machines wind tape more neatly than others, even when very old. When they cease to be useful for recording, such machines should be reserved for respooling duty.)

Many sources recommend the periodic respooling of tape in storage, for example 'tape should be inspected once every two years, measured from time of last playback, and rewound so that the curvature of the base is opposite to the direction of the previous curvature . . .[49] The objects of this are to redistribute tension in the tape pack so that potential distortions are released, and to lessen the effect of print-through. However the arguments relating to print-through are open to doubt (see below) and although ultimately tapes which have been correctly wound and stored may be damaged by pack tensions and sagging caused by the weight of the tape hanging on the hub, the risks seem small compared with the possibility of permanent damage caused by machine malfunction or human error during the respooling process. There is also potential for confusion in the 'reverse curvature' recommendation. In order to achieve this, tape which has been spooled (say) 'tail out' with the oxide layer facing the centre of the spool should be respooled 'head out' with the oxide layer facing the edge of the spool. This is done by respooling from reel to reel with one twist in the tape. It is not always easy to tell visually whether the oxide orientation has been reversed. In the busy, underresourced repository whose tapes are stored in good conditions, respooling programmes are a low conservation priority.

Print-through should not be a serious problem with standard-play polyester tape, properly used and stored, though the propensity for it varies between makes of tape.[50] Where it has occurred there are various suggested methods of removal which may be more or less successful, all based on the assumption that the unwanted printed sounds are held superficially by magnetized particles on the surface of the tape. The most frequent recommendation is that the tape should be spooled through, perhaps rapidly and several times, which will disturb its surface and reduce the strength of the print. This also lies behind the 'tail out' spooling recommendation: apart from the avoidance of pre-echo mentioned above, a 'tail out' (or reversed 'head out') tape needs to be spooled through before it can be played and this may help to break up the print. Regular respooling may reduce print, but it can recur, especially if the tape has been exposed to temperatures over 80 degrees F, and so respooling or other treatment will in any case be needed when the tape is wanted for playback.

Print-through can be prevented by recording with the DBX noise reduction system, the disadvantage being that all playback machines will need the capacity to decode DBX.

In severe cases where all else has failed there is an 'unofficial' way of removing print by passing the tape over an erase head having an extremely low current passing through it. No ready-made equipment for this appears to be on sale, and the technique can only work with the original print-affected tape, not a copy. The risks are obvious.

Whichever print-removal technique is chosen, it must be applied to the original tape. This is not always easy: thin-backed acetate tape is often affected but it is quite likely to disintegrate if subjected to repeated rapid spooling. Once the print has been rerecorded it cannot be removed 'physically' from the copy, though various electronic techniques such as the use of 'noise gates' or filtering may be successful in skilled hands.

(iii) *Cassettes*   No current cassette format is recommended for the long-term preservation of sound. Early formats are dependent on obsolete equipment, and digitally-recorded videocassettes on equipment which is already obsolescent. The R-DAT format is based on metal tape whose longevity is in doubt. Philips-type ferric cassettes are at least based on a reliable type of tape recorded by the analogue technique, but they rely on noise reduction electronics for adequate (though still limited) recording quality, and narrow, thin tape which is fragile in use and prone to print-through. However, good quality C60 cassettes based on polyester tape should not deteriorate more rapidly in storage than reel-to-reel polyester, which is why many poorly-funded oral history collections have adopted them as their only storage medium. Conservation recommendations for polyester tape apply equally to cassettes.

Copying   Provision for copying is such a basic requirement that the general requirements and standards have already been covered in Chapter 5 and in earlier parts of this chapter. This section is concerned with some more specialist aspects which the sound archivist may need to consider.

(i) *Undocumented track layouts*   Knowledge of the development of track layouts on quarter-inch tape is necessary when dealing with poorly documented recordings, particularly from amateur sources. It is quite possible to make worse-than-necessary copies simply through ignorance of contemporary practice. The following notes may help to increase awareness.

(a)   Full-track and half-track recordings
Early quarter-inch tape machines recorded only one track from the head to the tail of the tape, occupying its full width. If such tapes are played back with a half-track head, the tape hiss will be about 4dB higher.

Once half-track recorders became available, it was possible to record two mono tracks along opposite halves of the tape, but amateur users often failed to indicate which end of the tape was which or whether the whole (or even any) of both tracks had been used. Playing a half-track recording with a full-track head also increases the tape hiss by about 4dB.

Early stereo tapes, with both halves of the tape recorded simultaneously in the same direction, may be difficult to distinguish from full-track mono using conventional meters. If repeated listening fails to resolve the issue a 'sum-and-difference' meter may be needed.

From the early 1960s 'twin-track' machines became available enabling the two half-tracks to be recorded in the same direction independently. Studios found advantages in recording the 'vocals' and 'backing' for pop records separately. Twin-track and half-track stereo recordings may be virtually indistinguishable: the only physical difference lies in the distance separating the tracks, which is greater on a 'two-track' machine than on a stereo machine in order to avoid 'cross-talk' between the tracks. If a twin-track tape is replayed on a stereo machine and vice-versa, a slight increase in hiss may be the only consequence unless it was made for television and a 'timecode' band was recorded in between the two tracks, enabling it to be synchronized with video equipment. This may be audible on a full-track or stereo machine as a continuous chirping or warbling sound.

(b) Quarter-track and four-track recordings

Quarter-track machines were available from the late fifties and enabled cost-conscious amateurs to record four independent mono tracks instead of two and later two stereo tracks instead of one. On 'four-track' machines which came out in the 1970s, up to four tracks could be recorded and played back simultaneously: four-track machines therefore have four sets of record and playback electronics, quarter-track machines have one set if mono, and two sets if stereo.

The domestic role of quarter-track recording has been superseded by cassettes, so quarter-track machines in good working order are obsolete and becoming less common. The configuration is not used in modern studio or archival work, so a suitable playback machine will need to be acquired and preserved especially for these tapes. It may be the only non-standard provision for tape which the UK sound archivist finds he needs to make. Four-track machines were used for a time by small semi-professional studios and specialist amateurs but were never common.

The numbering of tracks on quarter-track recordings can be very confusing. In Europe machines were labelled so that the tracks were numbered in their physical order across the tape. A mono machine would start with track one from the head, recording along the top edge of the tape. At the tail the tape was turned over and the track switch pressed to change to the other head three-quarters down the head stack, which (with the tape now reversed) recorded the second track across the tape. Back at the head the tape would again be turned over but the track switch left in the same position. At the tail the tape would be turned over for the final time and the track switch returned to its original position to record the fourth track on the other edge of the tape. On a mono recorder the switch would therefore be labelled '1 & 4' and '2 & 3'. In America 'track 4' was numbered as 'track 2', so the switch, which was numbered '1 & 2' and '3 & 4' only had to be pressed once as the tape was being filled up or played back, and the tracks appeared in the order 1-3-4-2 across the tape. The track numbering for stereo is similarly complex, especially as no other mono and stereo recordings could be made on the same tape.

(ii) *Equalization* The playback head on a tape recorder responds to the rate of change in magnetic fields on the tape. The more rapid the rate, the greater the output from the head: so the 'frequency response' to higher frequencies on the analogue tape is better than that to lower frequencies because of the higher rate of change. For most of the frequency range, output increases steadily by 6dB per octave. But output drops off again at high frequencies when the wavelength of the magnetic variations (which depends on frequency and tape speed) begins to approximate to the width of the 'head gap',[51] and when the wavelength is identical to the head gap (or multiples of it) output falls to nothing.

To compensate for this 'non linear' response, the lower and high ends of the frequency range can in theory be boosted either during recording or playback, though in practice most of the compensation takes place at the playback stage. This form of 'equalization' is governed by international standards established by the NAB, IEC and DIN (see above under 'Elements of conservation policy – recording standards') relating to each tape speed. The 'curve' (i.e. the range of equalization across the frequency spectrum as represented on a graph) established by each organization is to a greater or lesser extent incompatible with the others. Equipment set to European standards will not play back American tape recordings as they were intended to sound, and vice versa. There has also been a revision of the European standards: the dullness of early tape recordings may not be due simply to the less efficient equipment of the time but also to incompatibilities between the old and new standards.

Tapes recorded in the course of commercial disc production are usually marked with the equalization standard used, as all three standards are likely to be encountered in what has always been an international industry. Broadcasting organizations such as the BBC tend to opt for a single standard and so do not need to mark tapes for internal use. This form of equalization relates only to the magnetic properties of tapes and recording machines are preset to one of the standards. Sound archivists or their engineers must ensure that a machine set to the same standard is used for playback. Subjective equalization used in recording and restoration work is a separate issue.

(iii) *Azimuth* The 'head gap' in the recording and playback heads of a tape recorder should ideally be perpendicular to the centre line of the tape travel. If the tape has been recorded on a machine with 'azimuth' misalignment, the effect will be a loss of high frequencies, and (in stereo) a lop-sidedness in the perceived stereo image because of the 'Haas precedence effect'. It can happen if the head, particularly on portable recorders, receives a knock; or there might be some asymmetry in the tape guides or in the way the tapes are loaded on the machine. In order to check whether it has been recorded 'off-azimuth' the tape should be played on a machine with an easily accessible head-block and the upper edge of the tape touched on either side of the playback head while in motion. If either results in a perceptible increase in high frequencies, the azimuth of the playback head is different from that of the original recording head, and the only cure is deliberately to misalign the playback head for maximum treble. This is easy enough, but of course the head has to be realigned again afterwards using a test tape and possibly a meter. On stereo machines and cassette recorders the effect is made more noticeable by paralleling the two tracks or switching the amplifier to mono.

(iv) *Noise reduction* The use of noise reduction on field recordings is often poorly documented. This applies especially to Dolby B, perhaps because it has become so commonplace on cassette machines and has the least noticeable effect on the raw recording. For this reason it may be difficult to tell subjectively whether Dolby B has been used, since all cassette systems enhance treble sounds. With the other systems (seeAppendix IV) the effects are quite conspicuous, and operators will soon learn the characteristic sound that each system gives.

Storage of tape (i) *Spools and hubs* Blank quarter-inch tape for professional use is often supplied in ten-inch diameter pancakes on flangeless hubs which are cheaper than professional and archival quality spools. Normally technicians spool up the tape as required, on spools of appropriate size for the length of recordings. It is also fairly common for studios and radio stations to store recorded master tapes, which will not be needed often, upright on the original hubs in individual boxes. This practice is not recommended for archival storage because any movement (e.g. on relocation of the repository) may loosen the windings and cause the pancake to split into an outer ring of tape, connected by loose and extremely vulnerable tape to the core which remains on the hub. (On spools this occurrence is prevented by the flanges.) It is impossible to reconstitute the pancake without serious damage to the loose tape at the break point, and very difficult to respool it. There is also the implication that in order to minimize these risks, spooling tension must be higher than normally recommended levels.

Spools should have rigid flanges with only sufficient clearance between them to avoid fouling on the tape. In the UK the only readily available spools which approach this standard are the very widespread metal-flanged 10½-inch spools manufactured to the NAB standard, which are used with separate plastic centres incorporating a rotating clamp mechanism which holds the spool firmly on the capstan of the tape machine. Currently available plastic spools, particularly in the 7-inch and smaller sizes, are normally quite flexible and fragile, and allow up to ⅛ inch of space between the flanges and the tape pack. This makes neat spooling more difficult and allows individual layers in the tape pack to spread laterally if it is moved or jolted, leaving these layers very vulnerable to edge damage. Steve Smolian's apparently daft suggestion that all ¼-inch tape for archival storage, however short in length, should be spooled on good quality 10½-inch spools, is actually the only logical practice while satisfactory smaller sizes remain unavailable.[52] And tape which has been stored on 7-inch and smaller spools with small hubs emerges with a pronounced curvature at the inner end indicating considerable pressure on the oxide layer at the centre. Spools with warped, bent or damaged flanges should never be used and should be substituted if discovered. Spools with radial threading slots should be avoided. The slot weakens the flange and its use results in unevenness at the centre of the tape pack.

(ii) *Containers* As discussed earlier, many storage problems can be avoided by enclosing tapes in sealed lightweight polyethylene bags within their individual boxes. The essential requirement is that the tapes must be placed in the bags under dry conditions, with 30 per cent RH or lower, in order to reduce as far as possible the presence of moisture which is detrimental to all types of tape. By this means the risks of damage by flooding or failures in climatic control are much reduced.

Plastic boxes of the type formerly supplied with 7-inch spools of tape by some manufacturers are probably the most suitable in that they are tough and long-lasting. But they are currently difficult and expensive to obtain in any size, so most repositories use cardboard boxes as supplied by tape manufacturers or on special order. Boxes should ideally be made from acid-free materials as tape is vulnerable to migrating acids, but the high extra costs involved will rarely seem justified, particularly as the manufacturers' boxes are included in the price of the tape and the acid problem, so far as it exists, must be greatly reduced by using inner plastic bags. However boxes of acidic board can fall apart within ten years and certainly within thirty, so the far-sighted, well-off repository may consider the extra expense worthwhile. Others will pay later when they have to rebox.

These 'others' should find it worthwhile avoiding the widespread practice of writing tape documentation on the boxes. Perhaps the best plan is to create a system in which no documentation except reference numbers needs to be stored with tapes; but if this is not possible, details should be compiled on a separate sheet of acid-free paper (for certainty in this respect obtain supplies from a reputable 'archival' stockist) placed inside the inner plastic bag. This can be transferred when reboxing is required.

Boxes are shelved upright and most sources recommend that spools be supported by a fixed drum inside the box so that the weight is borne by the centre, not the flanges. Manufacturers' boxes supplied with 10½ inch or larger NAB spools are usually equipped with these. Other spool types and sizes are not provided for in this way, which is perhaps another reason for not using them for archival storage.

Wire recordings

Wire recordings do not appear to have received serious attention from sound archivists or repositories. They are not covered by Pickett and Lemcoe or in any of the recent conservation studies referred to elsewhere in this book. Initially in the 1940s the most widespread use of wire was for signalling purposes in the armed forces, principally in the US (with machines based on designs by the Armour Research Foundation or the Brush Development Company's 'Navy Wire Recorder'), but also in the UK, where the Wirek machine was the most common. Post-war domestic machines were often designed to play discs as well as record on wire (such as the Columbia Silvertone model in the US and a similar Kloster-Brandes [KB] recorder in the UK). Miniature wire recorders, notably the Minifon sold by EMI in Britain, enjoyed a short vogue, while ultimately the most widespread use was in various types of dictating machines, some with built-in continuous-loop systems, others with removable spools. Wire was little used by recording studios or broadcasters, or for commercial publication, and perhaps as a result surviving wire recordings of any consequence are rare.

In some respects wire deserves more attention as a permanent recording medium than it has received. Stainless steel wire is a very long-lasting, extremely durable material. So long as strong magnetic fields are kept away, patterns of magnetization on it do not lose strength. It is not subject to problems related to short-lived backing materials and binders. Its performance was potentially little worse than that of contemporary tape and could perhaps have been improved had it received the attention since devoted to tape coatings. It is extremely compact to store[53] and is not affected by print-through because of its round surface and random distribution on the spool.

Another reason for the relatively poor performance of wire was the very fine gauges used. The most commonly found diameter is .004-inch (0.1mm) but gauges as low as 0.0015 or 0.002-inch were used on the miniature Minifon recorders. After years of storage on small spools it assumes a helical shape and will kink and snap if pulled tight. Some tendency to stretch is also reported. Playback is normally at around 20 ips and at this speed any tensioning problems can result in tangles which are difficult to undo and cause permanent damage. Joins are made and breakages repaired by tying the ends together, so accurate editing is not possible. Some non-stainless wire was issued for use onWirek machines by the forces. By now this has often been irrevocably damaged by rust.

There appears to have been little standardization in spool design between makers. The forces had their standard issue; domestic and office machines were no doubt supplied with a few spools of wire which would be used and reused. Long-term shelf storage was perhaps not envisaged.

All examples of recordings on stainless wire received by and reported to the NSA have survived in good condition. They have been treated like other obsolete or impermanent media and transferred to tape for preservation. Working wire recorders are very rare

Figure 6.23.   A range of wire recordings from the NSA's collections.

and it has been found easier to adapt a standard tape machine for playback than to try and coax old machines back into action. Modern electronics are likely to produce better results anyway. Advice on this can be had from the NSA conservation section.

Sound on film

Historical summary

This section is not concerned with the conservation of moving picture soundtracks but with the use of modified cinefilm and similar media for sound recording. None of the various systems was ultimately able to compete with magnetic tape, but in the period 1935-1960 they provided a successful technique for making recordings of longer duration than was possible on disc.

The earliest systems employed two or more optical soundtracks which were recorded and played back using essentially the same technology as talking pictures.[54] These included the British Oza-phane Company's 'Duo Trac' system (two optical soundtracks) and the Austrian 'Selenophone' double-sided 4-track paper tape system, recordings for which were also made using the optical soundtrack of cinefilm.

The earliest of these systems to achieve serious use was the Dutch Philips-Miller equipment marketed from 1935. A 7mm celluloid film was coated with transparent gelatine under an opaque black surface. Using a technique similar to lateral-cut electrical disc recording, a groove was cut along the length of the film with a stylus. This translucent track was then reproduced by methods akin to film sound reproduction, using a photo-electric cell. In 1939 the BBC experimented with the system and found it generally superior to the Blattner machines then in use for extended recording, but wartime shortages and the rise of tape recording after the war prevented much further development. Such Philips-Miller recordings as the BBC wished to preserve were transferred to disc.

A further technique which owed nothing to optical soundtrack technology was developed in Germany by Karl Daniel. In his Tefiphon (later Tefifon) system 35mm cinefilm was coated with gelatine and a series of parallel grooves cut in it which could be played back with a replay stylus, much as in conventional disc recording. The film moved through the machine in a continuous loop at 17¾ ips; a 50-metre loop could hold six hours of unbroken recording. The recording and replay machine, though mains operated, was light and compact; the NSA holds an extensive collection of field recordings made on such a machine in India in 1939. At that time it was probably the best technique available for making recordings of long duration.

The similar Amertape and Memobelt systems were used by the US army in the years after World War II, notably to record proceedings at the Nuremburg Trials. Whereas these belts were recorded on one side only, the Tefi loops were joined with a twist in them so that, on the 'Möbius's loop' principle, both sides were recorded.

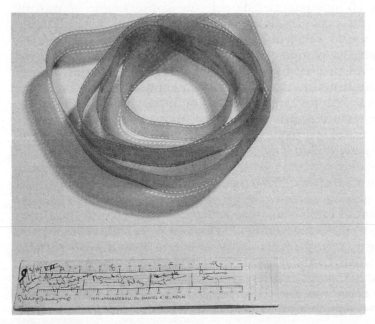

Figure 6.24   A Tefifon belt with track indicator as supplied.

In the early 1950s Daniel developed a smaller version of the Tefi system using ⅝-inch wide cassetted film which could play for up to four hours continuously at 7½ ips. There were no recording facilities in the new machines: the cassettes contained prerecorded film and were intended to rival the emerging LP as an entertainment medium. Duplication was by a pressing process based again on disc technology. The system worked well enough to enjoy a following in Germany: it benefited from constant linear speed, instant track selection without having to spool through, and long playing time which was popular with places of entertainment where continuous background music was required. But its minority status led to obsolescence after ten years.[55]

Further systems on the same principle but capable of recording as well as playback, such as the German Selectophon (a cassetted system) and the Dictaphone company's Dictabelt which used a short, broad belt capable of being flattened and sent through the post, survived rather longer, mainly in offices. But they could not rival the Philips cassette system for convenience and the film loops, along with all the sound-on-film types, could not be wiped and reused.

Conservation

Film adapted for sound recording shares characteristics with contemporary cinefilm and is therefore not a good long-term prospect. Amertape and Tefiphon belts held at the US National Archives, the UK Public Record Office and the NSA were loosely packed in cardboard containers at the time of recording and all remain in reasonable condition, though in the process of stiffening with age they have conformed to the shape of their containers, which can hinder smooth running through playback apparatus.

All the systems are completely obsolete. For practical and conservation reasons these recordings should be copied onto tape if their contents are thought worthy of permanent retention. The recordings based on film soundtrack technology are almost certain to be on nitrate stock and are unlikely to have survived in playable condition. Advice on replaying any which have might best be sought from film archive technicians, though it is likely that modern equipment would have to be specially constructed. This course has also been followed in attempting to replay Amertape. Charlie Mayn of the US National Archives has been unable to locate an adequate contemporary machine, and has therefore been working for several years on a new machine incorporating parts rifled from old machines and modern electronics. Amertape has a very narrow groove pitch, and tracking problems with modern lightweight styluses and cartridges were still preventing complete success with the project in 1989.

So far as is known this is the only work currently in progress on the conservation of the 35 mm formats. Offers of recordings on the more recent dictation formats should perhaps be turned down if a workable playback machine does not accompany them.

References

1. British Standards Institution, *Recommendations for the care and transportation of magnetic tape*, BS 4783, BSI, London.
2. C. V. Horie, 'Preservation of audio-visual archives: a framework of ethics' in *Newsletter of the International Association of Sound Archives UK Branch*, 12, 1986, pp. 9–10.
3. An advantage of digital recording is that deterioration can be monitored without control data. Defects in digital recordings are automatically rectified by the simultaneously recorded checkdigits on the tape; and the rate at which such dropouts and replacements occur can be monitored.
4. The less robust character of 'amateur' equipment has been brought home to the NSA by its experience of digital audio recording on domestic video recorders. In this case fully acceptable 'professional' recording standards are obtainable from comparatively cheap equipment, but the rate of mechanical failure is much higher than is characteristic of professional analogue equipment.
5. For example in UK and most of Europe: IEC (International Electrotechnical Commission); USA: NAB (National Association of Broadcasters); Germany: DIN (Deutscher Industrie Normen).
6. The RIAA (Recording Industry Association of America) standard. The UK version is available as BS 1928.
7. L. Stickells, 'The Packburn noise suppressor' in *Recorded Sound* 79, January 1981, pp. 23–4; A. Tuddenham and P. Copeland, 'Record processing for improved sound, pt. 3: noise reduction methods' in *Hillandale News* 164, October 1988, pp. 89–97.
8. A specialist in this field is George Brock-Nannestad of Denmark. See 'A concerted approach to historical recordings' in *The Gramophone*, January 1984, pp. 925–927; 'Horn resonances in the acoustico-mechanical recording process and the measurement and elimination in the replay situation' in *Phonographic Bulletin* 38, March 1984, pp. 39–43.
9. W. D. Storm, 'The establishment of international re-recording standards' in *Phonographic Bulletin* 27, 1980, pp. 5–12; 'The implementation of proposed standards for copying audio recordings' in Orbanz, *op. cit.*, pp. 105–108.

10. E. Brady et al., *The Federal Cylinder Project. Vol. 1: introduction and inventory*, Library of Congress, Washington, 1984, and subsequent volumes.
11. C. S. Myers, 'Music' in A. C. Haddon (ed.), *Reports of the Cambridge Anthropological Expedition to the Torres Straits*, vol. IV, CUP, Cambridge, 1912, pp. 238–269.
12. For one tale on this theme see A. H. Fox Strangways, *The Music of Hindostan*, Clarendon Press, Oxford, 1914, p. 90.
13. c/o the Secretary, 33 Derwent Drive, Maidenhead SL6 6LE.
14. c/o Elwood McKee (Secretary), 118 Monroe Street no. 610, Rockville, Maryland 20850, USA.
15. G. L. Frow, and A. F. Sefl, *The Edison cylinder phonographs*, G. L. Frow, Sevenoaks, 1978, p. 186.
16. J. C. Fesler, 'Electrical reproduction of acoustically recorded cylinders and disks, part 2' in *Journal of the Audio Engineering Society*, vol. 31, no. 9, September 1983, pp. 674–694.
17. The term 'threads' relates to the pitch of the feed-screw which guided the progress of the recording head along the cylinder.
18. J. A. Gray and D. S. Lee (eds), *The Federal Cylinder Project, vol. 2: Northeastern Indian catalogue; Southeastern Indian catalogue*, Library of Congress, Washington, 1985.
19. However the Pitt Rivers Museum in Oxford does hold an unusual series of metal moulding shells derived from a collection of field recorded wax cylinders and presumably intended for the production of duplicates for distribution to researchers or other museums. The more normal UK method of making small runs of copies was by means of a one-to-one direct-cut duplicator – see A. Ward, 'The Frazer Collection of wax cylinders: an introduction' in *Recorded Sound 85*, January 1984, p. 6. A number of European research institutions, such as the Berlin University Psychological Institute, from which the well-known Hornbostel research collection emanated, preferred to produce metal masters and mould their duplicates once this technique with its superior results was available.
20. Brady et al., *op. cit.*, pp. 9–12.
21. *Ibid.*, pp. 12–15.
22. For example the 'Owl cylinder reproducer kit' from Owl Audio Products Inc., P.O. Box 3122, Linden, New Jersey 07036, USA.
23. A notable UK maker is Joe Pengelly, 36 Thorn Park, Mannamead, Plymouth PL3 5PD.
24. L. F. Stickells, 'Evolution of a new cylinder reproducer' in *Recorded Sound 86*, July 1984, and 'The construction of cylinder replay machines' in Orbanz, *op. cit.* pp. 81–83; F. Lechleitner, 'The construction of cylinder replay machines', *ibid.*, pp. 79–80; T. Owen, 'Electrical reproduction of acoustically recorded cylinders and disks, part 1' in *Journal of the Audio Engineering Society*, vol. 31, no. 4, April 1983, AES, 1983, pp. 266–275.

25. T. Iwai et al., 'Reproduction of sound from old wax phonograph cylinders using the laser-beam reflection method' in *Applied Optics*, vol. 25, no. 5, March 1986, pp. 597–604.

26. W. A. Deutsch, *Restoration of historical recordings by means of digital signal processing*, paper presented at the 75th AES convention, Paris, 1984, AES reprint no. 2091; W. A. Deutsch and A. Noll, 'The restoration of historical sound recordings by means of digital signal processing: psychoacoustical aspects' in Orbanz, *op cit.*, pp. 113–116; S. J. W. Rayner, S. V. Vaseghi, L. F. Stickells, 'Digital signal processing methods for the removal of scratches and surface noise from gramophone records', *ibid.*, pp. 109–111.

27. The NSA holds what appears to be the largest and most significant collection of ethnographic research cylinders in the UK. It was assembled by Sir James Frazer in Cambridge before the First World War, but had been badly stored since. By the early 1980s when serious work on the collection began, any original order had been lost, and the chronology and provenance of each item could only be established from the scanty notes on containers and lids. In many cases successful identification was made using only the paleographic evidence of a few scribbled words. Since the recordings on these cylinders were often of primitive music or obscure language and dialect, the task of reorganizing the collection would have been virtually impossible without the notes on the boxes.

28. G. D. Gibson, 'Decay and degradation of disk and cylinder recordings in storage' in Orbanz, *op. cit.*, p. 48.

29. *Ibid*.

30. The custodial history of these discs provides an early example of the value of good archival practice. The wax discs and the stampers generated from them were stored in separate locations. During World War II all the waxes were destroyed by bombing but the metal parts survived and were later used to produce a new set of discs in a modern hardwearing material. See E. Aschinger, F. Lechleitner, D. Schüller, 'The old phonograms of the Vienna Phonogrammarchiv: re-recording principles and practices' in *Phonographic Bulletin*, 35, March 1983, pp. 16–20.

31. Sir W. Bragg, *The world of sound*, G. Bell and Sons, London, 1919, pp. 161–172. I am indebted to Peter Copeland for these references.

32. The disc contained two hymns from the service and was pressed by the Columbia Graphophone Company for sale in aid of the Westminster Abbey Fund; see H. O. Merriman, 'Sound recording by electricity, 1919–24' in *Talking Machine Review*, vol. 40, June 1976, pp. 666–681.

33. Michael Biel described a number of obscure early electrical recording experiments in an address at the 1977 annual conference of the Association for Recorded Sound Collections, and I am grateful to Mr Biel and to the archivist of ARSC for enabling me to consult a tape recording of it.

34. A. H. Watts, *Cecil E. Watts. Pioneer of direct disc recording*, A. H. Watts private publication, London, 1972.
35. J. H. Vickers, 'Private recording studios: a listing for 1948' in *BASC News*, no. 2, 1987, pp. 14–15.
36. See, for example, B. Fox, 'Early stereo recording' in *Studio Sound*, vol. 24, no. 5, May 1982, pp. 36–42.
37. Modern matrix numbers can be complicated. EMI, for instance, issue a small guidebook to assist with the interpretation of theirs.
38. The study, now 30 years old, is not available through commercial channels, but may be obtained in copy form through the British Library Document Supply Centre. The British Library Information Sciences Service (formerly the Library Association Library), and the NSA also hold copies.
39. In Orbanz, *op. cit.*
40. See McWilliams, *op. cit.*, pp. 36–43 and 57–68.
41. N. S. Allen et al., 'The nature of the degradation of archival cellulose-ester base motion-picture film: the case for stabilisation' in *Journal of Photographic Science*, vol. 36, no. 2, 1988, pp. 34–39, provides an introduction to this work. Further information is available from Dr Allen at the Chemistry Department, Manchester Polytechnic, Manchester M1 5GD.
42. See J. Stratton, 'Crackle' in *Recorded Sound*, 39, July 1970, p. 655.
43. F. K. Engel, '1888–1988: A hundred years of magnetic sound recording' in *Journal of the Audio Engineering Society*, vol. 36, no. 3 March 1988, pp. 170–178, and in *Phonographic Bulletin* 51, July 1988, pp. 8–19.
44. See R. Müller, 'On improvements of magnetic tape shown by measurements on early and newer tapes' in *Journal of the Audio Engineering Society*, vol. 36, no. 10, October 1988, pp. 802–818.
45. With consequent distortion; see S. Smolian, 'Preservation, deterioration and restoration of recording tape' in *ARSC Journal*, vol. 19, nos. 2–3, 1987, p. 39 and his sources.
46. See reference 41.
47. Statement by Dr. M. Edge during address to the IASA international conference, August 1989.
48. See for example 'A care and handling manual for magnetic tape recording' in Kalil, *op. cit.*, p. 137.
49. *Audio preservation: a planning study. op. cit.*, p. 199.
50. A. McKenzie, 'Magnetic tape' in J. Borwick (ed.), *Sound Recording Practice*, OUP, London, 1980.
51. See for example G. Alkin, *Sound recording and reproduction*, Focal Press, London, 1981, pp. 100–105.
52. Smolian, *op. cit.*, p. 44.
53. This was one of its main selling points. See S. J. Begun, *Magnetic Recording*, Murray Hill Books/Thermionic Products Ltd., London, 1949, p. 100. (This is a very informative and apparently authoritative

book on wire and very early tape recording in the US. There is now a photocopy in the NSA library but no other copies appear to be easily available.)

54. For which see, for example, *Photographic sound recording and reproduction*, British Kinematograph Sound and Television Society, London, 1975.

55. See P. Czada and F. A. Jansen, 'Tefifon' in *Hillandale News* no. 130 (Feb. 1983) pp. 168–171; F. A. Jansen, 'Non-magnetic sound recording on tape', *ibid.*, no. 133, Aug. 1983, pp. 239–243.

Chapter 7

FURTHER READING

This is a brief list with some annotations. Most of the books included are 'standard works' or general works of good all-round usefulness which are worthy of attention. Books already cited in chapter references as illustrating particular points only are not included.

With one exception, journal article citations in chapter references are not repeated, but a few additional articles which have been found useful in providing background information are included.

Bibliographies

Gibson, G. D., 'Bibliography – Working Draft' in AAA Committee of the Association for Recorded Sound Collections, *Audio preservation: a planning study* (Appendix III-D), Rockville, MD, 1988 (obtainable from Elwood McKee, 118 Monroe Street, no.610, Rockville, MD 20850, USA). Drawn up with the resources of the Library of Congress and includes information on various aspects of sound archive work. With 2430 entries and a detailed index it is the most comprehensive listing available.

Harrison, H. P., *The archival appraisal of sound recordings and related materials: a RAMP study*, ref: PGI-87/WS/1, UNESCO, Paris, 1987, pp. 69–86. Includes a useful list based on much larger bibliographies held by Rolf and Ann Schuursma, and by Helen Harrison at the Media Library of the Open University, Milton Keynes. Many aspects beyond appraisal are covered.

Lance, D., (ed.), *Sound archives: a guide to their establishment and development*, IASA, Milton Keynes, 1983. Appendix A, 'Suggestions for further reading', is a very useful and wide-ranging (if

195

rather outdated) review of articles and books, arranged under subject headings.

General

Phonographic Bulletin, Journal of the International Association of Sound Archives. Many useful articles have appeared in this publication over the years. The present IASA treasurer who handles subscriptions is Marit Grimstad, Norsk Riksringkasting, Programarkivet, Bjørnstjerne Bjørnsons Pl.1, Oslo 3, Norway. The present journal editor is Grace Koch of the Australian Institute of Aboriginal Studies.

Weerasinghe, L., (ed.), *Directory of recorded sound resources in the United Kingdom*, British Library National Sound Archive, London, 1989.

Acquisition

Harrison, H. P., (ed.), *Selection in sound archives*, IASA, Milton Keynes, 1984. A very useful collection of essays by authors from many different backgrounds.

Raspin, G. E. A., *The transfer of private papers to repositories*, Information Leaflet no. 5, Society of Archivists, 1988. Most of the considerations which apply to private papers also apply to deposits of recordings.

Copyright

Copyright, Designs and Patents Act 1988, HMSO, London, 1988.

Guides issued by the Performing Right Society Ltd, 29/33 Berners Street, London W1P 4AA; the Mechanical Copyright Protection Society Ltd, Elgar House, 41 Streatham High Road, London SW16 1ER; and Phonographic Performance Ltd, Ganton House, 14-22 Ganton Street, London W1V 1LB.

Information leaflets on various aspects of copyright published by the Library Association, 7 Ridgemount Street, London. WC1E 7AE.

Information sheets on copyright published by the National Council for Educational Technology, 3 Devonshire Street, London W1N 2BA.

Merkin, R., *Copyright, designs and patents: the new law*, Longman,

London, 1989. One of several new or revised books taking in the new Act.

Documentation

Cook, M. G. and M. Procter, *Manual of Archival Description*, 2nd ed., Gower, Aldershot, 1989.
Society of American Archivists, *Archival forms manual*, Chicago, 1982.

Accommodation

British Standard 5454, *Recommendations for the storage and exhibition of archival documents* BSI, London, 1989.
Buchanan, S. A., *Disaster planning: preparedness and recovery for libraries and archives*, ref. PGI–88/WS/6, UNESCO, Paris, 1988.
Cunha, G. M. and D. G., *Conservation of Library materials . . .*, 2nd ed., 2 vols., Scarecrow Press, Metuchen NJ, 1983.
Duchein, M., *Les bâtiments d'archives: construction et équipment*, Paris, Archives Nationales 1985.

Conservation

Audio preservation: a planning study (as above under 'Bibliographies'). An 860-page compilation covering many aspects of conservation strategy. The study includes a few articles (which are also printed elsewhere), but its main interest lies in the range of raw data presented, including the bibliography referred to above, the glossary which appears as Appendix V of this book, and the results of a worldwide questionnaire on conservation practice in sound archive repositories.
Geller, S. B., *Care and handling of computer magnetic storage media*, NBS Special publication 500–101, National Bureau of Standards, Washington, 1983.
Kalil, F. (ed.), *Magnetic tape recording for the eighties*, NASA reference publication 1075, NASA, Greenbelt MD, 1982. Aimed at the high standards and specifications required in the field of instrumentation tape recording, this collection provides a very useful series of research-based recommendations.
'Magnetic tape deterioration' in *The Australasian Sound Archive*

(Journal of IASA Australasian branch), no. 4, December 1987, pp. 48–61. An up-to-date and well-informed report and bibliographic survey.

McWilliams, J., *The preservation and restoration of sound recordings*, American Association for State and Local History, Nashville TN, 1979.

Orbanz, E., (ed.), *Archiving the audio-visual heritage*, Stiftung Deutsche Kinemathek, West Berlin, 1988.

Pickett, A. G. and Lemcoe, M. M., *Preservation and storage of sound recordings*, Library of Congress, Washington, 1959. Still the classic study.

Technical

Aldred, J., *Manual of sound recording*, 3rd ed., Fountain Press Argus Books, Watford, 1978.

Alkin, G., *Sound recording and reproduction*, Focal Press, London, 1981. A stage-by-stage idiot's guide.

Borwick, J. (ed.), *Sound recording practice*, OUP, London, 1980.

Pohlmann, K. C., *Principles of digital audio*, H. W. Sams, Indianapolis, 1985.

Smolian, S., 'Preservation, deterioration and restoration of recording tape' in *Journal of the Association for Recorded Sound Collections*, vol. 19, no. 2–3, 1987. An excellent, street-wise survey of current research and practice. Includes material more recent than 1987.

Historical

Dearling, R. and C., *The Guinness Book of Recorded Sound*, Guinness Superlatives Ltd., London, 1984.

Ford, P., 'History of sound recording', pts. 1-5, in *Recorded Sound*, vols. 1–2, British Institute of Recorded Sound, London, 1962–3. These articles give a clear, detailed, introductory account of events up to the 1960s.

Godfrey, J. W. and Amos, S. W., *Sound recording and reproduction*, Iliffe and Sons, London, 1952. Contemporary instructional manuals of this kind are difficult to find but provide much insight into the world of recording before tape became common. They describe techniques long forgotten in modern studios but essential to the informed processing of older recordings.

Journal of the Audio Engineering Society, passim. The AES journal has included the odd retrospective or historical article for many years, but recent issues in volume 36 (1988) have featured a series of articles dealing with the history of tape recording, the retrospective assessment of tape characteristics, and other matters of particular interest to the sound archivist. It is probably the most accessible and useful of the technical journals from the archivist's point of view.

Sound archives and oral history

Lance, D., *An archive approach to oral history*, Imperial War Museum and IASA, London, 1978.

Moss, W. W., and Mazikana, P. C., *Archives, oral history, and oral tradition, a RAMP study*, ref. PG1-86/WS/2, UNESCO, Paris, 1986.

APPENDIX I

NSA GENERAL CODE OF PRACTICE ON THE STORAGE, HANDLING AND PLAYBACK OF RECORDINGS (1988)

Note: 'Recording' means a recorded medium of any kind which is a possession of the National Sound Archive.

I General security

1 Preservation takes precedence over exploitation.
2 No recording may be removed from the premises of the NSA without the director's authority. Any proposed removal must be referred initially to the coordinator, Archival Services (see note 1 below).
3 Recordings must be kept in the NSA's designated secure storage areas and may only be taken out by staff for the specific uses described under I.4. All other proposed withdrawals must be referred to the coordinator, Archival Services.
4 Authorized uses for which recordings may be withdrawn from storage are:
   (a) playback in Listening Service;
   (b) playback and study by curators or cataloguers;
   (c) assessment and copying by Conservation Section or curators.
5 Non-members of staff *may not* handle NSA recordings, though they may handle related documentation (e.g. LP sleeves), with due care, at the discretion of staff.

II Access to stores; withdrawal and return of recordings

1 Subject to the above provisions, any established member of staff may enter the storage areas in 29 Exhibition Road and 47 Princes Gate.

2 The director, assistant director, coordinator, Archival Services, subject curators and assistants, and staff of the Acquisitions and Storage, Conservation, Cataloguing, Information, and Education/Publication sections may withdraw any recordings except (*a*) unaccessioned recordings, (*b*) recordings under lock and key within the storage areas, (*c*) tape recordings outside the main series.

3 Wildlife Sounds staff may withdraw wildlife species tapes. Requests for recordings falling outside this and the categories listed under II.2 (e.g. C Series tapes) should be made to the vaultkeeper. Staff working on special projects should consult the coordinator, Archival Services, if they require regular access to restricted material.

4 Access to all storage areas not mentioned above is restricted to the director, assistant director, coordinator, Archival Services, and members of the Acquisitions and Storage section. Requests for recordings shelved in these stores should be made to the vaultkeeper.

5 Except for Playback Service staff making short-term withdrawals for use in the service, staff withdrawing recordings should complete a triplicate staff application form for each recording required. The top copy should be placed in one of the jackets provided and placed on the shelf in lieu of the withdrawn item. The second copy should be given to the vaultkeeper and the third retained for reference.

6 Staff may not retain recordings out of storage for longer than one month. Requests for this period to be extended should be made to the coordinator, Archival Services. Acquisitions and Storage staff are not authorized to accede to such requests.

7 All recordings for return to storage should be given to the vaultkeeper or placed for his attention. Other staff *must not* return material to the shelves.

III Playback

1 Where two or more copies of a recording have been accessioned, one will be designated the archive copy and the other(s) the playback copy/ies. The archive copy will be stored separately and should never be played back except when it is being copied for conservation or other special purposes authorized by the coordinator, Archival Services.

2 Where only one copy of a recording is held, it must not be used

for playback (*except* as under 3(*a*) and 3(*g*) below), but a playback copy should be made if required. In the case of recordings on impermanent carriers (e.g. acetate discs), two copies will be made for use as archive and playback copies (see note 2 below).

3 *Permitted playback*

(*a*) Single copy vinyl and compact digital discs: 3 plays, after which a playback copy must be made.

(*b*) Playback copy vinyl and compact digital discs: unlimited (but see notes 3 and 4 below).

(*c*) Single copy shellac discs: must be copied for playback.

(*d*) Playback copy shellac discs: unlimited (but see note 3 below).

(*e*) Single copy tapes (all types including compact cassettes except as under (*g*) below: must be copied for playback.

(*f*) Playback copy tapes: unlimited (but see note 3 below).

(*g*) Single copy Betamax off-air recordings: 3 plays, after which a playback copy must be made.

(*h*) All other carriers: must be copied for playback.

4 The date when a recording is played back must be noted on its container (see note 5 below).

5 Playback may be carried out:

(*a*) in the Listening Service;

(*b*) by curators and cataloguers on equipment in their offices for the purposes of assessment and study;

(*c*) by the Conservation Section.

6 Casual listening to recordings by staff is not permitted.

7 Playback equipment will be checked regularly by the engineer. Do not use unchecked equipment, or equipment which you suspect may be faulty.

8 Never lower the stylus onto, or lift the stylus off a disc by hand.

9 Fast-wind monitoring of single or archive copy tapes is not permitted. Playback copy tapes may be monitored in this way but the practice should be kept to the minimum.

IV Handling and storage of discs

1 Handle discs by label and outer edges only – *never* touch the grooves with fingers or any other part of the hand.

2 Never leave discs out of their sleeves or containers when not in use.

3 Never leave discs on turntables or in CD players when not in use.

4 Never leave a disc stationary on a turntable with the stylus resting in the groove.

5 Always clean or arrange cleaning for dirty discs (see V below) before playing or returning to storage.

6 Always store discs in sleeves (CDs: plastic containers). When a disc has an inner and an outer sleeve, the openings of the two sleeves should be arranged at right angles, with the inner sleeve opening at the top. Damaged inner sleeves and disc bags should be replaced.

7 When carrying or stacking a pile of discs, make certain that all sleeve openings are facing in the same direction.

8 Never mix discs of different types or sizes in a pile.

9 Never carry more than ten 78 rpm discs in a pile.

10 If, as a temporary measure, discs have to be stacked horizontally, never stack them more than five high.

11 Shelve shellac, acetate and vinyl discs upright without great lateral pressure but enough to prevent sliding or warping. Never stack a single disc for any length of time in an upright position with the edge leaning against a vertical surface.

12 Never leave discs near a radiator or other source of heat (e.g. computer equipment), or in direct sunlight.

13 Never place uncovered discs on dirty, greasy, or uneven surfaces, or in places where they may be accidentally knocked or stepped on.

14 Do not eat, drink or smoke in the vicinity of any disc, whether uncovered or in its container.

V Cleaning discs

1 Do not attempt any form of cleaning on CDs. If cleaning appears to be required, refer to the conservation manager.

2 Superficial dust should be removed from shellac and vinyl discs before playing, using only cloths and brushes approved by the conservation manager. Always wipe or brush in the direction of grooves, never across them.

3 Vinyl discs which appear to be affected by a static charge should be stabilized using an anti-static gun approved by the conservation manager.

4 Dirty discs should be submitted to the Conservation Section for cleaning.

5 When cleaning discs conservation staff should follow estab-

lished procedures only. Other staff must not use liquids to clean discs.

VI   Handling and storage of tapes

1   All tapes should be handled with the greatest care as they are easily damaged by physical and magnetic forces.
2   Do not play any NSA tape on any machine before receiving full instruction from the Conservation Section.
3   When handling tape and threading it through machines touch only the leaders attached to each end and not the tape itself. When attaching leaders touch the tape as little as possible.
4   The following guidelines used in the technical preparation of tape recordings are included for the guidance of all staff.

(a) *NSA original recordings*
NSA recordings of live events, interviews etc. destined for inclusion in the C series may be made on any equipment or format considered appropriate by the conservation manager. Compact cassette recorders (e.g. Marantz CP 430) or Uher 4000 series reel-to-reel machines may be used to record interviews but should not be used for other types of recording without the approval of the conservation manager.

(b) *Formats for NSA main series recordings*
NSA off-air recordings are made digitally on Betamax videocassettes. Where an archive and playback copy of a recording are being made, the archive copy may be on Betamax. All playback copies should be on reel-to-reel tape. Current spool sizes acceptable in the main series are 10-inch (T tapes), 7-inch (no prefix tapes), and 5-inch (0 tapes). All videorecordings are made on VHS, *not* Beta. No other formats are accessioned in the main series (see note 6 below).

(c) *Speed*
The standard speed for all reel-to-reel recordings and copies made by the NSA for internal use is $7\frac{1}{2}$ *ips*. Recordings must not be made at slower speeds without prior arrangement with the coordinator, Archival Services.

(d) *Tape specification*
Standard play tape should be used for all reel-to-reel

recordings unless this presents insurmountable difficulties, in which case long play tape may be acceptable. If double play tape is the only real time option, a duplicate copy on standard play should be produced subsequently.

(e) *Track configuration and leader colours*
White (W): track one of a 2-track mono tape
Red (R): track two of a 2-track mono tape
Yellow (Y): start of a 2-track stereo tape
Red and white vertical stripes (RW): end of a 2-track stereo tape.
At present no other configuration or colours are normally used in the NSA (see note 7 below).

(f) *Editing*
Archive and playback tapes produced for permanent retention by the NSA must not be cut-edited or spliced.

(g) *Reference tones and announcements*
Reference tones are applied at present only to recordings made on NSA premises by the Conservation Section. Announcements should normally precede all recordings added to the main series except off-air recordings; staff should seek guidance from the conservation manager on the conventional form of announcements.

(h) *Subjective filtering and equalization on NSA produced tapes*
Archive copies: flat.
Playback copies: may be filtered and equalized. A record of equipment and settings used should be made in the tape register and on the tape container.
Original NSA recordings: filtering and EQ should be kept to a minimum and a record kept of equipment and settings used.

5 *Storage of tapes*
(a) Tapes are shelved upright in individual boxes.
(b) Do not leave tapes unboxed or exposed to any physical hazard (e.g. near sources of heat, in direct sunlight, on the floor) when not in use. Do not eat, drink or smoke near tapes.
(c) Never leave a tape near a magnetic field source such as a loudspeaker, television receiver or, most seriously, any kind of magnet (e.g. magnetic door catches or the magnetic letters and discs used with steel display boards).
(d) All NSA open-reel tapes are being placed in plastic bags within their outer containers. Care should be taken to

replace tapes in these bags after use, and to replace damaged bags.

(e) Store WR (mono) tapes tail in.
Store Y (stereo) tapes tail out.

(f) Rewind tapes carefully to avoid spillage and misalignment of individual layers. Do not fast-wind tapes immediately before return to storage; use 15 ips. Rewind any tape which has been dropped or subjected to rough handling. Replace any damaged or distorted spools. If in doubt refer to the vaultkeeper or conservation manager.

7 *Equipment*

Recording and playback equipment will be checked and serviced regularly by the engineer. Do not use unserviced equipment, particularly if the recording heads have not been demagnetized recently. Report all technical problems immediately. If tapes become jammed, twisted or tangled in equipment, switch it off and refer to the Conservation Section.

Tape machine performance is seriously affected by the accumulation of dirt and debris on recording heads etc. Staff will be instructed in cleaning procedures by Conservation Section staff and are responsible for cleaning the machines which they use. Machines should be covered when not in use.

VII Documentation

1 Great care should be taken to preserve all documentation relating to and accompanying recordings.

2 Disc sleeves and labels may be marked with accession numbers and other filing information (if necessary) by accessions staff, according to established procedures (which are designed to obscure as little as possible). No further marking except date stamping should occur (see note 5 below).

3 Tapes recorded by the NSA should be annotated according to established procedures on their containers, which should not then be marked further except for date stamping (see note 5 below). Spools *as well as* containers should be marked indelibly with reference numbers when tapes are accessioned.

4 Original containers and labels received with or fixed to privately made recordings must be preserved. *Do not* write indelibly on such containers and labels.

VIII   Damage to recordings

All newly-discovered or newly-caused damage to recordings or their containers must be referred to the coordinator, Archival Services.

Notes

1   The 'premises of the NSA' include the NSA van. Recordings in transit between NSA buildings and storage areas are not regarded as 'removed'.
2   Reference numbers of playback copy tapes of commercial discs should be passed to the acquisitions officer for noting in the accessions registers, before they are placed in storage. Playback copies of C series tapes should be passed to the Conservation Section AO for accessioning before being placed in storage.
3   'Playback' means one uninterrupted play of the whole or part of a recording. If repeated playing is envisaged, a copy should be made. Playback copies have a security and conservation function and should not be subjected to heavy use. The Listening Service may only play whole banded tracks of discs, or whole sides of unbanded discs. If repeated plays are required by listeners, this should be arranged via the locked-in cassette facility.
4   BBC Archive vinyl LPs should be treated as playback copies.
5   *Date marking*
    Tapes: stamp inside of box lid.
    Shellac discs: stamp back of bag (remove disc first).
    Vinyl discs: mark inside edge of outer bag or sleeve.
6   Obsolete sizes no longer added to the main series are on 8¾-inch spools (P tapes) and 5¾-inch spools (M tapes).
7   Blue and white vertically striped (BW) leaders were formally used at the start of stereo tapes but are now obsolete.
  As a temporary measure, green and red leaders supplied with some reel-to-reel tape currently in stock may be retained in storage.
  Leaders should not be attached or changed on tapes destined for the C series received from outside the NSA.

APPENDIX II

MANUAL OF ARCHIVAL DESCRIPTION (2ND EDITION): SPECIAL FORMAT FOR THE DESCRIPTION OF SOUND ARCHIVES*

Introduction

1A   This descriptive format, like the other special formats, has been designed for use in a general repository, and is concerned with descriptions of sound materials which are to be included in general finding aids.

1B   It is probable that no administrative system is based on sound recordings alone. Therefore, in a general repository, sound material will be found enclosed with or dependent on paper-based archive material. Some of this sound material will be archival (i.e. produced in the course of business and retained for business reference by an individual or organization); some will be collected material.

1C   An example of clearly archival material might be that produced by radio stations and record companies in the course of their work; these emanate from administrative systems and are consequently transactional in character. On the other hand, interview recordings resulting from oral history projects are a common form of collected material and they have more in common with collections of private papers, correspondence or research notes conventionally held by record offices.

1D   Commercially published recordings may be received in general repositories as part of an archival accumulation. These too may be described using the format, although the archivist may decide, as an alternative, to use an appropriate form of bibliographic description. Where commercial or published recordings with no archival context are concerned, standard *AACR2* bibliographical descriptions should be used, following the practice of the repository or the data provided by the publishers.

*In MAD2 the paragraphs reproduced in this appendix appear with the prefix 23: paragraph 1A is 23.1A, 1B is 23.1B and so on.

1E The *MAD2* format is suitable for use in the description of, among others, the following forms of sound recording which may be found among archival materials in a general repository and elsewhere:

- radio broadcasts
- interviews e.g. oral history recordings
- recording of events such as concerts, plays, conferences, panel discussions, meetings, debates etc.
- 'actuality' recordings (live recordings of e.g. demonstrations, riots etc.)
- recordings emanating from (scientific) monitoring apparatus
- 'masters' and other material used in the production of published records and tapes.

GENERAL RULES

2 Depth of description
2A A full range of data elements for technical description has been included in the format though many data elements will be inapplicable to the requirements of a non-specialist repository. However sufficient technical information must be included in any description to allow for conservation, retrieval and use.

2B Because users can only have access to the sound materials by means of an appropriate machine, the accuracy and completeness of the content and character area of the description is particularly important.

3 Levels of description
3A The general multi-level rule (secton 6) applies to the special format sound recording finding aid, in that a macro description giving background, context and provenance, together with information common to the set of descriptions covered, must be given as a headnote or title page at the beginning of the special format finding aid. This macro description should also appear as an entry in the general finding aids, or be cross-referred to a relevant entry there.

3B Outside the macro description referred to, the special format finding aid to sound recordings forms a distinct entity linked to but distinct from the central finding aid system of the repository. We would expect the special format descriptions to represent level 3 (where sets of recordings are a class), level 4 (where there may be related recordings in a single complex unit) or level 5 (individual recordings). Items are series of recordings produced in the course of a project or activity and forming a physical unit. Pieces are single recordings, which may not be physically independent.

3C Sound recordings are usually extracted physically in general repositories and kept in a sound recordings room or specially designated area, for ease of conservation and access. There are often dedicated lists of sound recordings (or sound recordings indexes).

3D Archival sound recordings are not often self-explanatory and may be particularly dependent on the evidence of their provenance and context. Consequently it is important to preserve links which may exist between the sound recordings(s) and their associated papers. Because of this, both the general (group/class) finding aid and the sound recordings index should contain cross-references and background information.

4 Summary table of data elements for sound archives

Identity statement area
    Reference code
    Title
        Simple term for form/type/genre
        Name element
        Simple date of recording

Context and provenance area
    Context, provenance
    Archivist's note

Content and character area
    Content
        Date recording made or compiled
        Purpose and aims
        Performer, subject, circumstances
        Fuller caption or title
            Creator of work
            Performer(s)/speaker(s)

Authority by which recording made
  or compiled
Participation criteria
Copyright
Subjects covered
  Periods covered
  Site or place
  Personal or corporate names
  Events, activities
  Subject keywords
Recording:
  Date and location of recording
  Recordist
Physical and technical description
  Carrier
  Material
  Size
  Extent
  Duration
  Playback speed
  Other technical data
    Cross-reference to conservation sub-area

Management information area
  Process control sub-area
    Copies record
      Number and format of copies made
      Original recording retained/destroyed
      Processing carried out
        Cross reference to conservation sub-area
      Copyright record
  Conservation sub-area
    Previous history
    Repairs required
    Level of priority
    Routine processes required
    Other conservation data
      Cross-reference to administrative record

5   Rules for the use of data elements

This section contains a fuller explanation of the content of each data
element used in the description of sound archives.

5A *Identity statement area*
Reference code
As for general format.

An additional call number or reference may be needed if the sound materials are kept separately in specialized storage.

Title The title sub-area may contain three data elements:

(i) a simple term indicating the form, type or genre of the materials; generally 'sound recording'. A more detailed descriptive term, necessary for technical management, should be entered in the physical and technical description sub-area.

(ii) a name element, briefly identifying the principal subject, participants or project. E.g.

'Peggy Archer's recollections of the Second World War, 1985'.

(iii) a simple recording date
The purpose of the simple date in this element is to help give a clear immediate means of reference. It will usually be a simple year date, but day or month may be added if these are significant. More complex dates appear in the abstract.

The simple date refers to the date of the recording. A date which is part of the subject description should appear either in the name element of the title, or in the content sub-area.

The simple date should be omitted if it is not significant.

Examples:

Sound Recordings of House of Commons Debates, 1983–1985
Bolton Sands Oral History Project recordings
Recorded dialects of South Yorkshire, 1969
Sussex Bird Song recordings, 1934–1953
Recording of 'The World at One' (Radio 4), 17 June 1987
Week Ending (Radio 4) 1983–1986
Cassettes of 'Aida' rehearsals, 1937–1955
Cassette of 'Aida' rehearsal at Royal Festival Hall, 1951 June 7

5B *Context and provenance area*
Context and provenance
This area is provided in order to record the context of the sound recording and its relationship with other recordings or documents

which were associated with it because of the circumstances of their origination.

The provenance of the sound recording includes not only the circumstances of its creation but also its subsequent custodial history and its transfer to the repository (though if preferred this may be recorded in the management information sector).

Circumstances of recording

Date: give the full date if this is not provided in the identity statement.

The *purpose and aims* of the recording are given in a series of linked data elements:

Give the identity of the creator or originator of the material or project.

Record the authority, project or scheme responsible for the work: title, statement of aims and purposes. Note important features; e.g. if the recording was made for a specific reason not necessarily connected with the material recorded in the content summary e.g. recording of language or dialect, musical forms etc.; where research use may be related to the sound, nature or style of the recording rather than, or as well as, the information content. Include information on the intended audience of the recording.

Record the criteria which were laid down for participation in the creation of the work or in the project.

Archivist's note
Include information on the relationship of sets of sound recordings and of their arrangement in relation to the rest of the group or class, including special arrangements made by the repository.

Note the existence of any transcripts and their length in pages.

Note the existence of other finding aids to the recordings e.g. indexes or lists of broadcast material compiled by radio stations.

5C *Content and character area*
The content and character area has two sub-areas: content, and physical and technical description.

5C1 *Content sub-area*
The content sub-area is an abstract which contains data on the production of the recording, and its subject matter.

If the title element of the identity statement area is not sufficient to indicate the scope of the contents, a fuller or more complex caption or title should be given at the head of the abstract. This may be a derived title, with a note to explain the circumstances. After this initial sentence, the abstract continues with a summary of the content of the recording.

The sub-area is normally a free text entry, without limitation as to length. However, a contents analysis may serve to structure the information which would normally be given. The following structure demonstrates the use of the data elements supplied for this format.

The *subject coverage* of the recording is summarized in a series of linked data elements, as follows. The rule of information retrieval applies: that is, the text should contain all keywords required for indexing or searching. Authority files should be used if available.

Chronological period covered by the information. Full or complex dates may be used, or a general term for period, such as 'the Depression'; 'the Cold War period' etc.

Site, locality or place dealt with or mentioned in the recording. Local authority lists should be used if possible. (The place where the recording was made should appear in the context and provenance area).

Personal or corporate names mentioned in the recording; if not recorded with the contextual information, give the identity of the performer(s), the circumstances under which he, she or they were working, and/or the name of the occasion or project.

Events or activities mentioned in the recording;

Other subject keywords for retrieval or indexing.

Part description:
    express a fractional extent in forms such as:
      'on side 3 of 2 sound discs',
      'on reel 3 of 4 sound reels'
    and express the duration of the part as noted above e.g.
      'on 1 side of 1 disc (13 min.)'

Location of part/item on carrier.

Indicate where on the carrier the subject of the description is to be found. Use terms such as:

disc: side, band, cut
tape: reel, track, cut

5C2 *Physical and technical description*
This sub-area is intended to provide for information on the physical shape, size and character of the medium carrying the original sound recording (not copies). The general rule that any data element, sub-area or area may be left unused, still applies. Much of this information can be cross-referenced to the conservation sub-area. The technical part of the description should be precise enough to allow the materials to be played on suitable equipment.

Carrier: describe the material or object which contains, supports or presents the sound recording. Use terms such as:

cartridge
cassette
cylinder
disc (compact, direct-cut, optical)
tape (magnetic, video [used for sound])
wire

Other carriers should be specified, with detail if rare.[1] The adjective 'sound' should be inserted before the type of carrier if this is not obvious from the context.

Material/medium: indicate the substance from which the carrier (or that part of it which actually holds the message) is manufactured. Use terms such as:

Cassette: ferric oxide; chrome dioxide; metal particle coated.
Cylinder: brown wax; black wax; celluloid.
Disc: shellac; vinyl; aluminium.
Tape: paper; cellulose acetate; PVC; polyester.
  Cross-reference to conservation area.
Size: give the size, capacity or length of the carrier (not the length of the recorded sound).
In the case of a cassette, indicate the total possible playing time; for a

1. Examples are Tefitape and Amertape (sound on film); early magnetic discs; direct-cut metal discs; early non-Philips cassettes. Also encountered are tape of greater widths than standard quarter inch, and recordings with individual specifications produced by dictating equipment.

cylinder, give physical length and diameter, and (if known) total possible playing time; for a disk, give the diameter in centimetres; for a tape, physical length, spool diameter, or total possible playing time.

Cross-refer to the location record.

Extent: this data element refers to the total extent of the entity, which may extend over more than one carrier unit. Use terms such as number of sides, cassettes, reels.

Duration of recording   If readily available, give the exact total playing time of the recording in hours, minutes and seconds. Give an approximate duration in hours and minutes if the precise duration is unknown.

Playback speed.

Disc: rpm (revolutions per minute).
Open reel tape (and wire): ips (inches or centimetres per second according to in-house practice).
(cassettes play at a standard speed.)

Playback mode.

Give the information needed to identify the appropriate machine or method. Use terms such as:

monaural ("mono")
binaural
stereophonic ("stereo")
quadraphonic

Give any further technical data useful for the preservation or use of the materials. Not all this data is necessarily of interest to lay users. There may be cross-references to the conservation sub-area.

Precise technical details of disk pressings are unlikely to be available or necessary; the headings given below relate mainly to tape recordings, though it may be useful to give technical information on direct-cut disks and other media where available and appropriate.

Additional technical data elements may include:
Method of recording.
Use terms such as:

acoustic or electrical
analogue or digital

Quality of recording
Note the quality of the original recording before any filtering has taken place.

Make and model number of machine used to make recording.

Recording equalization standard e.g. IEC, NAB.

Machine settings e.g. Dolby B, DBX, limiter, (on Nagra) music setting, etc.

Recording speed.

Track configuration and recording mode.

Other recording equipment used (e.g. mixer, filtering device, noise reduction system).

Microphone details: make and model number; accessories (e.g. windshield, parabolic reflector (for wildlife recordings); microphone placement e.g. tipclip mike on lapel, crossed stereo pair, dummy head mounting, suspended overhead).

Other signal source e.g. direct input from house public address system; original recording played on <specification> tape or disk machine.

Tape details: make, type (e.g. single play, double play, or give manufacturer's reference number) and date of manufacture.

Manufacturer's trademark, catalogue number (including prefix and suffix, and, if considered of value to users) matrix number.

5D *Management information area*

5D1 *Process control sub-area*
Copies record
The original recording which came into the archivist's custody is not likely to be the one used to provide access. Record details of the archival copying process, including:

the number of reference or conservation copies made;

the transfer of the original recording into a different format;

whether the original recording has been retained or destroyed;

any processing (e.g. filtering) carried out.

Cross reference to conservation sub-area.

Indicate as clearly as possible the copyright position.

5G *Conservation sub-area*

This area contains further physical and technical details not within the public domain. Cross-reference to the physical and technical description sub-area may be necessary.

Entries in this sub-area may apply either to the carrier or to the recording, or to both.

Describe the previous history of the materials, including a note of storage conditions prior to transfer to the repository.

Record the current state of carriers and containers, and note any repairs or conservation measures needed.

Indicate the level of priority accorded to the group/class or item.

Record routine processes to be carried out, including inspection, rewinding, cleaning, or the creation of conservation copies.

The conservation record may follow that of the general finding aids, including a record of the identity of conservators responsible for work, start and finish dates, the nature of any conservation activity, and recommendations for future action. A record of materials used may be added, and a record of any specific funding.

APPENDIX III

NSA CODE OF PRACTICE FOR TRANSFERRING 'ACETATE' DISCS

Introduction

This paper describes the operational principles to be followed by freelance operators undertaking work for the National Sound Archive in the financial year 1988–9. The work will comprise transferring sound from so-called 'acetate' discs (actually cellulose nitrate) to quarter-inch magnetic tape.

1 General principles

1.1 Operators are reminded that the purpose of the exercise is to ensure the preservation of the *sound*, and nothing should be done which destroys any audible part of the wanted sound.

1.2 Each item should be considered from the point of view of the producer of the original sound. For example, if the item is a radio programme, you should attempt to reproduce the radio programme in its entirety so that it runs continuously without any breaks; the original dynamic range and frequency response should be conserved; but any interference to these ideals caused by the recording or reproduction processes should be undone as far as possible.

1.3 Operators should make every effort to get those parts of the reproduction process which cannot be adjusted later right first time. They must use the correct stylus-shape and dimensions, the optimum playing-weight, and a turntable without any audible vices. Electronic groove-wall selection cannot be applied to a copy, so you should use this facility if you have it; but you may be tempted to use other tools such as declickers or filters. If so, these tools must not be applied in such a way as to prevent better tools being used on the copy at a later date, and such tools must only be used according to 3.3 below.

1.4 Operators should not restrict the frequency range except in the following circumstances. You may occasionally come across discs with a great deal of rumble, or excessive high-frequency noise. Analogue tape-recording can result in intermodulation distortion, which in effect adds noise to the middle of the frequency range. (You may be familiar with the effects under the names 'blasting', 'quockling', or 'breakup'.) You are permitted to apply high-pass or low-pass filters to reduce such effects. The frequency of cutoff should be chosen by careful listening, preferably using headphones in the case of low-frequencies. The ear can hear sounds behind background-noise which cannot be separated by any present-day electronic filters, so if you can set a filter so that it does not affect the audible wanted sound, you may do so. (And see 3.3. below.)

1.5 Every effort should be made to ensure accurate documentation of the copies, both by the written word and in spoken announcements. Assume we have not listened to the discs; we are relying on you to extract all the definite information you can from the content. Many are off-air recordings, for example; listen for the BBC announcer or characteristic off-air quality, and log the fact.

1.6 Operators are free to take any steps to ensure faithful reproduction (e.g. correcting speed errors), but if the techniques vary from the norm to be described later, they must always be recorded in the documentation.

1.7 Operators are free to decide how to use their time, but I shall not look favourably upon a lot of time being spent on refining the sound or the documentation. If you are tempted to spend more than twice the original running-time doing work over-and-above what this code of practice deems essential, please consult me first.

2   The source material

2.1 Most of the acetates will be coarse-groove 78 rpm, with a few microgroove 33s. They will all have been cut by commercial studios. They will be supplied in numerical order as they come off the shelf, the numbers being in the range 1 to 1300, written upon large rectangular labels attached to the top righthand corner of the sleeve. Please return them in the same order; but you should actually copy them in the order which most satisfies 3.5 below. Gaps in the numerical sequence are caused by the appropriate discs having already been copied at the NSA.

2.2 The following suggestions will be valid for most of the 78s. They should be reproduced to the so-called 'Blumlein' equalization curve, which has no treble de-emphasis, and bass-lift of 6dB/octave starting at 300Hz. (Operators are free to vary this if it sounds wrong, but must document the fact.) If listening tests show that inadequate radius-compensation was used on multiside items, causing an abrupt change in treble response at the side-change, the response may be tweeked empirically to minimize this without being documented, provided the outside edges of the discs meet the norm.

2.3 Unless you are very used to handling acetates, you should follow this procedure for dirty records. Brush any loose matter away. Make a transfer of the disc complete with its remaining dirt using the lightest possible playing-weight to minimize pressing the dirt into the grooves. This provides a safety-net if the disc should be damaged in the cleaning process. The disc can then be washed in lukewarm water with a little detergent added. Do not scrub the surface in any way, the lacquer is very soft. Remove large particles (which might cause a pickup to jump) with manual assistance, otherwise dirt should be dislodged only by the flow of the water. Do not allow lime to form on the disc as it dries. This can be avoided by rinsing with demineralized water, drying between sheets of blotting-paper, or by playing the record while it is still wet. Once the record is free from particulate matter, the playing-weight should be increased to optimize the signal-to-noise ratio, and another tape-copy should be made. Compare the two, and submit the better one to the NSA. If you wash a disc, don't put it back in a dirty sleeve! New inner sleeves will be provided, and if the whole thing will then fit inside the original, please repack it that way; if not, return the disc in its new bag and throw away the original (unless it has documentation on it). If you are unable to wash the disc without the risk of the label coming off or the ink running, note down the documentation before you start! If a label *does* become detached, always enclose it with the disc.

2.4 I am aware that there are many acetates which are copies of commercial gramophone records, but I am also aware many might be alternate takes or 'pilot performances' which we shall definitely want copied. May I ask you to act intelligently and listen out for the characteristic noise of a shellac 78 dubbed to acetate and ring me if you think it's a dubbing of a published disc so I can check we already have two originals? There are also many transfers, of rare acoustically-recorded material; here we are unlikely to own two copies so we *shall* want transfers.

2.5 As you complete each disc, please stick a small yellow label (supplied) to the bottom righthand corner of its sleeve. We shall add the tape number later.

3 The tape copies

3.1 All tapes should be recorded on NSA-supplied Zonal Type 675 at 7.5 inches per second, recorded to the IEC (70 microsecond) characteristic. An NSA level/frequency response/azimuth tape will be loaned if required, but it may be sufficient to note that NSA levels are exactly 4dBs below current BBC levels.

3.2 Copying should be done in duplicate. The monitored copy should be called the 'archive copy' and the other the 'Playback copy'. It is preferable that one tape should not be a dubbing of the other, but if this is unavoidable the original should be designated the 'archive copy.'

3.3 If you wish to perform de-clicking or filtering, you should apply them only to the playback copy. The archive copy must not carry these processes, but you may reduce the signal volume to prevent side effects as long as the volume is kept constant for the whole item and you log it.

3.4 Twin-track recording should be the norm, starting at the head on the upper track, and returning from the tail on the other track. All the source material is mono, and the only exception concerns items which cannot be fitted onto two tracks for one reason or another, e.g. a long continuous item, or the end of a batch of items which do not fill the last reel. In these cases, the recording should be done on both tracks in parallel.

3.5 Operators are free to choose the reel size (7-inch or 10½-inch) according to the following principles:1 Continuous items should not be broken up unnecessarily. 2 Items of a similar character should be put on the same spool; do not intermix wildly different items. (The broad principle is to keep each reel relevant to a particular NSA curator.) 3 Do not put so many items on a single track that it is difficult to find an item or to write the details on the tape box. 4 Do not waste time attempting to use every inch of tape. If the tape runs out while you are dubbing an item, you must then erase the incomplete version and start again on another track.

3.6 Tapes should have a white leader at the head and a red trailer at the tail. Apart from the splices for these, there must be no splices in the tapes; all editing must be done by drop-in procedures. When there are 'overlap' changeovers, choose the disc with the better quality as far as possible. If you cannot do drop-ins, you may cut and splice a previous-generation tape (preferably 15ips full-track), which should be copied to form the archive and playback copies. We should like to take delivery of any such previous-generation tapes as well, but they require only minimal written documentation.

3.7 All playback and archive tapes should commence at the head with the following tones : 5 seconds or so of 1kHz, two or three seconds of 6kHz, and not less than ten seconds of 10kHz. These should all be at NSA level.

3.8 Spoken announcements should precede each item. (An 'item' in this context may be considerably less than, or more than, a disc side. Put yourself in the position of the original producer. Is it supposed to run continuously or not?) The announcement should include any titles and reference numbers read verbatim from the label, the NSA acetate number(s), and any dates. Feel free to add further information if you know it, e.g. from playing the record or from scribblings on the sleeve or from any accompanying cue sheets, but say where it came from. This must especially be done where the information differs from what the label says, and where the copies may become confused later if such extra information is not given.

3.9 After each item has been copied, it should be followed by about five seconds of low-frequency tone at fairly high level. This provides a 'blip' which will cross the gap between the spooling tape and the rep-head so that playback staff can find where each item begins.

3.10 The tape box should carry as much documentation as possible, and it is vital to show what is on each track. NSA practice names the two tracks W and R, depending upon the colour of the leader they start with.Write in black non-fugitive ink; we shall be photocopying the boxes for our accessions registers, so do not sprawl your writing so that it won't fit onto an A4 page. You may use 'Snopake' if necessary. Do not write anything on the tape-box spine; we will be allocating reference numbers. Twin-track tapes should be supplied head-out, single-track tapes tail-out.

APPENDIX IV

NOISE REDUCTION

The noise-reduction systems most commonly used for magnetic recording are listed here without going into technicalities. There are two types of noise reduction. 'Single-ended' systems are used only for playback, taking advantage of various psychoacoustic phenomena to cut background noise while leaving the wanted sound as undisturbed as possible. Nevertheless, the wanted sound always *is* affected, so archivists should avoid single-ended systems on principle. The other type of noise reduction, 'double-ended' or 'reciprocal' systems, involves both 'encoding' and 'decoding' processes to make the signal less liable to noise. Since the encoding process always alters the wanted sound, decoding must be by means of the correct circuitry in order to recover the original.

'Reciprocal' methods work by increasing faint sounds when they are recorded so that they tend to drown the background noise. If the sounds are restored to their original strength on playback, the noise will go down as well. But psychoacoustic phenomena must still be utilized even when the wanted sound is successfully reconstituted. This is because the noise should not be heard to rise and fall distractingly in time with the sound, an effect known as 'modulation noise'. There are many parameters to be considered, such as different quantities of variation taking place at different points in the dynamic range, with different speeds of action, and affecting different frequencies, all to different tolerances; and cost is yet another factor!

The systems most commonly encountered will now be considered in chronological order of their introduction.

Dolby A

When Dolby A was introduced in 1966, great attention was paid to a design which affected the wanted sound as little as possible, since if the circuit had any audible side effects (for instance, because of a misaligned recording machine), sales would be considerably harmed. The effect on the recording was therefore somewhat subtle, and the casual listener might not realize the tape had been encoded

224

at all. However, all but the very first units incorporated a line-up tone generator whose output was recorded for calibration purposes, and the tone included a characteristic warble suggesting to the inexperienced ear that the tape had been catching on the flange of the spool. This tone is a sure sign that the following recording is Dolby A. The system has always been confined to professional recording environments, especially where multi-track tape was liable to multiply the effect of tape noise. For archivists, it also has the advantage that it mitigates incipient print-through, although it would be powerless to combat the disastrous print-through which might occur if a magnet were placed on top of the reel.

Dolby B

A simplified version for combating only high-pitched hiss, Dolby B was introduced in1970. Originally intended for domestic open-reel tape, licensees were prevented from using it for machines recording at 15ips to prevent confusion with Dolby A; but in 1971 its future was assured when manufacturers of prerecorded cassettes started using it to overcome the powerful hiss of slow-moving cassette tape. It has now become the *de facto* standard for cassettes, and most cassette-recorders now incorporate Dolby B circuitry. There are very few audible side effects, but some wildlife recordists do not like it because it works on high frequencies (which are needed more in wildlife recording than music or speech), and because it has proved difficult to maintain the performance of field recorders to a high enough standard. It has no direct effect on print-through levels; on the contrary, it may make print-through seem worse, because it removes hiss which might otherwise mask it.

Dbx

Dbx is a completely different system introduced in 1971 in which subtlety is sacrificed to power. No-one can mistake an uncoded tape for a coded one; both the frequency response and the dynamic range are radically affected. Tape hiss and print-through are virtually eliminated, but the wanted signal is rather prone to be accompanied by 'modulation noise', and any misalignment of the recording or reproducing machines is magnified twofold. The latter problem is particularly noticeable with low, almost subsonic, frequencies. In 1973 a modified version, Dbx II, was introduced. The new system ignored sounds at the extremes of the frequency range and was therefore more suitable for non-professional applications such as cassette tapes and LP discs. A Dbx I unit should decode a Dbx II tape and vice versa if there are no subsonics involved.

ANRS (Audio Noise Reduction System)

This is the Japanese Victor Co.'s answer to Dolby B, and very similar to it so far as decoding prerecorded tapes is concerned.

Dolby HX-Pro

Not in fact a noise-reduction system at all, Dolby HX-Pro is a piece of circuitry included in a tape recording amplifier to reduce distortion on high frequencies. It needs no action upon replay.

Dolby C

A modification of Dolby B, Dolby C was introduced for cassettes in 1982 to eliminate more hiss. When it works, it does so very successfully; but there have been cases where incompatibilities between machines result in disastrous failure of the system's 'transparency'. Dolby C does not affect print-through.

Dolby SR (Spectral Recording)

A more powerful noise-reduction system, Dolby SR was introduced in 1985 as an improvement on Dolby A, and aimed at the same market. Instead of the line-up tone with the warble, there is a loud hissing sound, which the decoder analyses to determine whether the intervening machinery was correctly aligned, and adjusts itself accordingly. This results in the most powerful and transparent noise-reduction system yet devised, which also virtually cures the symptoms of print-through.

APPENDIX V

GLOSSARY

Introductory note

This glossary of terms relating to sound recordings was first published as appendix III – tab B1 of *Audio preservation: a planning study*, compiled by the Associated Audio Archives Committee of the Association for Recorded Sound Collections. The need for a glossary in the present book was apparent from an early stage, but it seemed pointless to produce a separate and no doubt inferior compilation once the AAA's work had become available. Fortunately the Committee very generously agreed to the inclusion of their glossary here, subject to the points made in the third paragraph of this note.

The glossary has been reproduced as it appeared in the AAA study except for anglicized spellings and a few very minor textual changes introduced by the present publishers. It does not therefore relate directly to the terminology used in the main text of this book, though needless to say the variations are minor. Perhaps the only significant discrepancy is found under 'cellulose acetate' where the use of this medium as a coating for instantaneous discs is possibly overstated. Whereas 'reel' and 'spool' are used interchangeably in Britain under the definition given for 'reel', 'spool' appears to have a more specialized meaning relating to wire in the US. British readers seeking 'thermohygrograph' should look under 'hygrothermograph'.

The AAA Committee published the glossary as a work in progress, and allowed it to be reproduced here in the hope that readers might contribute comments and suggestions, so that the final version, when issued, would be truly comprehensive and international in it scope and usefulness. All contributions will be welcomed by the audio preservation project coordinator Elwood A. McKee, 118 Monroe Street no. 610, Rockville, MD 20850, USA.

Key: The number(s) following each term in this glossary refer to the following list (not alphabetical) of sources. The numbers mean that the term is listed and defined in that source. No numbers present imply that no sources listed the term.

Alphanumeric characters enclosed in brackets [] following each definition indicate the source(s) of the definition as in the following examples:

[6]   =   direct citation of definition in source no. *6*

[M6, 8]   =   *multiple* definition derived from source no. *6* and *8* combined

[O]   =   *original* definition provided by one or more participants in this study

[P6]   =   *paraphrase* of definition in source no. *6*

Sources

1 American National Standards Institute, *USA Standard: Acoustical terminology*, ANSI, New York, 1960.
2 Angus, Robert, Feldman, Leonard and Eisenberg, Norman, *The New world of audio, a music lover's guide*, Howard W. Sams & Co., Indianapolis, 1982.
3 Borwick, John (ed.), *Sound recording practice*, 2nd ed., Oxford University Press, London, 1980.
4 Canby, Edward Tatnall, Burke, C. G., and Kolodin, Irving, *The Saturday Review home book of recorded music and sound reproduction*, Prentice-Hall Inc., Englewood Cliffs, New Jersey, 1952.
5 Cooper, Jeff, *Building a recording studio*, 4th ed., Synergy Group Inc., Los Angeles, 1984.
6 Davis, Gary *et al.*, *The CAMEO dictionary of creative audio terms*, Creative Audio & Music Electronics Organization, Framingham, Mass., 1979.
7 Hurst, Walter E., and Delson, Donn, *Delson's dictionary of radio and record industry terms*, Bradson Press, Thousand Oaks, California, 1980.
8 Keene, Sherman B., *Practical techniques for the recording engineer*, Sherman Keene Publications, Hollywood, California, 1981.
9 Lowman, Charles E., *Magnetic recording*, McGraw Hill, New York, 1972.
10 Nisbett, Alec, *The Technique of the sound studio*, 3rd ed., Hastings House, New York, 1972.
11 Tall, Joel, *Techniques of magnetic recording*, Macmillan Co., New York, 1958.
12 Tremaine, Howard M., *Audio cyclopedia* 2nd ed., Howard W. Sams & Co., Indianapolis, 1969.
13 Woram, John W., *The Recording studio handbook*, Sagamore Publishing Co., Plainview, NY, 1976.
14 Alten, Stanley, *Audio in media*, 2nd ed., Wadsworth Pub. Co., Belmont, California, 1986.

15 Read, Oliver, *The Recording and reproduction of sound*, H. W. Sams, Indianapolis, 1949.
16 Frow, George L., and Sefl, Albert F., *The Edison cylinder phonographs*, George L. Frow, Sevenoaks, Kent, 1978.
17 Pickett, A. G., and Lemcoe, M. M., *Preservation and storage of sound recordings*, Library of Congress, Washington, D.C., 1959.
18 Rust, Brian, *Brian Rust's Guide to discography*, Greenwood Press, Westport, CT, 1980.

Glossary

abrasiveness 9
A relative measure of the roughness of tape and its effect on the wearing of a magnetic tape recorder head. [9]

AC bias 9
See **bias**

accidental erasure
The demagnetization of an already recorded magnetic tape through accidental means, causing loss of sonic content. This is usually brought about by mistakenly recording over a tape which has been recorded earlier, sometimes simply because the 'record' switch on the tape machine is activated instead of the 'play' switch. It can also be achieved by bringing an external magnetic field (from a motor, a vacuum cleaner etc.) into too close contact with stored tapes. [O]

acetate
See **cellulose acetate**

acetate base 6, 10, 13
Cellulose acetate, a material used as a tape base (i.e. the backing on which the magnetic oxide is carried). Tends to break rather than stretch when subjected to excessive stress. As a break can be mended easily and cleanly, whereas a tape which has been stretched beyond its elastic limit can only be cut out of the tape, acetate backings offer some insurance against mishandling. [10] However, the properties of polyester, especially Mylar, when used as a backing, offer many more benefits and acetate is no longer used. [O]

acetate disc 1, 3, 7, 10, 12
See **lacquer disc**

acoustical or **acoustic recording** 12
The earliest commercially practical method of recording by causing the sound waves to actuate a diaphragm to which is attached a stylus. The stylus bears on the recording medium and mechanically engraves or embosses a sound track corresponding to the impressed sound waves. This was the method used before the advent of electrical recording in the 1920s. Acoustical recording is also called mechanical recording.

Because the output of most of the instruments used for acoustical recording is low and a considerable amount of energy is required to obtain a satisfactory level on the record, horns were used to reinforce the acoustic output. [12] An acoustic recording also refers to the disc or cylinder produced through this method. [O]

additives 9

Materials added to the basic coating composition of discs and tapes to foster specific desired effects such as lessening friction, softening or plasticizing the binder, retarding fungus growth or making the coating conductive. [O]

air check 12

A recording made from a radio broadcast by means of a radio receiver. [12]

album

For sound recordings, a container for records or a container with one or more records. Prior to the introduction of long-playing (LP) microgroove records in 1948, recordings containing multiple-disc sets were frequently sold in book-like albums containing sleeves or envelopes for the individual records. Empty albums of different sizes with varying numbers of sleeves were also available to afford better appearance and protection for individual records which were usually sold in comparatively flimsy paper sleeves. Some (mostly) early long-playing, multiple-record sets were issued in albums, but most such sets have been issued in various types of sleeves inserted in boxes or slipcases. Starting about 1950, the term album has increasingly come to be used for single-disc record issues with multiple selections as well as multiple-disc sets. [O] *See also* **album number; box; set; slipcase**

album number

Manufacturer's/Producer's issue/catalogue/order number for most multiple-disc sets; the term is also used for some 'post-78 rpm' single discs. For multiple-disc sets, the album number was/is used instead of the individual record issue numbers for ordering purposes in most, but by no means all, cases. Sound archivists need to be aware also that during the '78 rpm era', particularly in Europe, even major manufacturers did not always assign album/set numbers to multiple-record sets or issue them with albums. [O] *See also* **issue number**

alignment 2, 3, 6, 12, 13

For tape recorders, refers to the correct adjustment of the tape head position with respect to the magnetic tape's path, and also adjustment of the recorder's electronics for the best frequency response. [6]

alignment tape 6, 13

A special tape recording for use in alignment and calibration of tape recorders and containing test tones at specified frequencies. [6] Also known as test tape.

aluminium disc

A form of direct or instantaneous recording in which the grooves containing the signal are cut directly into the metal base which has no coating (by the indentation method, not engraving – *see* **indentation recording**). Playback is usually attained with shaved wood, fibre or cactus needles. Used frequently in field recording before acetate discs and magnetic tape became the normal medium. [O]

Amberol 16

Trade name for a four-minute cylinder, made of a brittle, waxen composition, introduced by Edison in 1908. Too fragile for extensive repeated playing, they were not commercially successful and were replaced in 1912 by the very durable Blue Amberol cylinders which were moulded from a celluloid-like compound. [O]

ambience 2, 3, 5, 6, 14

The distinctive acoustical characteristic of a given concert hall, recording studio etc. It results from reverberations (multiple sound reflections) from the walls and ceilings. Rooms that lack ambience are said to be 'dead'. [6]

ambient noise 5

The average amount of noise in an environment, measured in decibels. [5]

Amertape

Trade name for sound recordings made by embossing fine grooves on 50-foot belts of clear 35 mm acetate film. Used by US armed services 1945–50. [O]

amplifier 6

A device in a sound system which alters the level of a signal (usually increasing, but not always) for recording purposes or for playback through speakers. [O]

amplitude 3, 5, 6, 7, 14, 15

Another term for 'level' or 'volume' of an electrical or acoustical signal. A measurement of the height of a waveform. [6]

analogue recording 3, 6, 7, 9, 14

1   Every sound recording is an analogue of its source sound pattern no matter how the recording was made or reproduced. An analogue is 'a thing or part that is analogous,' i.e. 'similar or comparable in certain respects'. Sound is emitted through a pattern of pressure variations which vary in pitch, intensity and duration. The capture, storage and reproduction of a source sound pattern involves the physical application of analogy – 'an explaining of something by comparing it point by point with something similar' – to the original sound and results in a reproduced sound pattern which is an analogue of the original source sound. [O] (Quotations from *Webster's New World Dictionary*, 2nd College ed., World Publishing Company, New York, 1972.)

2   A recording made by one of various methods of capturing and storing a continuous replica of the source sound pattern by tracing an analogous pattern in another medium. The most commonly used storage methods have been engraved or embossed modulated grooves, magnetic particle patterns, and optical film patterns. [O]

231

analogue-to-digital converter (ADC) 3, 6

An electronic device used at the input of digital audio equipment to convert analogue signals to digital values whose numbers represent the amplitude and frequency information, at each calculated time interval sampling, contained in the original analogue signal. [P6]

anchorage 9

The adhesive quality of the magnetic oxide coating to the tape base film. It can be measured by checking how easily the coating can be lifted from the backing with adhesive tape or a specially designed knife. [P9]

antibloom agent 9

An agent that prevents the magnetic coating of tape from shedding excess powdery residue. [9]

antifungus agent 9

An agent added to the coating compositions of discs and tapes to retard the growth of fungus. [P9]

anti-skating compensation 2

A method of centring the stylus in the record groove during playback of a disc by applying a force against its natural inclination to ride inward against the inner groove wall. This prevents the pickup and stylus from 'skating' (climbing over or riding on the top of the groove walls), and not tracking in the grooves. [P2]

antistatic element 9

A material, usually carbon black, used to make the coating of a disc or tape recording (blank, master or pressed) conductive, in order to prevent the buildup of electrical charges due to friction which lead to 'static' (distortion in playback). [P9]

asperity noise 6, 13

Literally, roughness noise. Hiss, caused by minute imperfections (asperities) in the surface of recording tape. [6]

audio spectrum 6, 7

The audible (to humans) portion of the electromagnetic wave spectrum that ranges approximately from 15 Hz to 20,000 Hz. [P7]

azimuth 3, 6, 9, 10, 12, 13, 14

Alignment of the recording and playback heads on a tape recorder so that their centre lines are exactly parallel with each other [9], and the angle of the head gap is at right angle to the direction of the tape travel. This is to obtain optimum high frequency response. [6]

backing (base) 6, 9, 10, 13

The base on which the magnetic oxide coating of tape is carried. It gives strength and permits flexibility, and its thickness insures that the physical separation of successive layers of the magnetic coating is sufficient to hinder print-through. Common materials are acetate, polyvinyl chloride and polyester (Mylar); paper was used in the early days of tape, and stainless steel has been tried. [P10] The base of a laminated disc is known as the core. [O] *See also* **core**

backing thickness 9

Thickness of the tape backing material: 1.5 or 1 mil is usual for audio, instrumentation, digital, and video; audio cassettes use down to 0.25 mil. [9]

bakelite

A synthetic resin developed in the early part of this century and widely used as a substitute for hard rubber or celluloid. It was used in the production of some phonograph records, and is almost identical to 'Condensite' used by Edison in the coating of his 'Diamond Discs'. [O]

band

See **cut**

base-film backing 9

See **backing (base)**

bass boost 6

An accentuation of lower audio frequencies in recording or rerecording, normally provided by an equalizer or tone control. [6] This is a questionable practice in archival rerecording. [O]

bias 2, 6, 9, 10, 12, 13, 14

A high frequency signal or current, several times that of the highest frequency to be recorded, that, when applied to magnetic tape along with the audio signal, results in a signal of low distortion and a considerable increase in the signal-to-noise ratio. It mostly vanishes from the tape soon after recording, by a process of self-demagnetization. [M10, 12]

biasing 1, 3

See **bias**

binaural 2, 3, 6, 12, 13, 14

A sound system consisting of two microphones at the point of sound pickup, placed in the same relationship to each other as the ears of a listener. The microphones are connected to separate amplifiers and transmit the sound to the listener through headphones. Each headphone is connected to its own amplifier. True binaural sound cannot be achieved with loudspeakers, only headphones. When loudspeakers are used, it is two-channel stereophonic sound. [12]

binder 1, 9, 12, 13, 15

A substance used to help the basic materials of a record compound (disc or tape) to adhere together. In magnetic tape, it is also used to keep the magnetic particles on the coating separate from each other. [M1, 9]

bit

As used in magnetic recording or computer technology, this represents one recorded information cell. [O]

blank groove 1

A groove made in a recording with no signal applied to the cutter, hence it has no sound content, also known as unmodulated groove. [1]

blank tape

Magnetic tape with no magnetization applied, and hence no sound, to be used for making a tape recording. The term 'blank' also refers to unrecorded cylinders and discs upon which modulated grooves will be cut. [O]

blocking (layer-to-layer adhesion) 9

The tendency for adjacent layers of tape on a reel to stick together, usually due to long-term storage under high humidity and temperature conditions. [9]

Blue Amberol

See **Amberol**

boomy 6, 10

Subjective description of a sound quality which has resonances in the low frequencies. Expressions with similar shades of meaning are tubby or, simply, bassy. [10]

box

As applied to sound recordings, the container for cylinder and piano roll recordings, later for tape recordings, and currently a jargon term for a multiple-disc set of records. [O]

boxy

Subjective description of a sound quality which fails to create an impression of the space and ambience of the original sound source and its environment. Usually applied to speakers, particularly small, inefficient systems with poor bass and off-axis response. [O]

bright 6

A subjective expression that usually describes a large amount of high frequency energy in a recording or playback system, or a sound reinforcement system. Sound which is too bright is considered to be shrill. [6]

bubble

Commonly used defect term for disc recordings. It is most often the result of faulty pressing. [O]

buckling 9

Deformation of the circular form of a roll of magnetic tape caused, generally, by a combination of adverse storage conditions or improper winding tension. Such deformation has a seriously detrimental effect on the quality of sound during playback. [P9]

buildup

A term referring to the accumulation of debris and magnetic particles deposited by magnetic tape on the heads of a tape recorder, which causes head-tape separation and an increase in friction. Solvent cleaning of the tape recorder heads will usually remove such buildup. [O]

bulk eraser 3, 6, 9, 10, 12, 13, 14

Also known as a degausser, this removes all traces of previously recorded signals from the magnetic emulsion of a tape and leaves it in a completely demagnetized state, quite important from the standpoint of minimizing both noise and distortion in reusing tape. Erasures made using a bulk eraser generally result in greater signal-to-noise ratio than those erased on a tape recorder through the erase head. [P12]

bump

Commonly used defect term for disc recordings, implying a raised surface on a portion of the playing area of the disc which could cause sonic distortion or groove jumping by the stylus. [O]

buzz 12, 15

A rasping noise heard in the background of a sound recording (disc or tape) that is generally caused by hum or noise in the playback system. [P12] In disc playback it can also be caused by imperfect or discontinuous contact of playback stylus in groove. [15]

calibrate 14

To adjust equipment, for example, a console and a tape recorder, with a standard so that their measurements are similar. [14] It usually refers to the technique of adjusting the VU meters on two pieces of audio equipment, for instance, a tape recorder and a control board, so that they will respond identically to a signal at a given voltage, or to the loudest portion of a recording to be dubbed. [O]

capstan 2, 3, 6, 9, 10, 12, 13, 14

A rotating shaft connected to the motor of a tape recorder that moves the tape at constant speed across the heads. [6]

carbon black 9, 17

An inert filler used to protect the basic resin in a record compound from the action of light by absorbing radiant energy. It is also used as an antistatic element in magnetic tape. [M9, 17]

cartridge 1, 2, 3, 4, 10, 14

1 The portion of a record player which contains the reproducing stylus and the electromechanical translating elements which convert the vibrations of the stylus into electrical energy for amplification and playback. Sometimes used interchangeably with the term pickup. The cartridge is usually attached to a removable portion of the record player's tone arm known as a head shell. [M1, 2, 14]

2 An endless loop of tape, sealed in a plastic container for use in tape players and recorders. Eight-track cartridges were popular for a short period of time until being successfully overtaken commercially by audio tape cassettes. [0]

cassette 2, 3, 7, 10, 12, 14

A compact tape-recording system that utilizes a length of recording tape (audio or video) and two hubs inside a sealed plastic shell. The best known versions are the compact cassette introduced in1964 and, today, the most frequently used form of tape for home recording and playback, and the video cassette for recording and playback over television. The tape used in the compact cassette is narrower and thinner and runs at a slower speed than the normal tape used in reel tape recording. [P2]

catalogue number

See **issue number**

cellulose acetate 10, 13, 14, 15

A material used as a tape base and also as the coating on a direct-cut lacquer disc. It is the most fungal resistant of the cellulosics, and, although the best instantaneous recording medium for many years until magnetic tape on a polyester base, it is an unstable medium with a limited storage life. [P15] The term 'acetate' is commonly used as a synonym for an instantaneous or direct recording as well. [O] *See also* **acetate base; lacquer disc**

cellulose nitrate 10

The first of the modern plastics which replaced cellulose acetate as a disc or cylinder recording medium. Also used in motion picture film, it is highly unstable and subject to oxidation and denitration. [P10]

centre (of disc)

That part of the surface of a disc recording circumscribed by the inmost part of the playing area and, when there is a label present, can be further defined as inside margin and label. [O]

centre start disc

This is a disc recording (usually vertically cut) which requires the pickup and stylus to move from the centre of the disc outward (having the beginning of its modulated groove at the outer edge of the inside margin). It is commonly abbreviated as C/S. [O]

centring of disc

1   The act of placing a disc on a turntable and lining up the centre hole with the central pin on the turntable. [O]
2   The accuracy of the location of the centre hole in a disc or tape reel or hub. [O]
3   The act in the manufacturing process for discs (during which the centre hole of the master is lost) in which a centre hole is located for the finished pressings. [O]

channel 1, 2

A single path for recording or reproducing sound. Independent recorders in a recording system, or independent tracks on a recording medium. For stereo sound, for instance, a separate left and right channel of information must be supplied to the listener. [M1, 2]

channel separation 2, 6

The degree to which sound signals on one channel are not picked up by an adjacent channel; electrical isolation. Good separation implies very little leakage (crosstalk). [6]

chatter 15

An erratic 'spotted' pattern in record grooves with short alternate light and dark strips. It is caused by a poor cutting stylus or one set at a wrong angle. Too deep a cut in thin disc coating may also produce a similar effect, which is most likely to occur close to the centre of the record. [15]

chief source of information

For cataloguing purposes, 'the chief source of information' for each container or major type of sound recording is set out here:

TYPE	CHIEF SOURCE
Container	Container

Cylinder	Embossed edge, rim or inside margin
Disc	Label on disc
Drum	Label on drum
Roll (piano, organ etc.)	Label on roll
Sound recording on film	Label on reel
Tape (cartridge)	Label on cartridge
Tape (cassette)	Label on cassette
Tape (reel-to-reel)	Label on reel
Wire	Label on spool

For types of sound recordings not listed above, the chief source of information is the label or label-equivalent on the sound carrier. 'If information is not available from the chief source of information, take it from the following sources (in this order of preference), specifying in a note the alternate source: container (sleeve, box etc.); accompanying textual material; other sources; sound data on the recording.' Quotations from: *Rules for Archival Cataloging of Sound Recordings*, Association for Recorded Sound Collections, copyright 1980.

chip
Commonly used defect term for disc or cylinder recordings. It usually refers to a small missing piece from the edge or rim of the recording, while dig or gouge refers to a pit or small break in the horizontal surface further in from the rim. [O]

chrome tape 6
See **chromium dioxide**

chromium dioxide 3, 12, 14
A compound of magnetic particle oxide used as a coating on some magnetic tape, especially cassette tape. Such tape has significantly better signal-to-noise ratio and response to short wavelengths at lower speeds than that usually employed for a given type of recording. It is also used in video recording and computer tapes. [P12, 14]

cinching 9
Longitudinal slippage between the layers of magnetic tape in a tape pack when the roll is accelerated or decelerated. This can cause tape breakage or permanent deformation. [P9]

clipping 3, 6
Form of very audible distortion produced by the capabilities of an amplifier being exceeded (known as overload). [M3, 6]

coarse groove
Term used to describe the type of groove size prevalent in cylinder and most 78 rpm recordings, as opposed to the 'microgroove' used in contemporary LP recordings. [O]

coating 9, 10
1 The layer of finely divided magnetic material, bonded in plastic and polished to allow smooth flow over the tape heads, that carries the magnetically recorded signal in tape. Ferric (iron) oxide and chromium dioxide are both used as the recording medium. [10]

237

2   The outer layer on a laminated disc or cylinder in which the grooves are cut. [O]

coating thickness 9
The thickness of the coating applied to the base of magnetic tape or the core of a laminated disc or cylinder. In general, thin coatings on magnetic tape have excellent resolution at the expense of reduced output at long wavelengths. Thick coatings give high output at long wavelengths at the expense of resolution. [P9]

coating transfer
Refers to the transfer of material from one layer of tape (front side) to another layer (back side) during storage in a wound pack or reel. This can cause loss of sound during playback or excess deposit (buildup) of the transferred material onto the tape heads. [O]

coefficient of hygroscopic expansion 9
The relative expansion in dimension of a disc or tape (or base material of a tape) per percent increase in relative humidity, measured in a given humidity range. [P9]

coefficient of thermal expansion 9
The relative increase in dimension of a disc or tape (or base material) per degree rise in temperature, measured in a given temperature range. [P9]

coercivity 6, 9, 12, 13, 14
The magnetic force field necessary to reduce a tape from saturation to full erasure, expressed in oersteds. [14]

compact disc 14
A new recording medium, introduced commercially in 1983, consisting of a disc, 4¾ inches in diameter, made principally of plastic, coated with a reflective layer of microthin aluminium and a protective layer of lacquer. It is recorded and played on one side only and can yield up to 72 minutes of playing time per side. The sonic content consists of digitally encoded sets of numbers translated into minute pits that are etched into the reflective layer of the disc and 'read' from inside to outside by a laser light beam as the disc revolves at constant velocity at speeds ranging from 500 to 200 rpm. Claims for this new format include greater dynamic range, elimination of surface noise, wow and flutter, and immunity from wear caused by direct contact, dirt and scratches. [O] *See also* **laser disc**

compliance 2, 10, 12, 14
The ease with which a stylus moves from side to side and up and down in the record groove. [14]

component demagnetization
See **demagnetization**

concentric groove 1
Also known as locked groove or end groove. A blank (unmodulated) and continuous groove in a disc at the end of the modulated or recorded groove(s) whose function is to prevent further travel of the pickup (tone arm) toward the centre of the disc by creating a lock or block to end the

travel of the pickup in the revolving groove. [P1] *See also* **eccentric groove**

Concert Cylinder 16

A large-diameter cylinder record made by Edison-Columbia, Edison Bell and others under various designations from 1899. Having a higher linear speed, these records emitted a greater volume. Although rendered obsolete by Edison's Gold Moulded process, they continued to be made by dubbing until 1907. Their approximate size was 4¼ inches in length, external diameter of 5 inches, the inside tapering from 4¼ inches to 4 ⅜ inches. [16]

conductive coating 9

Coating that is treated to reduce electrical resistance and thus prevent the accumulation of static electrical charge. Carbon black is often used for this purpose. [9] *See also* **antistatic element**

constant torque winding/spooling

Winding magnetic tape at a steady controlled tension to eliminate a buildup of tension on the tape that could cause deformation. This is in contrast to fast winding or rewinding which creates an uneven and steadily increasing tension on the tape. [O]

core 1

The basic support or central layer of material in a laminated disc or cylinder. In acetate (lacquer) discs, for example, it can be metal, glass or fibre. [P1]

cps (cycles per second)

See **hertz (hz)**

CR

'Created role': commonly used designator in discographical writing to indicate a named artist was the first performer of the work cited. [O]

crack

Commonly used defect term for disc and cylinder recordings. It usually refers to a complete fissure through the entire recording visible on both sides and will cause noticeable distortion or faulty tracking in playback. A patina crack is a smaller fissure which does not penetrate through the recording but probably causes a break in the modulated groove. [O]

crackle

The distorted sound created usually because of a buildup of electrostatic charge on the surface of a sound recording, but also because of dust or foreign material permanently embedded in the grooves, or on the surface of the tape. [O]

crazing

The deformation of a laminated disc coating layer through cracking. Can be caused by loss of plasticizers, by excess heat and/or humidity etc. [O]

created role

See **CR**

creep

1 The physical deformation of disc recordings due to continuous load

pressure either from improper storage or from the force of gravity. It results in both surface imprint from packaging materials, which can impair fidelity by the deformation of the groove walls, and disc warpage.

2   In magnetic tape this refers to the residual deformation of the tape such as curling or longitudinal curvature which remains even after removal of tension caused by improper winding and storage. [O]

cross linking 17

The binding together of adjacent chain molecules in polyvinyl chloride (vinyl) by primary valence bonds which is manifested by embrittlement, warping and cracking. Usually caused by exposure to ultraviolet light or to heat. [17]

crosstalk 1, 3, 6, 9, 10, 11, 12, 13, 14

Undesired signal appearing in one channel as a result of leakage from another channel [6]. In magnetic tape, it is the leakage of signal from one track to another track. [O]

C/S

Commonly used defect indicator for disc recordings. [O] *See* **centre start disc**

cupping 9

See **curl**

curing 7

A manufacturing process whereby blank acetate discs (lacquers) are gradually cooled. These 'green' and 'unripe' discs are stored in such a way so as to allow the thinner on them to evaporate properly. They are placed in a temperature-controlled environment to achieve a uniform hardness and flat even surface. [7]

curl

The transverse warping of magnetic tape, or literally 'curling', usually caused by the difference in properties between the base and the coating which react separately to heat, humidity or simple ageing. This can cause improper contact between the tape and the playback heads leading to signal loss. It can also cause cracking or flaking of the coating. [O]

cut 3, 14, 15

1   To make a disc recording. [O]

2   To decrease the level of amplitude in recording. [14]

3   Portion of the recorded surface on a disc separated by a marker space or scroll (increased groove pitch to mark the separation of two successive bands of recording), and containing a rill, or linking groove. Also known as 'band', or 'selection'. [P3]

cutting through 15

Refers to the stylus cutting through the coating of a disc and into the base material. [15]

cycles per second 3, 6, 10, 12, 14

See **hertz (Hz)**

cylinder 16, 18

The recording format invented and patented by Thomas Edison. Originally made of grooved brass around which a sheet of tin foil was wrapped (the signal was embossed into the foil), then wax, and later celluloid. Hollow, tube shaped, with vertically modulated grooves containing recorded material on the outside surface. The inside was usually ribbed and slightly tapered to grip the mandrel of the playback or recording machine. Playback speed was approximately 160 rpm (sometimes 180 rpm). Those with 100 tpi (threads or grooves per inch) lasted two minutes, and those with 200 tpi lasted four minutes. No longer produced after 1929. There were many different types or makes of cylinders produced during the life span of the Edison Phonograph Company, including White Wax, Brown Wax, Gold Moulded, Concert, International Correspondence Schools Cylinders, Amberol, and Blue Amberol. [P16]

DAT
See **digital audio tape**

data density
The number of data characters stored per unit length of tape. [O]

DBX 3, 7
A trademarked noise-reduction system designed to eliminate 'hiss', a noise inherent in the tape-recording process. This allows for increased recording levels without increased tape 'hiss', resulting in higher fidelity recordings. [7]

decibel 2, 3, 4, 5, 6, 7, 8, 10, 13, 14
The measuring unit of sound pressure and hence loudness (abbreviated as dB). The decibel is actually a numerical ratio between the sound pressure of a given sound and the sound pressure of a reference sound. Common decibel levels encountered vary from the rustling of grass (15 dB) to conversation (50 dB), to live rock groups (110 dB) to jet plane engines at close range (130 dB). [5]

de-emphasis 3, 6, 12
Also known as post-emphasis or post-equalization. Refers to altering the frequency characteristics (i.e. equalizing) of a signal during recording or playback. [P12]

degaussing
See **demagnetization**

delamination
The loss of adhesion between layers of a laminated cylinder, disc or tape caused by poor fabrication, exposure to fungal attack, or extremes of temperature and humidity, i.e. the peeling or flaking of the acetate layer on a lacquer disc. [O]

demagnetization 13
1 The erasure of magnetic tapes by neutralizing the oxide particles in the tape coating, achieved through a high frequency current passing through an erase head over which the tape passes, or through the use

of a bulk eraser. Accidental demagnetization can occur when stray, external magnetic fields come into contact with the tape.

2 The neutralizing of the heads and other parts of a tape recorder which come into contact with the tape to prevent magnetic buildup which can erase or demagnetize the tape. [O]

demagnetizer 6

An AC electromagnet used to neutralize magnetism in recorder heads, guides, tape etc. [6] *See also* **bulk eraser**

denitration

Degradation of cellulose nitrate materials due to the conversion of nitrogen peroxide into nitrous acid by moisture, which in turn has a further autocatalytic reaction on the original compound. [O]

Diamond disc 16

The name given to a double-sided record, marketed by the Edison Company from 1913 to 1929 and intended for playing solely on one of the range of Edison Disc Phonographs, supplied with a diamond stylus reproducer made especially to play the vertical-cut records. They revolved at 80 rpm and were mostly 10 inches in diameter. They were surfaced with an early type of plastic called 'Condensite' and were claimed to be resistant to warping. Weighing 1 pound apiece and being ¼ inch thick, they are readily recognizable. [16]

dig

Commonly used defect term for disc and cylinder recordings, used interchangeably with 'gouge'. [O] *See* **needle dig**

digital audio tape (DAT)

Refers to magnetic tape which can be digitally encoded with sound from a source using the digital recording process and played back on a machine capable of 'reading' or decoding the tape. DAT is most commonly interpreted as a new cassette format introduced in 1987 for the mass consumer market which makes it possible to make and play back digital recordings in the home. [O] *See also* **digital recording**

digital optical recording (DOR)

Refers to a recording made through the digital recording process onto a disc which has the digital data stored on its surface as a series of tiny pits that can be detected by a focused laser beam for playback purposes. It is capable of storing both audio and visual material. Both digital audio tape and digital optical discs employ similar encode/decode techniques. Their differences are in the manner and density of data storage and playback technology. Primarily intended for archival storage at this time, digital optical disc recording has the potential, for challenging digital tape recording for general purposes in the future. [O] *See also* **digital recording; laser disc**

digital recording 3, 6, 7, 14

A sound recording made by the digital recording process whereby the source sound (or in some instances its analogue) is transduced/transformed into continuously variable voltages; the voltage amplitude is measured upwards of 44,000 times per second; each measured sample is converted into a binary number; the binary number string is stored, most commonly on magnetic tape, although other digital storage devices may be, and have been, used. For dissemination purposes the number string may be duplicated on digitally formatted magnetic tape, or laser disc (*see* **compact disc; laser disc**), or converted back into continuously varying voltages which drive a disc-record cutting stylus or analogue tape-recording head. Reproduction of any of these recording formats involves tracing or 'reading' the stored pattern and converting it to varying voltages which cause a speaker diaphragm to emit a pattern of sound pressures which resemble the original sound. [O]

digital-to-analogue converter (DAC) 3, 6

An electronic device used at the output of digital audio equipment to convert digital numbers representing level and frequency information back to a continuously varying analogue electrical signal for playback. [6]

direct recording 15

See **instantaneous disc**

direct-to disc recording

Refers to a type of contemporary record production which eliminates intermediate taping stages and other procedures (multichannel taping, mixdown, special equalization etc.) and returns, in a sense, to the form of disc recording in use before World War II, engraving the analogue of the signal directly onto a blank master disc. There are claims of improved sonic quality in this method. [O]

discography

Derived from the Greek words meaning disc and to write, this is 'a term concerned with the description, listing and study of sound recordings. It may be defined as the method and practice of describing sound recordings; a listing of sound recordings according to the procedures of this method and practice; or the study of one or more aspects of sound recordings in historical or other context. In current usage the term may be applied to all types of sound recordings: disc, tape, wire, cylinder, piano and organ rolls, and audio-visual media.

In order to define a sound recording sufficiently, a full discography contains the details of the music, performance, recording, etc., details of the type of recording and sometimes comments on the actual content.' Although most discographies provide a varying degree of information on the listed recordings, the ideal discography would contain composer/author of selection, title (including edition details), performer(s), name of label, name of manufacturer, name of series, issue number, matrix number, take number, patent and copyright information, date of recording and issue, duration, language of text, location of recording studio, and full physical description of the artifact itself. Some types of discographies are subject groupings by type of music, listings of recordings of the works of one composer or performer, listings of a country's recordings, listings of a manufacturer's output etc. (The above quoted or derived from *The New Grove Dictionary of Music and Musicians*, vol. 5, Macmillan Publishers Limited, London, 1980; article on *Discography* by Edward E. Colby.)

distortion 2, 3, 4, 6, 7, 9, 10, 13, 14

Unwanted changes of sound quality, in the frequency response, or by the generation of unwanted products. [10] There are many different types of distortion (harmonic, intermodulation, transient etc.). In general it can be caused by inadequate playback or recording equipment, by the poor manufacture of a sound recording, or by factors during the recording process. [O]

documentation

The following definition is quoted from Appendix I TAB B-4: 'For the purposes of this study the term documentation, when applied to sound recordings, is understood to comprise all available information which purports to identify or make more fully comprehensible the audio event(s) captured on one or more sound recordings. For the purposes of preservation of sound recordings, such documentation should be:
- factual insofar as the preservation and conservation of the artifact is concerned, and
- available without recourse to playing any sound recording even when the identifying or explanatory information was originally communicated verbally by means of a recording.'

Dolby 3, 7, 10, 12

A noise reduction system named after its inventor. It is used primarily in tape recording to provide a higher signal-to-noise ratio to be used partly to reduce hiss, hum and rumble, and also (by lowering recording levels a little) to produce less distortion and to lower the danger of print-through. [10] The original Dolby A system was designed for professional use. Later systems (Dolby B and Dolby C) were developed for the consumer market as well. They all operate by increasing the volume of the passages that are closest to the noise producing frequencies and are lowest in level during recording, and, during the decoding, bringing these increased passages back to their original levels, which reduces the noise. [O]

drive holes 1, 15

Three holes, usually in instantaneous disc recordings, spaced around the centre hole, which engage the drive pins on a turntable to prevent a disc from slipping. [15]

dropout 2, 3, 6, 9, 10, 12, 13, 14

Any tape-caused phenomenon that results in temporary or permanent loss or reduction of signal (sound) for a specified length of time. The most prominent cause of dropouts is surface contamination, where a piece of oxide shed or foreign particle adheres to the surface of the tape and lifts the tape from the head. [9] Dropout can also refer to loss of signal during a radio or television broadcast, or to temporary loss of signal for electronic or electrical reasons during recording or playback. [O]

D/S

A commonly used abbreviation to describe a double-sided disc recording. [O]

dub (dubbing) 1, 2, 3, 6, 7, 10, 12, 14, 15, 18

A copy of a sound recording, e.g. a transfer of sound from a disc recording to magnetic tape. It can also refer to the combining of two or more recordings into a single recording, or several tracks recorded at different times into a single recording. Before the introduction of electrical recording in 1925, dubbing was accomplished by one of two primary methods: (1) a mould was taken of the source recording and new manufacturing parts generated from the mould – in the case of discs, this method was used almost exclusively by early record pirates; (2) the source recording was copied pantographically (mechanically) with further copies generated from the initial copy. Early cylinders and discs generated from master cylinder recordings (e.g. Pathé) used this latter technique. It was also used on occasion to generate new masters and stampers from copies of lateral-cut recordings as the result of damage or loss of original manufacturing parts. Obviously, it too was used by early forgers and record pirates. After the introduction of electrical recording, dubbing was accomplished by feeding the signal from the source recording directly to a disc-cutting head, or still later, to a magnetic tape recording head. [O]

Durinoid

A semi-flexible shellac composition manufactured by the Durinoid Corp. of New Jersey and used by Emil Berliner as a substitute for vulcanite in his disc stamping process. [O]

Dust bug

A well known record cleaning product manufactured by Cecil Watts Ltd., of England. It consists of a podium, a carrying arm, and two brushes (rolling and stationary) which track the disc during playback ahead of the stylus. [O]

dust jacket

See **slipcase**

dynamic range 3, 6, 9, 10, 12, 13, 14

The range of volume of a sound recording or a program. It may be measured as the range of peak values (the difference between maximum and minimum volumes) or the range of average volume. [10]

eccentric groove 1

A locked groove whose centre is other than that of the disc generally used to trigger mechanical operation of the pickup or tone arm. [P1] *See also* **concentric groove**

echo (pre and post)

An 'echo' of a particular sound signal which, on a disc, may appear in the groove before or after that which carries the playing signal. This is due to the gradual relaxation of molecular tensions which occurs after the record has been pressed, and causes plastic deformation of the groove walls. On tape it occurs one turn of the tape before or after normal signal, and is caused by print-through. [10]

edge (of disc or cylinder) 10
In a disc recording, the edge is the narrow vertical surface at the circumference of the horizontally held disc. In a cylinder recording, it is the end with the larger diameter. [O]

edge flake
Commonly used defect term for disc or cylinder recordings. Refers to the peeling or flaking of coating material from the vertical edge of a disc or cylinder. Edge flake can occur more easily than surface flake and causes no damage to the sonic content of the recording. However, it is a signal that the remainder of the coating layer is in danger of deterioration. It is commonly abbreviated as EF. [O] *See also* **flaking**

edge fluting
A rippling deformation along the edges of magnetic tape brought about because the edges of the tape are exposed to the environment while the centre is not. It is similar to curling and can be created by heat or humidity, or by the tape rubbing unevenly against the containing reel sides (flanges) during playing, winding or recording. [O]

EF
Commonly used defect indicator for disc and cylinder recordings. *See* **edge flake**

elasticity 14
The capacity to return to the original shape or place after deflection or displacement. [14] In tape, this would be the material's capacity to 'unstretch' after handling or winding; in discs, the capacity of the groove walls to return to their original shapes after playing. [O]

electrical or electric recording 12, 18
The system of recording introduced on a large scale in 1925 by the major labels (Victor, Columbia, and later Brunswick) that involves the use of a microphone and amplifier. It replaced acoustical recording. Simply put, it is the conversion of acoustical sound waves from a source into electrical energy, an image of which is transduced into a modulated groove of the recording and later reconverted into acoustical sound waves through the playback system. All sound recording since that date has depended on some form of electrical recording. [O]

electrostatic charge
The buildup on tape or disc surfaces of electrical charges through friction, or the combination of heat and dryness, which results in static distortion in playback. It also causes dust to be attracted to the disc surface and, if severe enough, can seriously interfere with the performance of the cartridge/pickup. [O]

embossed recording 12, 15
A form of cylinder, disc, belt, or film recording in which the coating material is displaced by the cutting stylus and shoved upward, appearing as two small ridges at the edges of the grooves. The frequency response

of such recordings is rather limited, and the signal-to-noise ratio will vary with different types of recording materials. [P12]

engraved recording 12

The most common form of disc recording in which some of the disc-coating material is removed from the disc as the cutting stylus is making the grooves. [12]

equalization 1, 2, 3, 6, 10, 12, 13, 14, 15

The process of modifying the amplitude/frequency response in a recording and reproducing system to produce flat overall characteristics, minimize noise or give an 'artistic' effect. [3] There are different types of equalization such as frequency correction, diameter etc. [O]

equalizer 4, 5, 6, 7, 12, 13, 14

A signal processing device that can boost (amplify), cut (attenuate), or 'shelve' portions of the audio frequency spectrum during recording. It can be used to alter the sound of a recording when making a copy. [P6, 14] There are many kinds of equalizers, serving different functions: fixed frequency; graphic; paragraphic; parametric; peaking; shelving, etc. [O]

erase head 1, 2, 3, 6, 10, 12, 13, 14

A device on a tape recorder used to obliterate any previous recording or magnetic field on the tape. It is activated when the tape recorder is in the 'record' mode. [O]

erasure

See **bulk eraser; demagnetization**

etching

See **fungal etching**

extender

Organic material blended with basic resins in recordings usually for economic reasons; natural waxes, wood resins, plant fibre resin etc. [O]

See also **filler**

exudation

The process, or the product of the process, in which material is emitted or oozes from an object, usually applied to the decomposition (and its products) of disc or tape material. [O]

fast wind 9

The winding of tape at high speed, usually done to remove a partially-played tape from a playback machine in faster time than simply letting it play out at a constant playback speed. This creates a tension in the tape which may cause deformation (i.e. stretching) that could be permanent if stored in this condition. [O]

ferric oxide 6, 9, 13

A form of iron oxide (rust), whose chemical formula is $Fe_2 O_3$. Also known as magnetite. The magnetic particles in most open-reel recording tapes are composed of finely ground and graded ferric oxide. [P6]

fidelity 6, 7, 11

A subjective term used to describe the degree of faithfulness with which recorded and reproduced (or broadcast) sound copies the original. [O]

field recording 18

A recording made under abnormal conditions, such as with a portable recording instrument (cylinder phonograph, wire recorder, disc cutter, or tape recorder). Much valuable recording of folk music, blues, jazz, and other forms has been done 'in the field', that is, in the homes of the artists, outdoors, in dance halls, church halls, back rooms etc. [P18]

filler 1, 12, 15

An added substance used to modify the physical properties of a resin in sound recordings in order to create a specific effect, or simply for economic reasons. Some examples are limestone, clay, cellulosic by-product flours, plant fibres, carbon black etc. Often used in processed records to provide colour and weight. [O] *See also* **extender**

filter 2, 3, 6, 10, 12, 13, 14, 15

An electronic circuit designed to remove or attenuate (lessen) certain frequencies during recording or playback. It is frequently used to remove distortion from record scratch or wear or turntable rumble in re-recording. [P2] There are many types of filters, such as high pass, low pass, band pass etc. [O]

filtering

Removing or lessening unwanted sound during recording, for example, scratches on a record. [O]

flagging

Marking the place of a sound recording on a shelf when it is being removed, to facilitate reshelving. [O]

flaking

The loss of bonding or adhesion between the base and coating of laminated discs or magnetic tape, resulting in pieces of the coating breaking loose from the base. It is essentially the same as peeling but more localized in effect. [O]

flange

See **reel flange**

fluting

See **edge fluting**

flutter 1, 2, 3, 6, 9, 10, 12, 13, 14, 15

Rapid speed variations in tape or disc playback, causing pitch and/or amplitude variations. It is usually the result of faults in equipment or friction between the tape and heads or guides. [M6, 9, 10] *See also* **wow**

full track 13

A tape with a single track recorded across its entire width [13] implying monophonic recording. Mostly used in professional work because the greater recorded track width (as opposed to two or four tracks) retains more magnetism, producing a higher output and better signal-to-noise ratio. [O]

fungal etching
1 The degradation or scarring of the base material in a disc or tape as a result of enzymes and acids excreted by fungi during attack on the additives in the coating.
2 Surface etching on discs or tapes resulting from excretions of fungi growing on the packaging that is in contact with the recordings. [O]

fungicide
Material added to tape and disc coatings to retard the growth of fungus. [O]

gamma ferric oxide
See **ferric oxide**

gap smear 9
The erosion of the edge of a tape recorder head gap caused by abrasive tape. The eroded material gets into the gap, causing a magnetic short. [P9]

generation loss 8
Any time an analogue recording is re-recorded or copied, the degradation of signal from the first recording to the copy constitutes a generation loss. [O]

gouge
Commonly used defect term for disc and cylinder recordings. It is used interchangeably with dig and needle dig. [O] *See* **needle dig**

gramophone 16
Word derived from Greek: gramma=letter; phone=voice/sound. Used after 1887 to describe a machine that reproduced sounds from incised disc records (as contrasted with Edison's 'phonograph'). [16]

graphophone 16
Reproducing machine invented by Chichester Bell and Charles S. Tainter in 1885, and the first phonograph to have a recording readily removable, transportable and replaceable for playing. By 1890, it had been adapted to play a brown wax cylinder of normal size, and became Edison's strongest competition in the cylinder world. [16]

greying
Commonly used defect term for disc recordings. It indicates widespread needle wear which results in a discolouration or 'greying' of a part or all of the playing area surface of the disc. It usually means that the disc has been extensively played, or that it has been played with too heavy a stylus tracking weight. Sometimes called steeling. [O]

groove 14, 15, 16
A furrow cut or embossed in the surface of a record (disc or cylinder), which can be a blank (unmodulated) or recorded (modulated) groove, or a combination of both. A cut recording contains only one groove cut (or embossed) spirally from the beginning to the end of the item, but it is more common to refer to this groove in the plural. [O]

groove jumping 15
Occurs when the pickup stylus will not remain in the groove track during playback but skips to an adjacent groove. Causes can be poor manufac-

ture of recording, uneven playback turntable, improper tracking pressure applied to pickup etc. [O]

groove skating 15

Occurs when the pickup stylus tends to climb or 'skate' the groove wall, either skipping some grooves or sliding over the disc without making contact with any grooves. Can be caused by improper vertical pressure of the pickup, or also by a natural inclination of the stylus to ride inward against the inner groove wall during rotation of the disc. Most playback turntables have a control which can be set to counteract this tendency. [O] *See* **anti-skating compensation**

guard band 3, 13, 14

A space of unrecorded tape left between the recorded tracks to prevent crosstalk or leakage of sound from one track to another. Its width is only slightly less than that of the recorded track. [O]

half-track 6, 10

A tape recording standard format in which two independent tracks (channels) are recorded in the same direction; also known as two-track. [O]

head

See **erase head, playback head; record head**

head shell

The removable portion of a record player's tone arm which houses the cartridge and stylus. [O]

heads out 14

Having the beginning of the programme information (recorded content) at the head or outside of the reel of tape or film ready for immediate playback or projection without the need to rewind. [14]

hermetically sealed

The airtight sealing of sound recordings in protective envelopes or sleeves, usually done in a controlled, dust-free environment. [O]

hertz (Hz) 2, 3, 5, 6, 7, 8, 10, 12, 13, 14

The measuring unit of frequency or the speed of vibration of a sound wave. Synonymous with **cycles per second (cps)**. Named after Heinrich Rudolf Hertz, a nineteenth-century German physicist. [M2, 5]

hill and dale recording 1, 3, 18

See **vertical cut recording**

hiss 6, 10, 13

An undesirable wide spectrum noise heard when a recorded tape is played back. It sounds similar to a leaky steam pipe. [P6, 10] It is caused by various factors, including taping at too low a speed, or poor quality tape. Various noise reduction systems have been developed to combat this. [O]

hold back tension 6

A tension (back force) purposely created in the magnetic tape during play, record or fast winding, by driving the supply reel motor in the reverse direction of the tape travel. This is most often applied to prevent tape breakage or stretching during fast winding. [P6]

horn 16

The conical tube which collected the sound in early acoustical recording machines for transmission to the sound box and recording stylus, or which amplified sound emission from the reproducing (playback) machine. [O]

hub 6, 13

The cylindrical object at the centre of a tape reel, around which the tape is wound. NAB hub refers to a standard set by the National Association of Broadcasters for all 10½ inch and 14 inch diameter reels of professional recording tape. [P6]

hum 2, 3, 4, 6, 10, 15

A low frequency noise, generally related to the power-line frequency of a sound system or its harmonics, that intrudes into reproduced sound and mars the listening quality. [2]

hygrothermograph

A device for determining or recording (usually on graph paper) the relative humidity and the temperature of the atmosphere. [O]

Hz

See **hertz**

inches per second (ips) 6, 7, 10

The measurement of the speed at which tape passes through a tape player. Tape speeds are all based on the early standard of 30 ips for coated tape. Successive improvements in tapes, heads and other equipment have permitted reductions to 15 ips and 7½ ips for professional tapes, and 3¾ ips and 1⅞ ips for home use. [M6, 10]

indentation recording 15

Term applied to recording on certain metal discs, e.g. aluminium, with a diamond stylus, in which the material is compressed to make grooves, i.e. no thread is removed or displaced. [15]

infrasonic 6, 12

Frequencies below audibility, i.e. below approximately 15 to 20 Hz. The opposite of ultrasonic. [O]

inner sleeve

See **sleeve**

inside margin

The space between the playing area and the circumference of the label on a disc recording. Discs with no discrete labels should be considered as having no inside margins but as having centres only. [O]

instantaneous disc 1, 12, 15

A recording intended for direct reproduction without further processing. [1] Refers to a disc recording made 'live' at an event, and not commercially produced or pressed. Also known as direct recording or spot recording. [O]

ips
  See **inches per second**
iron oxide 14
  See **ferric oxide**
issue number 18
  This is the number under which a record appears listed in the catalogues, leaflets and other publicity material issued by the company owning the rights to it. Usually common to both sides of the record, and appearing on the record label, this number may change when a record is reissued or released again at a later date. Recordings containing different performing events have from time to time been released with the same issue number, both inadvertently and deliberately. Dubbings are sometimes assigned the original issue number. Also known as catalogue number. It is different from the matrix number. [O]
jacket
  See **slipcase**
label
  1 'A Label is any permanently affixed paper, plastic, etc., slip or ribbon affixed to the item in a permanent manner at the time of production by the manufacturer, creator, or the individual responsible for its existence. If there is no affixed label, then performer, author, composer, title information embossed, printed, etched, or incised onto the surface of the item is to be considered a label equivalent.' (Quoted from: *Rules for Archival Cataloging of Sound Recordings*, Association for Recording Sound Collections, copyright 1980)
  2 Record label: normally used to mean a round paper disc affixed to the centre, unrecorded surface of a disc recording and containing some or all of the following artifact documentation/identifying information: manufacturer's/distributer's label name, trade mark/colophon/logogram of issuing company, issue number for the recording, contents title(s), identification of composers/authors, identification of performer(s), generic description of contents, place of recording, date of recording, publication and copyright data, alternate issue numbers, including album number as applicable, reiteration of matrix or tape transfer numbers, equalization/recording characteristic, engineer/producer, playing time, playing speed, and musical key signature. In cataloguing terms, the label constitutes the 'title page equivalent' and preferred 'chief source of information'. [O]
  3 Tape transfer label: a container label containing identifying information about the source recording and the technical transfer documentation necessary for users of the transfer copy to know precisely in what respects it varies in content and technically from the original recording from which it was dubbed. [O] ARSC/AAA is evaluating a proposed standard transfer label. Cf *Audio Preservation: a Planning Study*, Final report, Appendix IIC4, Tab E., 31 December 1987.
label name
  The publisher's name identification, as prominently displayed on the

252

record label, of the series of recordings to which a given sound recording belongs. Many, possibly most, sound archives shelve their commercial record holdings by label name and issue number; however, there is no commonly accepted list of label names or common, consistent practice. For example, Victor, Victrola, Bluebird etc., may be shelved as one, two or three different names in different collections. [O]

lacquer disc 1, 3, 7, 10, 12
A recording disc usually made of metal, glass or fibre and coated with a lacquer compound, usually acetate or cellulose nitrate, into which the grooves are cut. They can be one-sided or two-sided. Sometimes referred to as acetate disc. Intended for instantaneous recording. Subsequent to the use of a wax master and until the use of Direct Metal Mastering became prevalent, the lacquer master is also the original step in the record production procedure leading to final pressed recordings. [O]

laminate adhesion
The sticking together of layers of a laminated recording achieved through the use of a binder. [O] *See also* **delamination**

laminated disc 1, 18
A recording medium composed of several layers of material held together by a binder. Lacquer discs, for example, are laminated. [1]

land 1, 3, 4, 15
The uncut surface between two adjacent grooves on a disc recording. [1] Also known as a **scroll**. [O]

laser disc
Includes compact disc, video disc and digital optical recording. The first two are mass produced and prerecorded, the third is the only one on which the user can record and only one copy is produced. The content of these media is digitally encoded (except for video on a video disc which is in analogue form) and etched into a reflective layer on the disc in the form of holes or pits (depressions). A laser light beam is focused on the disc as it revolves. Where there are no depressions, the light beam simply moves on. Where there are depressions, the light beam is reflected back into the playback apparatus, which 'reads' the reflections and eventually converts them back into an analogue signal for playback. [O] *See also* **compact disc; digital optical recording; video disc**

LAST
See **Liquid Archival Sound Treatment**

lateral recording 1, 3, 12, 15, 16, 18
Sometimes called needle-cut recording. Invented by Emil Berliner, the recording process by which a stylus cuts a furrow or groove of constant depth but varying width into the disc – that is, the images of the sound vibrations are cut into the sides of the groove. With the advent of stereophonic sound, an added vertical compliance was required, but most commercial recordings have been lateral cut. [P16] *See also* **vertical cut recording**

layer-to-layer adhesion

See **blocking**

lead-in 1

A blank (unmodulated) spiral groove at the beginning of a disc recording, having a pitch much greater than that of the recorded (modulated) grooves, whose purpose is to guide the pickup or tone arm into the first recorded grooves. [P1]

lead-out 1

Same as a lead-in groove, except located at the end of a recording and connected to either the locked or eccentric groove. [1]

leader tape 3, 6, 10, 11, 13, 14

Non-magnetic tape spliced to the beginning and end of a tape and between segments to indicate visually when recorded material begins and ends. [14]

leakage 6, 13, 14

See **crosstalk**

level 3, 6, 9, 10, 13, 15

Intensity or amplitude of a sound signal measured in dBs. [O]

level indicator 6

A device which provides a visual display of the signal amplitude or level; it can be a meter or a series of light emitting diodes (LEDs). [6] *See also* **V/U meter**

liner

See **album; sleeve; slipcase**

liner notes

Commentary and explanatory information about the contents, performers, or recording circumstances printed on, attached to, or inserted in, the container in which a sound recording is distributed. [O]

Liquid Archival Sound Treatment (LAST)

A trademarked lubricant and preservative fluid that works by reacting with vinyl and shellac to alter the nature of the groove walls on a disc, thereby, it is claimed, reducing wear and eliminating distortion. [O]

locked groove 18

See **concentric groove**

longitudinal curvature 9

Deformation, usually warping or stretching, of magnetic tape along its length caused by pressure from winding the tape under tension and storing it in this condition. This is permanent deformation which impairs the reproductive sonic quality of the tape recording. [O]

lubricants 9, 15

Additives that minimize the abrasiveness (lower the coefficient of friction) of the binder and oxide particles in tape. [9] Also a once common practice of lubricating or waxing the surface of laquer discs to prolong playing life. This practice was abandoned because such applications collected dust and added to the surface noise of the disc. [M9, 15]

magnetic tape 1, 3, 6, 9, 10, 12, 13

Paper, acetate, steel or plastic based tape which has been coated with a layer of magnetizable particles, usually ferric oxide or chromium dioxide (some newer tapes use actual metal particles). These particles are held in a binder and lubricated. Standard size is ¼ inch in width, but compact cassette tape is ⅛ inch and video tape ranges from ½ inch to 3 inches. [M6, 10]

magnetic wire recording 1, 12

Patented by Danish inventor, Valdemar Poulsen, in 1900, and considered obsolete since the development of magnetic tape recording. This system utilizes stainless steel wire approximately 4 mils in diameter which is magnetized on one side as it passes over the wire recorder head. The life of the wire is limitless, except for mechanical breakage. However, the signal-to-noise ratio is considerably less than for magnetic tape because of the small cross-sectional area of the wire, as compared to tape. One of the principal drawbacks to wire recording is that it is not uncommon to have a 2-minute or more variation in a 10-minute program, resulting in sound and pitch distortion. This system led into the development of magnetic tape recording in Germany in the 1930s. [P12]

magnetite

See **ferric oxide**

mandrel 16

The part of a cylinder phonograph that carried the cylinder record, causing it to revolve under the reproducing or recording stylus. [16]

margin (of disc)

See **inside margin**

master disc 3, 6, 10, 12, 15, 18

A finished disc recording in edited or approved form from which copies can be made in the record producing process. It is used to produce a reverse copy or metal matrix which has ridges instead of grooves that is then used as a stamper for producing copies in the single-step process, or is used to produce a metal 'mother' in the three-step process. [P12]

master tape 3, 6, 7, 8, 13

A completed tape, used in tape-to-disc transfer, or from which other tape copies are produced. [13] In commercial record production, it is the equivalent of the master disc and is controlled as the original recording from which all records and tapes for distribution will come. [P7]

matrix

A metal negative (with ridges instead of grooves) of an original master disc. In the record production process, it can be used either as a stamper for producing pressings, or to create a mother from which the stamper is made. [O]

matrix number 18

The number allocated to each side of a directly cut record by a record company at the time of recording, or sometimes in advance. It is usually found etched, embossed or stamped on the inside margin or centre. It is usually a rough guide to the dating of the record, and sometimes indicates which take or performance of several done in one session the recording actually represents. The matrix number may also indicate, usually in the prefix or suffix portions, additional data such as method of recording, e.g. electrical or acoustical, dubbing etc., recording engineer identifier, place and, in the case of exchange of leased masters, original manufacturer. When dealing with records reissued under new issue numbers, the matrix number is the chief means of verifying whether the reissue is the same take or performance as an earlier issue. [O] *See also* **take** 15

mechanical recording
See **acoustical recording**

metal-particle tape 14
Tape specially made for cassette tape recorders with a high coercivity and sensitivity compared with other cassette tapes. [14]

microgroove 3, 12
A type of recording having 200 to 300 or more lines per inch, suitable for reproduction by a stylus having a tip radius of 1 mil (or less). Contemporary LP recordings are microgroove, as opposed to 'coarse' groove for older 78 rpm shellac recordings. At the same speed of playback, microgroove recordings permit longer playing time than coarse groove recordings. [P12]

mil 6, 9, 10, 13, 14, 15
A measurement consisting of one one-thousandth of an inch (0.0001"). [6] Used to describe the thickness of magnetic tape, the width of record grooves, and the size of the radius of the tip of a stylus. [O]

mint
Commonly used physical description term for sound recordings. It means that the recording appears to be new with no visible flaws. [O]

monitor 10
To check the sound quality, operational techniques, programme content etc., by listening to the programme as it leaves the studio in broadcast, or during recording or rerecording. [P10]

monitor speaker 5, 6, 10, 13, 14
Usually refers to the loudspeakers used in a recording studio or laboratory, and hence, of high quality. The term can refer to any loudspeaker used for listening to recordings. [P10]

Monk's record cleaner
A disc washing machine, in which the disc is washed with distilled water, or a solution of distilled water and ethyl alcohol, and then the solution and dirt are removed by vacuum suction, which prevents dust from being redeposited or trapped within the grooves during the drying process. [O]

monophonic/monaural 3, 5, 6, 10, 12, 13, 14
Sound heard from a single channel. This is defined by the form of recording or transmission, and not by the number of microphones or speakers. In monophonic sound the only spatial movement that can be simulated is forwards and backwards; there is no sideways spread. [10]

mother 12, 15

A nickel or copper plated positive copy of an original master recording (made from a metal matrix or negative copy) which is used to make a stamper for producing pressings in the commercial recording process. It replaces the original master which can then be stored for safety purposes. [P12, 15]

muddy 6

An expression that refers to a lack of definition or clarity in a recording, playback system or sound reinforcement system. Can be caused by many factors, including distortion, excess bass or deficient mid- and high-frequencies etc. [6]

Mylar 6, 12, 14

A polyester plastic manufactured by the Dupont Company, and currently used as the backing in many types of magnetic recording tape. [6]

National Association of Broadcasters (NAB) 3, 6, 7, 13

A national group of broadcasters who have voluntarily formed a regulatory body for television and radio. [7] Three of its standards have become widespread in the recording field: the NAB curve which is the standard tape record/playback equalization curve; the NAB hub and the NAB reel (and reel adapter). [O] *See* **hub; reel-to-reel tape**

ND

Common abbreviation for needle dig. *See* **needle dig**

needle dig

Commonly used defect term for disc and cylinder recordings, sometimes abbreviated as ND. It is used interchangeably with gouge and refers to a visible pit or break in the surface of the recording, most probably caused by the stylus having been dropped onto that portion of the surface. [O]

needle run

A spiral scratch caused by the pickup stylus leaving the modulated groove and skipping across the record surface during playback. When abbreviated as NR, it is a commonly used defect indicator for disc sound recordings. [O]

nick

Commonly used defect term for sound recordings. It is similar to needle dig, referring to a visible pit, dig or break in the surface of the recording which will probably cause some degree of sonic distortion. [O]

noise 14

See **ambient noise; random noise; white noise**

noise floor 6, 8

The level at which noise exists in an electronic device, audio system or tape recorder, measured in the absence of sound signal. [6] *See also* **quiescent noise**

NR

Commonly used abbreviation for **needle run**

oersted 9, 12, 13

A unit measurement of magnetic field strength. [O]

open reel
See **reel-to-reel tape**
optical disc
See **digital optical recording**
optical soundtrack
Photographic sound recording in motion pictures in which the sound-track is present on the photographic film and translated into an electrical signal for playback during projection. [P12]
order number
See **issue number**
original 18
Applied to sound recording, a much used – and misused – term which can be misleading if the reader is not intimately familiar with the context. Commonly used examples follow:
– *original album/box (or other container):* may refer to the container in which the recording was first issued, the sound recording itself, or both.
– *original cast:* refers to recordings made by members (not necessarily *all* members) of the cast of the first production of a stage work – frequently associated with place of production.
– *original label:* label used on the first published release of the sound recording in question.
– *original performance:* meant to distinguish recording in question from subsequent, sometimes revised, recorded performances
– *original pressing:* first issue of the recording in question.
– *original recording:* may refer to the first issued version of the recorded performance in question, or to an unedited or duplicated master recording, or to the source copy of a recording from which a copy is to be, or has been, made.
– *original take:* same as *original performance* above. [O]
oscilloscope 6, 7, 11, 13
An instrument which displays electrical signals as graphs on a screen, which can be used to analyse control room acoustics, for general trouble-shooting in a sound system, or to analyse a sound signal being recorded. [M6, 7, 13]
overload 14
Feeding a component or system more loudness than it can handle, and thereby causing overload distortion. [14] *See* **clipping**
oxidation 9
The degrading effect of oxygen on certain resins or plastic compounds dependent on environmental and time parameters, which can cause decomposition, loss of certain physical properties, etc. [O]
pack 6, 9
Refers to the form taken by tape as it is wound on a reel or around a hub. A good tape pack will be smooth and free of ripples, buckling, cinching, etc. [P6, 9]

pancake 6

A roll of magnetic tape that is wound onto a NAB hub. The roll does not have sides or flanges. Tape stored as a pancake must be handled carefully to avoid spillage as only friction holds the tape in a roll. [6]

peeling

Commonly used term referring to the widespread separation of the coating layer of a laminated recording from its base or core. It is used interchangeably with flaking, although the latter usually implies more limited or local deterioration. [O] *See also* **flaking**

perforated disc

A punched disc, usually made of metal, made to be played by a mechanical music box. As the disc revolves, the various holes activate a tuned comb-like instrument which reproduces the tones of the melody the disc was originally punched to play. In the late nineteenth century, companies such as the Regina Music Box Co. of New Jersey were manufacturing deluxe console models of such music boxes which were a popular parlour item. These machines had an early influence on the design of phonograph and gramophone consoles. [O]

phonograph 16

Derived from two Greek words: phone = voice/sound; graphos = writer/written. Edison applied this word to his first recording/reproducing machine of 1877. In general American terms, a phonograph was and is any machine reproducing sounds from indented, incised or engraved cylinder or disc records; in general European terms, a machine reproducing sounds from such cylinder records only. [16]

piano roll

A roll of paper containing perforations such that air passing through them actuates the keys of a mechanical player piano. Some of these were made by famous composers and musicians who did not make any other recordings, thus giving us at least a partial semblance of their technique and artistry. [O]

pickup 1, 2, 4, 6, 10, 12, 14, 15

Device that translates (transduces) mechanical motion of a stylus riding in the record groove into electrical impulses in a playback system. [P15] The term is used interchangeably with cartridge. It is also sometimes used to refer to the tone arm containing the pickup or cartridge. [O]

pinch roller 6, 12, 13, 14

On tape machines, a free turning wheel with a rubber surface which presses the tape firmly against the capstan to ensure consistent tape motion. [6]

pit

1 Commonly used defect term for sound recordings which is similar to 'dig' and 'gouge', although it might be a visible depression in the surface of the recording that causes no break in the modulated groove and, hence, no sonic distortion.

2 The term used to describe the depressions in the surface of a laser

disc which contain the digitally encoded program material to be 'read' by the tracking laser beam in playback. [O]

pitch 3, 5, 6, 8, 10, 12, 14

1 The subjective human perception of frequency, dependent on sound level as well as frequency, by which sound may be ordered on a musical scale. [P3, 5, 6]

2 The distance between the centres of the bottoms of two adjacent portions of the groove of a recorded disc or cylinder (can be fixed or variable, depending upon type of system used, variable pitch having come into general use in the 1950s). [O] *See also* **Tpi**

plasticizer 9, 15

An additive used to alter the properties of a basic resin such as cellulose nitrate, usually to soften or 'plasticize', which in turn could induce chemical degradation of the basic resin. Examples are camphors and castor oil. The loss of plasticizer can lead to shrinkage or hardening of the coating, causing flaking and peeling. [O]

playback 15

The reproduction of a sound recording on a sound system to hear its contents. [O]

playback head 1, 6, 13, 14

A device on a magnetic tape recorder that senses previously recorded signals on a tape as it passes over. Coils in the head convert passing magnetic fields on the tape, sensed at the head gap, into electronic audio signals for playback or reproduction. [P6]

player-piano roll

See **piano roll**

playing area

On a disc or a cylinder recording, this is the area from the position of the beginning to the position of the end of the recorded (modulated) groove. [O]

polyester 6, 9, 14

An abbreviation for polyethylene glycol terephthalate, a material commonly used as the base film for magnetic tape. It has a higher humidity and temperature stability than most other film-base materials. It also has greater strength and fungus and mildew resistance. [9]

polyethylene

A plastic material sometimes used as a protective liner or sleeve for discs and tapes. It furnishes a smooth fungi-resistant surface and is also a moisture barrier for both the disc or tape and the external packaging (jacket or box). [P17]

polymerization

The conversion of substances into a new compound by a joining together of their molecular structures. In recordings, additives are chosen to alter certain physical properties for a desired effect through polymerization. Sometimes these additives can also create undesired effects. [O]

polymerized vinyl chloride/polyvinyl chloride/PVC 10, 17

A synthetic resin which has been manufactured in the United States since the 1930s. In the sound recording industry it is used in the manufacture of phonograph discs, magnetic tape backing, and magnetic tape binder. It was used as a binder in 78 rpm shellac type discs, and is the primary ingredient in contemporary LP discs. [P17]

polystyrene 17

Another form of plastic used in the production of phonograph discs. Production costs for such discs are lower than PVC for large runs, but require a larger initial capital outlay. It has chiefly been used in the manufacture of seven-inch 45 rpm single records. [P17]

post-echo 10, 13

See **echo**

pre-echo 3, 10, 13, 15

See **echo**

presence 14, 15

Subjective term applied to a quality of naturalness in sound recording/re-production so that the illusion is such that the listener perceives the sound as close and realistic and not being produced at some remote location. [M14, 15]

preservation copy

A sound recording designated for archival preservation; such recordings are played only under exceptional circumstances. [O]

preservation duplicate

A duplicate copy of a sound recording designated for archival preservation. [O]

preservation transfer copy

A dubbing made for archival preservation of a recording which cannot be preserved due to ongoing deterioration; or a dubbing made to serve as a preservation duplicate of a preservation copy of a recording. [O]

pressing 1, 3, 7, 10, 12, 15

1   any disc phonograph record produced in a record-moulding process from a master or stamper.

2   A number of records produced at one time (e.g. the initial pressing order was 1000 records and the second pressing was 5000 records).

3   The process whereby a machine flattens, compresses and squeezes the vinyl and shapes the record grooves in record production. [7]

print-through 3, 6, 9, 12, 13, 14

The unwanted transfer of a magnetic field (and the sound signal) from one layer to another within a roll of tape. The magnitude of this induced signal tends to increase with the storage time and temperature and decrease with the unwinding of the tape roll. It is a function of the magnetic instability of the magnetic oxide on the tape. It causes echo or repeated sound from one layer of tape while the next layer is passing over the playback head. [P9] *See* **echo**

psychrometer

An instrument for measuring the amount of moisture in the air. [O]

quadrophonic or quadraphonic 3, 5, 14
System of recording and reproducing sound using four separate chan-nels and four separate loudspeakers in an attempt to recreate a 360 degree sound field around the listener. [M3, 5]

quarter-track 6, 10, 12
A tape format in which there are four separate tracks on ¼ inch tape. The tape runs from left to right and the top track is usually recorded first, and then the third. To record the other two tracks the tape is turned upside down and once again fed left to right. For stereo, the first and third tracks are recorded at the same time, using a stacked head (one with both gaps in line). Quarter-track recording has a signal to-noise-ratio which is poorer than that of half-track or full-track recording in proportion to the relative tape widths. Four-channel stereo uses all four tracks in the same direction. Quarter-track tape is primarily intended for the consumer market (home use). Also known as four-track. [P10]

quiescent noise 6, 13
The noise of an audio system in a static condition; that is, with no applied signal. [13]
See also **noise floor**

random noise 11, 12
Artificial noise which is intermixed and amplified with the program signal in a sound recording system, usually of electronic origin. [P12] *See also* **white noise**

record head 1, 3, 6, 12, 13, 14
A device on a tape recorder which converts audio signals from a sound source to magnetic fields that magnetize the oxide particles on magnetic tape, thus 'recording' the sound onto the tape. Audio signals are combined with high frequency bias during this process. [P6] *See* **bias**

recording channel 1
See **channel**

Recording Industry Association of America (RIAA) 6, 7, 10, 12
A non-profit trade association founded in 1952 to work for the interests and betterment of the sound recording industry. Members are US companies which create, manufacture and market sound recordings. It was responsible for establishing the RIAA curve, a widely used, standard phonograph disc record/playback equalization curve (recording charac-teristic). [M6, 7]

reel
Refers either to the plastic/metal container for a roll of tape, or to the roll of tape on such a container. [O]

reel flange 6
The metal sides for a reel of tape. Professional 10½-inch and 14-inch tape reels have flanges mounted on NAB hubs. [6]

reel-to-reel tape
Magnetic tape wound in spools or packs around a hub and not enclosed in any shell. So called because a full reel or spool unwinds onto an empty

reel (hub with flanges or sides) during the recording and playback processes. [O]

reissue 18

An issue of a commercial sound recording that has previously been withdrawn. Strictly speaking, the term should be confined to sound recordings manufactured by the process used for the prior issue. 'Reissue' is frequently used, however, to describe dubbings and re-edited performances issued in changed formats. [O]

remanence 6, 9, 12, 13

The magnetic induction (field) remaining in a magnetic substance after the applied magnetic force has been removed. Remanence is used as a reference number for comparing the relative output, distortion and response of the recording tape at low frequencies. [M6, 12] *See also* **retentivity**

repressing

In commercial record production this refers to a continued or additional pressing of recordings usually from the same stamper as an original pressing run (although occasionally a different or duplicate stamper may be used). These recordings may differ from the original pressings by having different labels, different logos, different imprints, different composition of materials, different recorded work(s) on the alternate side, or different packaging. [O]

rerecording

Used in some discographies to indicate the product of an acoustic vocal recording with a superimposed electrical accompaniment, in others to indicate simply a dubbing. [O]

retentivity 6, 9, 12, 13, 14

Measure of a tape's ability to retain magnetization after the force field has been removed. It serves as an indication of the tape's sensitivity at high frequencies. [M6, 14] Also called residual flux. *See also* **remanence**

revolutions per minute

See **rpm**

RIAA

See **Recording Industry Association of America**

RIAA curve

See **Recording Industry Association of America**

rill 18

The groove on a disc recording linking the end of one cut (band or selection) with the beginning of the next. [P18]

rim (of disc or cylinder)

In a disc recording, the rim is the area between the edge and the playing area, which can be sloped, concave, convex, flat, raised, lowered, etc. On a cylinder recording, the starting rim is the same as on a disc. The run-off rim is the area following the playing area. [O]

rpm

Revolutions per minute. The speed at which a disc or cylinder rotates or revolves on the recording or reproducing machine. Although most recordings are described as 78 rpm, 45 rpm, $33\frac{1}{3}$ rpm or $16\frac{2}{3}$ rpm, there were many variations in speed, particularly in the early half of the century for so-called 78 rpm recordings. [O]

RR
  See **re-recording**

rub (rubbing)
  Commonly used defect term for sound recordings which refers to a visible mark on the surface of the recording (usually caused by another item or material having come in contact with the surface) which may not actually cause any distortion in playback. It is used interchangeably with scuff. [O]

rumble 1, 2, 3, 6, 12, 13, 15
  Low frequency noise caused by the mechanism of a turntable or tape transport. Rumble sometimes can be heard from the discs themselves, having been induced during the recording or cutting stages. [2]

run-in and run-out grooves 15
  See **lead-in; lead-out**

run-off rim
  See **rim**

saddle warp 7
  Occurs if the paper grain of both labels on a record is not running in the same direction when the labels are affixed to the vinyl; the natural curl of the paper may put unequal stress on the record's centre surfaces and can result in record warpage when the record is first removed from the press. [7]

safety master 3, 11, 13
  A copy of a master tape, generally filed as a protection against the damage or loss of the master tape. Also known as protection copy. [13]

sample rate 6, 9, 14
  The rate or frequency at which an analogue signal is analysed during the digital conversion process. [P6, 14]

sampling 6, 14
  See **sample rate**

saturation 2, 6, 9, 12, 13
  In tape recording, the point at which no further signal can be accommodated by either a recording head or by the tape. Any additional signal beyond saturation causes distortion. [2] The term has other meanings when applied to power amplifiers, loudspeakers and microphones. [O]

scanning electron microscope
  An instrument used to analyse record grooves, both to determine deformation, and to determine the size and configuration. [O]

scrape
  Commonly used defect term for sound recordings which implies a visible marring of the surface of the recording that appears to be deeper or

more serious than a scuff or rub and may cause some degree of sonic distortion. [O]

scratch

Commonly used defect term for sound recordings which implies a visible marring of the surface of the recording in the form of a single, thin line or 'scratch' which will cause momentary distortion (usually referred to as a tick) when the stylus tracks over it. It is markedly less severe than a crack. [O]

scroll

The marker space on a disc recording indicating the separation of two different cuts or bands on the disc. It contains a linking groove known as a rill which carries the stylus into the next cut. [O] *See also* **cut; rill**

scuff

See **rub (rubbing)**

selective erasure 17

A curative measure for tape recorded at too high a level or which has been exposed to high temperatures or AC fields; in particular, just prior to rerecording. It is best accomplished by using a coil through which the tape is passed at recording speeds with reduced erase current from a recorder. Print-through decay can be accelerated by this process, however, and the process is justified only in unusual cases. [17]

self erasure 6, 9, 13

The process by which a piece of magnetized tape tends to demagnetize itself by virtue of the opposing fields created within it by its own magnetization. This effect becomes increasingly stronger at short wave lengths (high frequencies). It can be avoided by avoiding the use of excessive equalization boost at high frequencies, by avoiding extremes of temperature when storing tapes, and by using high quality tapes. [M6, 9]

service copy

A sound recording designated for repeated playback for listeners who use the collection. [O]

service duplicate

A duplicate copy of a service copy. [O]

service transfer copy

A dubbing made from another sound recording to be used for repeated playback for listeners who use the collection. [O]

set

In sound recordings this most commonly refers to albums of multiple 78 rpm recordings distributed as an album by the manufacturer. The album or set usually had an issue number distinct from the individual disc numbers. These were frequently sold in booklike containers, although some manufacturers, particularly European ones, sometimes distributed these sets in individual sleeves with no overall container or set number. [O] *See also* **album; box**

shaving 16

Erasing the playing grooves of a wax cylinder by paring the surface so that a fresh recording could be made on it. [16]

shellac 10, 15

Term sometimes used interchangeably with 78 rpm record. It is a thermoplastic resin used as the basic ingredient in the production of disc recordings until supplanted by various vinyl formulations with the advent of the microgoove LP disc. Shellac discs could be solid shellac stock or laminated onto a board, fibre, plastic or paper core. [O]

shrink wrap

Outer cellophane-type wrapper enclosing a commercial LP recording and its slipcase which is sealed thermally before distribution for sale. The material is stretched extremely snugly around the packaging and can contract under high temperature, causing disc warpage. [O]

signal processing equipment 6, 13

Any equipment or circuit that is used intentionally to change the characteristics of a sound signal (other than overall level or intensity). It consists of such devices as equalizers, limiters, phasers, delay lines, etc. [6]

signal to noise ratio (S/N ratio) 2, 3, 6, 7, 8, 9, 10, 12, 13, 14, 15

The difference in decibels between the signal and noise levels in a piece of equipment, its output, or a recording. The quoted S/N ratio is that available when the signal is as loud as it can be without significant distortion. During recording it is advisable to put as high an undistorted level as possible on the tape, which will minimize surface noise in reproduction, and also to use correct equalization. [M10, 15]

skating

See **groove skating**

slate 3, 6, 8, 14

A voice or talkback signal recording an announcement or identifying information directly onto a tape before recording any program or item. It consists of a low frequency tone with the recorder's voice mixed in. Its purpose is to identify material being recorded and to enable quick location of items on a tape by counting the beeps (sound of a 'slate' at rewind or fast forward speed) until the desired segment is positioned for playback. [M6, 8]

slate tone 6

The low frequency tone added to a slate announcement or used alone which creates a beep sound during high winding speed to aid in location of segments of a tape. [P6]

slating 13

See **slate**

sleeve

Usually refers to the inner paper, glassine, or polyethylene protective envelope for a disc within a cardboard/paper outer jacket (slipcase). There are also specially manufactured, acid-free sleeves used for record protection in archival situations. [O]

slipcase

The outer container for a disc recording usually made of paper/cardboard, and containing credits, pictorial information, titles, narrative information (sometimes referred to as liner notes), etc. It is usually open on one end only, for slipping the disc in and out of the container. [O] *See also* **album**

S/N ratio

See **signal to noise ratio**

softener

See **plasticizer**

sound recording

A working definition of this term was developed for this planning study: 'An artifact which has been constructed and used for the specific purpose of storing a representation of energy for the further purpose of reproduction in the audio portion of the spectrum.'

sound track 1

A narrow band usually along the margin of a sound film, which carries the sound record. [1] *See also* **optical soundtrack**

spiral groove

Usually refers to the lead-in or lead-out groove on a sound recording, and is so-called because it traces the pattern of a spiral on the surface of the recording. [O]

splicing 13, 18

The joining together of two pieces of magnetic tape using a short length of special adhesive-coated tape. Usually done to repair broken or snapped tape, to join two or more recorded programs onto one reel of tape, or to add leader tape. [O]

splicing block 6, 10, 13

A non-magnetic metal block with a channel that holds magnetic tape in precise alignment during the act of splicing. Additional straight and diagonal grooves provide a path for a razor blade to follow for cutting the tape precisely before splicing. [6]

splicing tape 3, 6, 13, 14

A special, pressure-sensitive, non-magnetic tape used to join two pieces of recording tape. In order to prevent dirt build-up on the recording heads or tape guide, and to prevent adjacent layers of recording tape from sticking together, splicing tape uses a special adhesive. [6]

spool

Refers either to the central (usually metal) hub around which a roll of magnetic wire recording is wound or to the roll of wire around that hub. [O]

spot recording

See **instantaneous disc**

squeal

See **tape squeal**

S/S

Commonly used abbreviation to describe a single-sided disc recording. [O]

stabilizers

Substances added to the basic compound of a disc or tape recording to prevent deterioration or the loss of desired physical properties. [O]

stamper 1, 3, 7, 12, 15, 18

A negative of a positive copy (mother) of a master recording (generally made of metal by electroforming) from which final pressings are 'stamped' in record processing. [P1, 15]

standard

For the purposes of this planning study, the following definition was adopted: 'The result of a particular standardization effort, approved by a recognized authority. It may take the form of: 1) a document containing a set of conditions to be fulfilled; 2) a fundamental unit or physical constant, for example, ampere, metre, absolute zero (Kelvin).' Quotation from *The Aims and Principles of Standardization*, International Organization for Standardization [n.d.]

starting rim

See **rim**

static

The distortion created in disc or tape playback when the recording has a buildup of electrostatic charge. Also refers to interference or distorted reception in a radio broadcast signal. [O]

stereophonic 2, 3, 7, 10, 11, 12, 13, 14, 15

A multiple-channel sound system in which each channel carries a unique version of the total original performance. When the channels are played simultaneously, they recreate the breadth and depth of the original performance, adding a dimension that is usually missing in monophonic sound. At least two channels are required for stereo operation, though more than two may be used. [2]

stroboscope 4, 10, 11, 12, 14

A device used to measure the speed of rotation. It contains a high intensity flashing light whose flashes may be adjusted to a frequency equal to or a multiple or submultiple of the rotation of the equipment under observation. This light can be used to illuminate a disc which has bars (or spots) on it. When the time between the light flashes is a multiple of the period of the rotating disc, the disc appears to be at rest. [P10, 12]

stylus (ellipitical/conical etc.) 1, 2, 3, 4, 10, 12, 14, 15

Commonly referred to as needle. Includes the cutting stylus or needle used in making a recording (disc or cylinder) and the playback needle which engages the groove of a recording and transmits the mechanical motion to the pickup or cartridge of the system for conversion (transduction). The different sizes and configurations of recording grooves through the history of recording obviously require different styli. Materials most used today for styli are sapphire and diamond. Wear on the stylus depends on playing weight and the record material; wear on the recording is obviously dependent on the tracking weight and proper form and size of the stylus as relates to the grooves. [O]

stylus drag 1

An expression used to denote the force resulting from friction between the surface of the recording medium and the playback stylus. [1]

stylus force 1, 12

The vertical or downward force the pickup (with stylus) applies to the record groove, expressed in grams. This force must be altered for playback of different types of recordings. [P12]

surface imprint 17

The transfer of material from the packaging containing a recording to the surface of the recording itself due to high contact stress (caused by high temperatures, wrinkled or uneven surfaces of the packaging material, or improper and uneven storage pressure). This can result in poor playback because the transferred material may interfere with stylus tracking. [P17]

surface noise 1, 15

In recording playback, surface noise is the noise component in the electric output of a pickup (cartridge) due to irregularities in the contact surface of the grooves. [1] Can be caused by many factors including dust and foreign particles in the grooves, improper stylus and pickup being used, poor manufacture, wear on the grooves caused by previous improper playback, etc. [P15]

swarf 16

The threads of waste material removed from the blank record face (disc or cylinder) by the recording stylus. Also includes the material pared off a cylinder during 'shaving'. [16]

tails out 6, 8, 14

A tape recording that is stored after recording or playback without being rewound, i.e. with the tail-end of the tape outermost on the reel. Tails out storage is preferable because the tape 'pack' tends to be smoother, hence safer, than if the tape had been rewound. [6] *See also* **heads out**

take 15

The making of a recording, namely, a good take, or a bad take. Record manufacturers usually assign a different indicator to each take (sometimes indicated in the matrix number of the recording but not the catalogue or issue number). Hence, the matrix number of a recording can often indicate whether a reissue of an earlier recording is actually the same take or a different take. [O]

take-up reel 6

The reel on a tape recorder that is on the right side of the head stack and which is empty prior to the beginning of the recording or playback. [6]

take-up tension 6, 13

The tension or pulling force which the take-up reel applies to the tape as it leaves the capstan/pinch roller area of a tape recorder. [6]

Talking Machine 16

Words attached early to the phonograph and gramophone but in time more especially to the latter, the terms 'phonograph' and 'graphophone' then implying cylinder reproducing machines. Until 1910 when the Gramophone Company lost exclusive use of the word Gramophone, other makers were not able to use it, and Talking Machine had been used in general for disc-playing machines; after 1910 the word began to drop out of use and now has something of precocity about it. [16]

tape hiss

See **hiss**

tape lifter 6

A device on a tape recorder which prevents tape contact with the heads during fast forward and rewind modes. This prevents wear of the heads and the tape through the elimination of needless contact and friction. [P6]

tape squeal

Commonly used term to describe the sonic distortion which occurs in playback of a tape recording which has a deterioration or loss of the lubricant in its coating, causing friction as the tape passes over the playback head of the machine. It can also sometimes occur when tape is played in an excessively dry environment. [O]

tape weave 6

Describes a condition in which recording tape makes unwanted up and down movement as it passes the heads. This may be caused by improper tape slitting, poor transport mechanical alignment, worn heads or tape guides, or improper winding of the tape before storage. [P6]

test pressing 18

A rough 'first off the press' record, usually with a plain or undecorated white label, made to assist in judging whether a recording/take is suitable for issue. Rejected or unissued recordings have often survived in this format only, because someone in the record company saved it. [P18]

test tape 6, 12, 13, 15

A tape containing a series of test tones at a standard reference fluxivity used to verify the performance of the tape recorder's playback system, and for 'alignment' and 'calibration' of the tape recorder. [M6, 13]

test tone

An alignment tone recorded on a magnetic tape, usually preceding the program information, which assists in adjusting the playback machine to correlate to the machine on which the tape was originally recorded. In professional and archival settings, there are general agreed standards for recording this tone. [O]

thermoplastic 12, 17

The general basic ingredient in most contemporary disc recordings which is synthetic or partially synthetic. This material will repeatedly soften when heated and harden when cooled. There is no abrupt change, at the surface temperatures of these materials, between the fluid and solid states, but, instead, a thermoplastic gradually becomes softer as the temperature increases. The properties of plastics can be altered remarkably by additives in order to achieve a desired result. [17]

threads per inch

See **tpi**

tick

1 Commonly used defect term for sound recordings which refers to a small, visible break in the surface of the recording. It is similar to but smaller than a nick or dig.

2 Commonly used term to describe the momentary sonic distortion created when the playback stylus tracks over a defect in the surface of a recording, such as a scratch, nick, dig, etc. [O]

timbre 3, 5, 6, 10, 12, 14

The subjective tonal quality of a sound. The timbre of any musical or non-musical sound is determined largely by the harmonic structure of the sound wave. Rich sounding musical tones tend to have a great number of inner harmonics which contribute to their lush timbre, while thin sounding musical tones tend to be lacking in the presence of harmonics. [5]

tone arm 15, 16

Originally the tube, usually of metal, that carried the sonic output from the sound box of a gramophone/phonograph to the neck of the horn in playback. [16] When it was invented, it was claimed that the tone of the reproduced sound was improved, hence its name. [P15] Today it is commonly used to refer to the pickup carrying arm on a turntable. [O]

tpi 16

Threads per inch. The number of adjacent portions of the sound groove found per longitudinal inch on the surface of a cylinder record, or per radial inch on the surface of a disc record. [16] *See also* **pitch**

tracing distortion 15

Harmonic distortion in record playback due to improper pickup stylus tip size. [P15]

track 14

The path on magnetic tape on which the signal is recorded. [14] Sometimes used confusingly and interchangeably with 'cut' or 'band' on a disc recording. [O]

transcription disc 12, 15

Disc recording, usually slow speed lateral or vertical cut type, specially made for broadcasting. It is often 16 inches in diameter. In the US, if not a direct (instantaneous) recording, it is generally a vinyl pressing. [15]

transferring 3

Copying by re-recording on a different or similar medium, e.g. making a tape recording from a disc. [P3]

transient 2, 3, 5, 6, 8, 10, 11, 13, 14

A signal of very short duration, such as those created by cymbal crashes, percussive effects, plucked strings, etc. Transient distortion occurs when a component fails to reproduce this kind of sound accurately. [2]

treble boost 6

An accentuation of higher audio frequencies, normally provided by an equalizer or tone control. [6] This is a questionable practice in archival sound recording. [O]

turntable 14, 15

The system that plays a disc recording, which will include a motor, a drive system of some kind (belt or direct drive), and a platter for holding the disc. [O]

two-track

See **half-track**

ultrasonic 6, 7, 12

A term which describes sound waves of frequencies too high to be audible to humans. [7] Ultrasonic cleaning of recordings is a system consisting of a tank, a cleaning solution, and an oscillator operating in the ultrasonic wave frequencies. [P12]

unmodulated groove

See **blank groove**

variant edition

A commercially issued sound recording which differs in any way from other copies of the same recording. It is similar to a **repressing** (*see above*), except that the difference might even occur in the course of a single pressing run. [O]

vertical cut recording 1, 2, 12, 15, 16, 18

A recording in which the sound is engraved in the bottom of the grooves instead of in the sides (lateral record), causing the stylus to move up and down within the groove. This technique was used in cylinder recording, in some early acoustic disc recordings, and in some transcription disc production. It is also known as Hill and Dale recording because of the ridges and valleys in the bottom of the groove. Its great advantage in early recording was that the depth of cut dictated the volume of sound, while in lateral recording, heavy engraving could cause the stylus to break into adjoining grooves. [P16]

video cassette 7

A prepackaged enclosed unit containing magnetic tape (either prerecorded or blank) for video recording or playback, usually ½ inch or ¾ inch width. [O]

video disc 7

A flat, circular platter on which both audio and video information can be stored for playback by means of a laser. [O] *See also* **laser disc**

vinyl 7, 12, 15

Short form of polyvinyl chloride (PVC). Also a contemporary slang term for a disc record. [O]

vinyl chloride

See **polymerized vinyl chloride (PVC)**

volatilization

The process whereby a material is altered into a vapour; vaporization, caused by a reaction to other materials with which it is combined or to environmental conditions. It can be applied to the decomposition of certain materials contained in a sound recording. [O]

V/U meter 2, 3, 5, 6, 12, 14

A meter designed to measure audio level in volume units during recording or re-recording in order to obtain maximum level without distortion. [O]

vulcanite

A type of hard rubber which was the first material used commercially by Emil Berliner in the manufacture of his Gramophone disc recordings. [O]

white noise 3, 6, 10, 12, 13

1 In acetate discs, this is the increase in playback noise caused by the drying out or loss of plasticizer which creates a shrinkage of the coating, exposing nodules of imperfectly dispersed carbon black as well as minute pores. [P17]

2 Also refers to a specific type of random noise in audio equipment or recordings. [O]

wire recording

See **magnetic wire recording**

wow 2, 3, 6, 9, 10, 12, 13, 14, 15

Slow speed variations on a tape machine or record player (usually less than ten times a second), which cause unwanted pitch changes. [6] *See also* **flutter**

zenith adjustment 6, 14

A mechanical adjustment of a magnetic tape head to obtain uniform contact with the top and bottom of the tape. Zenith refers to the forward-backward tilting of the head. [6]

APPENDIX VI

AUSTRALIAN NATIONAL FILM AND SOUND ARCHIVE: EXTRACTS FROM CORPORATE PLAN 1988/89 TO 1991/92

Part 2

Corporate vision

2.1 The Archive has an active, pioneering vision for the future. Like its counterparts overseas, it can take little for granted. As an institution it cannot define its nature by reference to traditional concepts of libraries, archives, museums or galleries (it is all of them); its very name only partially describes its role and is confusing in its connotations.

2.2 Current realities and priorities must be placed in a longer term context. Hence it is appropriate and historically symbolic to adopt the year 2001 (the centenary of federation) as the target year for achieving the following:

   (a) *Acceptance* – The Archive is a body whose time has come but this fact has yet to be translated into the provision of resources adequate for its task, and the development of full community awareness of the realities and importance of media preservation. By 2001, this will be achieved: the Archive's role and work will be widely understood, and it will be taken for granted as one of Australia's great national institutions.

   (b) *Funds and staffing* – The Archive will have completed the move from 'Cinderella' status to a responsible equality with other media. There will be significant sponsor and revenue support, but most of the Archive's resources will come from the taxpayer.

   (c) *Buildings and equipment* – the buildings foreshadowed in 'Time in Our Hands', and extensions of them, will be realities; buildings and equipment will equate in size and quality (relative to work volumes and collection size) with good northern hemisphere counterparts. The Archive will be a major tourist attraction of Canberra.

(d) *Skills and knowledge* – a distinctive philosophy and body of knowledge will have been built up. The Archive will be a centre of excellence, offering opportunities for research and development of skills.

(e) *Geographic* – the Archive will have offices or representation in all major population centres, with a mature, efficient and logical devolution of functions and services away from headquarters.

(f) *Corporate nature* – the Archive will be a statutory authority with a governing council, as described in 'Time in Our Hands'.

Part 3

Mission Statement

3.1 Against this background, and in view of the need to set policies and principles for the development of the Archive pending final government decision on the Advisory Committee and IDC Reports, the Archive's present mission statement is seen to be:

- *to acquire, preserve, research and provide access to the moving image and recorded sound heritage of Australia, and to express its cultural significance.*

3.2 The Archive's mission statement will be amended if necessary to take account of the government's response to the two reports. It will also be reviewed in the light of experience when this plan is updated.

3.3 It should be noted that in another context, with the introduction of program budgeting for the 1987/88 financial year, the Archive has adopted as its objective:

- *to increase the Australian community's awareness, appreciation and understanding of the nation's moving image and recorded sound heritage by the acquisition, preservation and presentation of relevant historical material of national significance.*

3.4 The two statements are seen as complementary and are expanded in 'Corporate Goals' (Part 4).

Part 4

Corporate Goals

4.1 To achieve its mission, the Archive pursues defined goals based on its understanding of its terms of reference provided by government (statement by the minister, April 1984) and the Prime Minister (October 1984).

4.2 The Archive's perception of its goals also has regard to the wisdom of internal and external experience over time, including the views of the former and current NFSA Advisory Committees as expressed in 'Time in Our Hands' and elsewhere.

4.3 Subject to approved policies and priorities, and within the limits of available resources, the Archive seeks to achieve the following goals:

- to identify, acquire, preserve, research and provide access to the recorded sound and moving image heritage of Australia
- to promote appreciation of that heritage, and to seek to establish full recognition of its cultural value
- to monitor Australian recorded sound and moving image production and to maintain a definitive national record
- to give effect to the national leadership, coordination, representation and service functions implicit in the Archive's role
- to develop in Australia the skills and facilities necessary to accomplish these goals.

Part 6

Key Issues

The following key issues need special managerial attention. Action on them is necessary to achieve the Archive's goals.

6.1 Improving the Archive's external environment, specifically:

- increasing resources (from government, sponsorship, revenue)
- building public profile, understanding and acceptance of the Archive's needs and tasks.

6.2 Improving the situation of the collection, specifically:

- increased quantity and quality of preservation work
- bringing collection control to an acceptable level
- bringing access services to an acceptable level
- transfer of material to suitable accommodation
- better quality and quantity in collection building.

6.3 Establishing policies and methods, specifically:
- determining the codifying of a full range of policies and operational guidelines
- determining the most effective structures and managerial practices.

6.4 Strategic planning, specifically:
- decentralization of Archive activities
- ADP development.

APPENDIX VII

AUSTRALIAN NATIONAL FILM AND SOUND ARCHIVE: DRAFT SELECTION AND ACQUISITION POLICY

Introduction

1.1 The range and nature of NFSA's collecting responsibilities are defined from time to time by government, and by NFSA's act and charter (when established). Briefly, they include:
   (a) recorded sound, film, radio and television productions made in Australia or having Australian relevance
   (b) ephemera, documents and artifacts relating to the moving image and recorded sound media.

1.2 The immense quantity of these materials produced or disseminated in Australia, compared to the finite resources of the Archive, precludes the possibility of acquiring everything. Selection is inevitable. It is better that it occur deliberately, rather than by default even though the difficulty of selecting from the viewpoint of the future is self evident.

1.3 *Selection* is the process of choosing works or items appropriate for addition to the NFSA's collection. *Acquisition* is the subsequent step of physically adding such items to the collection whether by donation or otherwise. *Selected* material might not be *acquired* immediately or even for a considerable time.

2   Selection principles

2.1 Selection judgements should reflect a balanced overview of tastes, trends and views of history and society.

2.2 NFSA seeks to acquire the maximum amount of material of enduring Australian cultural significance regardless of its country of origin. It applies the *'loss' principle: if there is any reason of form, content or external association why the loss of a particular item would be regretted in the future, there is a case for preservation.*

2.3 Priority will be given to materials of Australian origin or association. However, because Australian cultural values have developed in an international context, the collection must reflect Australians' right to permanent and ready access to overseas material.

2.4 The NFSA may choose to record events, statements, personal reminiscences, performances etc. to augment the national collection.

2.5 In general, works are preserved in their original and completed form, i.e. in the form in which they were released to the public or regarded as complete by their creators, with their content intact.

2.6 NFSA seeks to complement and cooperate with, rather than duplicate, the activities and emphases of other collecting institutions within Australia and overseas. It observes the relevant international standards and protocols, and the obligations of its membership in professional federations.

2.7 NFSA reserves the right to deselect material from its collections and dispose of it with due observance of the legalities involved.

3.   General selection criteria

The following criteria are principal factors against which the cultural value of material is measured:

3.1 *Content*: The work may have one or more of the following attributes:
- documentary social record, including:
  - actuality record of an historic event
  - aspects of contemporary life
  - important manifestation of national character and sentiment
  - people of historic interest
  - record of geographical places, especially related to stages of development
- art or entertainment in its own right.

The secondary characteristics of a work may be stronger argument for selection than its primary intent: for instance, a routine pop song recording or fiction film might be an eloquent document of social attitudes. Or these may be an argument against selection: for instance, the equivalent information may be better preserved in another medium, such as still photographs or the written word.

3.2 *Form*: the work may have physical, aesthetic or technical attributes of historic or educative importance.

3.3 *External association*: A work may be important because of its association with personalities, events or social phenomena. For example, it may be the object of an award, or have had wide social impact as exemplified by ratings or box office performance.

3.4 Material illustrative of the history, nature and dynamic of the screen and sound media themselves. This includes publicity and promotional materials, and extended 'slices' of radio and television programming, preserved as such.

3.5 *Range*: Recorded sound and moving image carriers of all technical descriptions predominate in the collection, and embody its central character. These are supplemented by paper-based materials of all types (known collectively as *documentation*), objects and artefacts.

3.6 The collection should include a representative and balanced sampling of programs, productions and materials by period, geographic location, type, and social impact.

3.7 Trends in demand for access to the NFSA's collection are, in themselves, an indication of cultural values and a legitimate factor in selection decisions.

4. Selection priorities

4.1 Insofar as it is not practical to give equal attention to all aspects of the recorded sound and moving image heritage at any one time, priority of attention is given, in order, to items:
   (*a*)   made in or about Australia
   (*b*)   made by Australians overseas
   (*c*)   manufactured in Australia or for the Australian market, and
   (*d*)   imported to Australia.

4.2 Subject to 4.1, prime attention shall be given to endangered, unique or rare items, material of highest heritage value, or material which other institutions do not acquire.

5.   Acquisition principles

5.1 *Acquisition* is the process of physically adding *selected* items to the collection.

5.2 Material is sought in the condition, format(s) and quantities which best meet preservation and/or access objectives.

5.3 Donation, as the strongly preferred means of acquisition, is encouraged.

5.4 Purchases may be made on the basis of market valuation for an artifact, or fair recompense for goods and services supplied. Surcharges (e.g. royalties, licence fees) which may be construed as payment for the right to acquire will not be accepted.

5.5 NFSA reserves the right to make, at any time, such copies as it considers necessary for preservation and access (subject to 5.6 below).

5.6 NFSA will honour the entitlements of copyright owners and donors in its subsequent dealings with collection items.

5.7 The beneficiaries of acquisition by NFSA are: (*a*) the Australian people on whose behalf the NFSA performs its functions and (*b*) the owners of rights in the material concerned. The NFSA can never be in the debt of its suppliers: it cannot respond to acquisition proposals which assert otherwise.

5.8 When NFSA accepts material on a custodial rather than ownership basis, it is on the understanding that it has been placed permanently in the national collection. Should the owner permanently withdraw the material, NFSA will be entitled to seek fair compensation for the cost of its custodianship.

6.   General acquisition criteria

6.1 All items must be available for inspection by NFSA before acquisition.

6.2 Formed collections are acquired in toto only if selected as such. Otherwise items are sought individually whether or not they are part of formed collections.

6.3 Because there is no such thing as a cost free acquisition, each transaction is assessed in relation to its total cost: including travel, overheads, packing, shipping, exchange copies, other obligations, and purchase price (if any).

6.4 Further, collection management and preservation implications are assessed beforehand: for instance, processing workload, storage space requirements, level of duplication with existing holdings, impact on preservation program and budget. The transaction proceeds only if the implications are acceptable.

7. Acquisition mechanics

7.1 All acquisitions, other than retail or wholesale purchase, or anonymous donations, will be documented with receipts and standard contracts which define the content and nature of the acquisition, the purchase terms (if any), and the obligations and rights of the parties involved. NFSA does not recognize open-ended, non-specific obligations to donors or suppliers.

7.2 Standing arrangements for the donation of material by producers or their representatives are encouraged.

7.3 NFSA recognizes the following types of acquisition transaction:
   (a) *donation*: involves no purchase price but donors may be eligible for taxation concessions
   (b) *bequest*
   (c) *exchange*: in some circumstances, NFSA may acquire new collection material by offering items in exchange
   (d) *purchase*: an agreed price is negotiated. The cost of providing the vendor with goods or services of any kind (including copies of any collection items) is construed as part of the purchase price
   (e) *deposit*: under some circumstances the NFSA accepts custody of material which it does not physically own
   (f) *duplication and off-air recording*: made to order copies, initiated by NFSA.

8. Responsibility

8.1 Responsibility for implementation of this policy rests with the director or his delegate. The director and minister have the benefit of advice from the NFSA Interim Advisory Committee on matters of policy development, and on major selection decisions.

8.2 Only the director or his delegate is authorized to conclude acquisition transactions.

9.   Guidelines

9.1   The NFSA may from time to time develop implementation guidelines relating to this policy.

INDEX

INDEX